INVISIBLE
NO MORE

INVISIBLE NO MORE

THE AFRICAN AMERICAN EXPERIENCE AT THE UNIVERSITY OF SOUTH CAROLINA

EDITED BY

Robert Greene II and Tyler D. Parry

Foreword by Valinda W. Littlefield
Afterword by Henrie Monteith Treadwell

THE UNIVERSITY OF
SOUTH CAROLINA PRESS

© 2021 University of South Carolina

Published by the University of South Carolina Press
Columbia, South Carolina 29208

www.uscpress.com

Manufactured in the United States of America

30 29 28 27 26 25 24 23 22 21
10 9 8 7 6 5 4 3 2 1

Library of Congress Cataloging-in-Publication Data
can be found at http://catalog.loc.gov/.

ISBN 978-1-64336-253-3 (hardcover)
ISBN 978-1-64336-254-0 (paperback)
ISBN 978-1-64336-255-7 (ebook)

Publication of this book is made possible in part by the
University of South Carolina Office of Diversity, Equity, and Inclusion.

Contents

Illustrations

Acknowledgments

The work of an edited volume is a collaborative project, which in many ways is a welcome departure from the traditionally solitary nature of historical work. Many hands have lifted this effort, and we are deeply grateful to acknowledge those who believed in this volume and brought it to fruition. Nearly one decade ago we each received a message from Valinda W. Littlefield, then Director of the University of South Carolina's African American Studies Program, about an endeavor to commemorate the university's two desegregations in 1873 and 1963. Alongside many others, including many contributors to this volume, Val oversaw a yearlong endeavor to commemorate the remarkable achievements and contributions of Black people on USC's campus.

Such events were made possible by the support of many faculty, administrators, students, and community leaders in both the university and Columbia community. We give special thanks to Harris Pastides, Mary Anne Fitzpatrick, Nikky Finney, Steve Benjamin, Chanal McCain, Tamerra McCrea, and Sean Pitt. We also gratefully thank each of our wonderful contributors, Brian Robinson, Ramon M. Jackson, Holly Genovese, Katharine Thompson Allen, Lydia Mattice Brandt, Evan A. Kutzler, Graham Duncan, Jason C. Darby, Marcia G. Synnott, and Christian Anderson, for offering their compelling work to this collection. Without their collective work, this volume would simply not exist.

Robert Greene individually recognizes several people at the University of South Carolina who shaped his academic career for the better. Marjorie Spruill, Greene's dissertation advisor, became a mentor for him as he delved deeper into the history of southern politics in the latter half of the twentieth century. Bobby Donaldson taught him what it meant to be a true public-facing historian, always giving back to the broader community that shaped him as a historian, a citizen, and as a human being. Friends and colleagues Jennifer Taylor, Candace Cunningham, Ramon M. Jackson, Brian Robinson, and Randy Owens all served as bedrocks during his time in graduate school. Jennifer Gunter has been his closest friend and confidant during and after graduate school at South Carolina. Also, Robert thanks his colleagues at Claflin University, especially those in the Department of Humanities, who have supported him during this endeavor. Finally, without his parents Robert and Cynthia Greene, he would not be the person or scholar he is today. Their reading to him at a young age and encouraging his curiosity about the world molded him into a historian. To them, he owes an everlasting thanks.

Tyler D. Parry, also independently, first thanks his wife, Shanelle, who has been with this project since its inception, and who, as a fellow Gamecock graduate, is excited about its long-awaited publication. Tyler remembers how she listened to his first presentation on this subject in the Gressette Room of Harper College in April 2014 and has steadfastly supported the work in its long road to publication. He also recognizes the important contributions of his daughters, Nazanin and Yara, who, although making sustained writing and editing sessions rather difficult, have provided welcome distractions by pulling "Dad" from his work area to view their latest block towers or, most commonly, a new drawing (usually on the wall). Tyler is also thankful for their energy and the positive force they continue to provide in his life. In addition, he is grateful to his parents, Stan and Carol, who remain bedrocks of support and always listen to his latest ideas with interest. Tyler also recognizes the many scholars and friends who are responsible for helping him to see this project from beginning to end. Most notably, Kevin Dawson, who first encouraged him to consider the University of South Carolina for graduate school; Daniel C. Littlefield, a mentor, adviser, and friend who always gives honest feedback on his work; Bobby Donaldson, a scholar and community advocate who always asked him the best questions and demonstrated the value of connecting the university to the community; and Matt D. Childs, who is not only a terrific scholar but also a genuinely good human being. A specific thanks goes to Erica L. Ball, Sharla Fett, Justin Gomer, and Robin D. Muhammad, each of whom read and commented on Tyler's Reconstruction research and helped push this broader project forward. He also gives a huge thanks to all of his wonderful University of Nevada, Las Vegas, colleagues, who have supported this project since his return home in the Summer of 2019.

Last, we both honor the remarkable Henrie Monteith Treadwell for accepting our request to write the afterword for this volume. Alongside James Solomon Jr. and Robert Anderson, Treadwell initiated the critical step toward desegregating USC, and we are deeply grateful for her continued activism and contributions to Black people in South Carolina and beyond.

Foreword

ROBERT   HENRIE   JAMES
ANDERSON   MONTEITH   SOLOMON

They arrive knocking at Osborne's great garnet door. They want to
study mathematics, join the debate team, and sing in the choir. They
are three in a sea of six thousand. With each step they pole-vault shards
of doubt, sticks of dynamite, and stubborn hate mail. With them arrives
the bright peppermint of change. The new laws of the new day can
no longer resist these three irresistible ones, in a sea of six thousand,
stepping through a door now garnet and black.

Nikky Finney, "The Irresistible Ones," 2013

For two and a half years I served as cochair, along with then Associate Provost,
Lacy Ford, for the commemoration of the 50th anniversary of the 1963 desegregation of the University of South Carolina, *Embracing Change, Fulfilling the Dream.*
Tiye Gordon, MA History graduate student, served as the graduate assistant for
this project, and much gratitude is owed to her for those long hours of service.

At the beginning of this journey, I wanted to accomplish three things. First,
I wanted to ensure we developed and completed a series of successful events.
Working with alum, colleges, departments, institutes, programs, corporations,
members of the at-large community, and an advisory board, we held a series of
events from September 6, 2013, through April 12, 2014. The university family was
so receptive, and several organizations provided crucial assistance in moving these
commemorations forward. The College of Education, McKissick Museum, and
the Thomas Cooper Library each hosted separate exhibits. Members of USC's
alumni also held events, and both undergraduate and graduate students were
fortunate to collect and preserve oral interviews they conducted with them. Civil
rights activists Andrew Young Jr. and Diane Judith Nash also spoke on campus
and met with students. Even when Nash was unable to visit on the originally

scheduled date, the late Don Fowler graciously arranged for Young to appear before the campus community. Fowler embodied those individuals who go above and beyond their required service to make such commemorations successful.

Other USC sponsors included the Black Alumni Council, Department of Athletics, Department of Facilities, My Carolina Alumni Association, Office of the President, and Office of the Provost. African American Studies sponsored John C. Brittian, Professor of Law at the University of the District of Columbia. The Athletics Department honored African American firsts in Athletics during halftime at the USC versus Kentucky football game. Other speakers during the year included Benjamin Jealous, former president and CEO of NAACP, and Jotaka Eaddy, founder and CEO of Full Circle Strategies and an alum of the university.

The list of supporters is immense, and the activities they produced are incomparable. The Dance Theater brought Alvin Ailey II Dance Group to campus, while USC Gospel Choir hosted a Festival of Spirituals. On September 11, 2013, we held a ceremony for the *Retracing the Steps and Commemorative Garden Groundbreaking,* and the university hosted the Garden Dedication on April 11, 2014, to honor the bravery of the "Irresistable Ones," Henrie Monteith, James Solomon Jr., and Robert Anderson, the first Black students to attend USC in the post-Reconstruction era. The closing ceremony was held the following day on April 12. Bert Ligon, Professor of Music and Director of Jazz Studies developed an original composition, *Our Journey Forward: Remembering Our Past, Celebrating Our Progress, Sharing Our Future.* Thaddeus Davis and Tanya Wideman-Davis, both from the School of Dance, presented an original choreographed dance with historical documentary vignettes titled, *We Hold These Truths.* The University of South Carolina Gospel Choir and "Carolina Alive" presented *Medley of Freedom Songs* arranged for the Commemoration. *We're At The Crossroads,* composed in 1989 by Bert Ligon and Melissa Gatchel North as part of Project Crosswords for KERA-TV in Dallas, Texas, concluded the program, and the evening ended with a public reception in the Koger Center Lobby. Taken together, the academic year, 2013–2014 was nine months of intense intellectual, cultural, and social exchange.

In my second wish, I hoped to produce a permanent physical space to remember this occasion, which eventually became the "Desegregation Garden." After checking with Elizabeth West, the university archivist, about the availability of space beside the Osbourne building located on the campus's Historic Horseshoe, I approached Emily Jones, University Landscape Architect, and Derek Gruner, University Architect and Associate Vice President of Facilities Planning, Design and Construction, to investigate the possibility. Working with Gruner and Jones was one of the most rewarding experiences of my 21 years at USC. Lacy Ford and

I then began to work with other university leaders to designate the specific area where "The Irresistible Ones" registered for classes as a commemorative space, though the location was largely unused and not particularly attractive. But our team believed in the value of this project. We discussed ideas about the space and in the final design created a place, as cultural theorist Isadora Stankovic articulates, "of cultural encounters . . . of heritage itself," combining "different cultures through the use of the past in the present and its preservation for the future."[1] Nikky Finney, an award-winning poet and the John H. Bennett, Jr. Chair in Creative Writing and Southern Letters agreed to write a poem that was etched in the granite monument, and Pearl Fryer, a South Carolina–based topiary artist and civil rights activist agreed to design the garden. Numerous corporate sponsors, including Bank of America, Columbia Green and Electric Cooperatives of South Carolina, and USC facilities, provided funding for the Desegregation Garden.

Finney noted about her short poem that she wanted "to find one word that would make readers of the poem slow down and linger a bit as they read it." Thus, Finney's "The Irresistible Ones" has a double meaning. "There is the Irresistible word, and there is also the Resist word embedded inside of it," said Finney. For this poem, "these students were 'Irresistible' because the laws of the country had finally changed in their favor." Attached to Finney's words, Fryer's vision for the garden's landscape exemplifies the power of the moment, creating one topiary of three connecting balls for the center of his creation, and two individual topiaries for each side that provided a "double three" imagery. In honoring the courage of Anderson, Monteith, and Solomon, this space gives sensory meaning to the experiences of the Irresistible Ones and preserves those memories for future generations. Jessica Allison and the Alumni Center facilitated a bricklaying ceremony at the Maxcy Monument for Anderson, Monteith, and Solomon.

The third and final wish was to involve students in researching and presenting information on African American Experiences at USC from 1865 to 1980. My stated suggestion to the students in 2013 was that they should continue this research and later publish their work. The seed is now bearing fruit with this volume *Invisible No More: The African American Experience at the University of South Carolina,* edited by Robert Greene II, Assistant Professor of History at Claflin University, and Tyler D. Parry, Assistant Professor of African American and African Diaspora Studies at the University of Nevada, Las Vegas. Both Greene and Parry were among this original contingent of researchers when they were PhD students in the USC History Department.

The original panel consisted of graduate and undergraduate students. All were affiliated with the African American Studies Program (AFAM) as majors/minors, teaching assistants, research assistants, or adjunct faculty. All students were an absolute joy to work with, and they have become the successful lawyers, professors, and archivists AFAM helped to nurture. Using archival resources, oral histories, interviews, and a wide swathe of secondary sources, eight students presented their findings on April 12, 2014. The list included the following: Brian Robinson, PhD candidate, Department of History, "Found and Lost: Reconsidering Education and Culture in South Carolina, 1865–1878"; Tyler D. Parry, PhD candidate, Department of History, "When the Mountains Were Brought Low and the Valleys were Exalted: African Americans at the University of South Carolina, 1873–1877"; Robert Greene II, PhD candidate, Department of History, "Before 1963: African Americans, USC, and the Fight to Desegregate Southern Universities"; Chanal McCain, undergraduate (2014), African American Studies, Political Science, "We Can't Be Mississippi: Some White Students' Response to Desegregation"; Sean Pitt, undergraduate (2015), American Studies and History, "From Desegregation to Integration: Early Race Relations at the University of South Carolina"; Holly Genovese, MA Candidate, Department of History, "After Desegregation: USC and the Office of Minority Student Affairs"; Ramon M. Jackson, PhD candidate, Department of History, "Peace, Love, Education, and Liberation: The Association of Afro-American Students and the Rise of Black Studies at USC"; Tamerra McCrea, undergraduate (2014), African American Studies and Health Promotion Education and Behavior, "'Let's Get Together': Harry Walker's Campaign." Of the eight presenters on Friday, April 11, 2014, in the Gressette Room at 2:00 P.M., two of them are the editors of this volume and three others are contributors.

In the ten chapters of *Invisible No More,* the writers collectively explore the experiences of African Americans on the campus from the inception of the university in 1801 to present. In doing so, Parry, Greene, and the ten other authors continue the long journey of ensuring that the contributions made by underrepresented and often oppressed people help us remember all of "The Irresistible Ones," those who have committed, and continue to commit, toward the long struggle for a more democratic society. For their efforts, I am eternally grateful!

Valinda W. Littlefield
Columbia, South Carolina
April 2021

INTRODUCTION

"Enslaved people were an integral part of the operations of South Carolina College, visible on campus yet invisible," said then–University of South Carolina (USC) president Harris Pastides in 2017. As part of a celebration of two new markers on campus dedicated to the enslaved at USC, Pastides' statement was intended to recognize how far the university had come to remember their contributions. However, the legacy of Black involvement at the school has, in recent years, been a curious and tumultuous one—springing from the complicated history of the institution.[1]

In August 2020, a curious event occurred on the campus of the University of South Carolina. As students returned to campus during a tumultuous year of the COVID-19 pandemic and a resurgence of Black Lives Matter protests, one individual decided to go to the campus in Columbia, South Carolina, to protest the existence of the social justice movement. He soon found not only opposition to his protest and his presence on campus, but he also caused what became a humorous response to his one-man crusade. Students began to play instruments —including a trombone—to drown him out. In the process, it showcased a renewed militancy among many students to oppose discrimination of any kind. The student body president at the university, Issy Rushton, said, "The Gamecock family is defined by passion, resilience and a community that celebrates diversity." She argued that he stood for everything that USC did not. "This is not what we stand for," she said, "and we will not let our family be divided."[2]

This statement would have been welcome news to African Americans who have been part of the university's fabric from its founding in 1801. Indeed, it would have been a balm to the African American students and faculty of the school during the Reconstruction era, and a comfort to the three brave African American students who desegregated the university for a second—and permanent —time in 1963. Of course, such resistance efforts by student activists are not unknown in the university's history. Even during the most dangerous periods of segregation when public rallies were held by the Ku Klux Klan (KKK) throughout the state, student activists resisted the foremost symbol of hate in the American

South. In one report from 1949, a group of USC students actually approached a KKK rally held in West Columbia to specifically challenge the event. They threw "stench bombs" into the crowd of five hundred Klan members and jeered as the grand dragon, Samuel Green, gave a speech against President Harry Truman's civil rights efforts. In a team effort, the police and a few "burly Klansmen" dispersed the student protestors, who continued to disrupt the event by jeering at them from the "fringe of the meeting."[3]

This 1949 case is important for what it does, and does not, reveal about histories of student activism. Throughout the duration of Jim Crow, USC reflected two contradictory identities. On the one hand it was a symbol of white supremacy and separatism as it prevented African Americans from entering its grounds. On the other hand, it was an institution that harbored liberal ideas that challenged past orthodoxies, which helped to gradually prepare many of its students to confront segregation and reject white nationalist organizations in the mid-twentieth century. Were these students reflective of the university's all-white student body or were they outliers? Did these white students form any coalitions with Black student activists throughout the city of Columbia, or was this a single event specifically rejecting the KKK and its dwindling power? Was this event at all significant in the larger effort toward desegregating the University of South Carolina fourteen years later? The lack of details in the report, alongside the reality that such stories are largely unknown in official university histories, reveals the need to further investigate histories of activism, specifically those centering the contributions and efforts of Black South Carolinians who led efforts toward social justice and placed their lives on the line to push for systemic change.

The continued reckoning with the legacies of white supremacy, the "Old South," and the largely suppressed histories of Black activism throughout the university's history serves to remind student activists of the tremendous work that needs to be done to make African American students at USC today feel that they are part of the campus community. In the winter of 2021, the USC chapter of the National Association for the Advancement of Colored People (NAACP) was reformed, sparked by both Black Lives Matter protests and the protests at USC against the numerous buildings on campus named after slaveholders, Confederate leaders, and segregationists. Caley Bright, an African American student at USC, said, "I think students are ready for change. I think people were looking for that one person to lead or that one organization, and now that we have the NAACP, I think they have found it."[4]

Invisible No More: The African American Experience at the University of South Carolina makes it clear that, to understand the history of the flagship university of the Palmetto State, one must look at the experience of its African Americans. This encapsulates *all* African Americans—from the enslaved who kept the university running in the antebellum era; to the Black faculty and students that were the mind, body, and soul of the institution from 1873 until 1877; to the students, staff, and faculty at the university today. Like the broader history of the state of South Carolina, the American South, and the United States of America, the history of African Americans at USC is about more than their mere existence at the institution. It is about how they molded the university into something greater than the sum of its parts.

The University of South Carolina's current debates over race, memory, and representation are but the latest phase in an argument that has taken place since the institution was created in 1801: What does it mean to be an African American at the flagship institution located in the capital city of the seedbed of the Confederacy? The chapters in this collection show this to be a variegated debate, one that has both matched similar queries about the place of Black people in South Carolina, the South, and across the United States—and, at the same time, often influencing those debates too. The chapters are a window into both a changing university, and a changing South Carolina.

Other universities have begun the process of reckoning with their own histories of race and racism at their campuses. Books such as *Ebony and Ivy: Race, Slavery, and the Troubled History of America's Universities* by Craig Steven Wilder and *Slavery and the University: Histories and Legacies*, an anthology edited by Leslie M. Harris, James T. Campbell, and Alfred L. Brophy, have led the way in the last decade in pushing the African American experience at institutions of higher learning across the United States to the forefront. Both works trace this troubled history back to the era of enslavement, going beyond the narratives of desegregation in the twentieth century—as does our volume.[5]

Our book also joins a growing list of volumes dedicated to the fight for access and equality for African Americans that took place at numerous universities in the twentieth century. Some of these schools, like the University of South Carolina, are schools based in the former Confederacy. Their desegregation in the 1960s represented progress, but these works also remind us that such progress did not come without cost for the African American students involved. Nor—and this is a critical point for *Invisible No More* as well—did the process of desegregation end when those students first registered at their campuses. Instead, the process of desegregation should be thought of as *ongoing*, which explains the decades of activism at universities across the country for the sake of greater acceptance of African American students, minds, and experiences. Books on institutions such as Georgia State, the University of Alabama, the University of Georgia, and numerous private institutions done by scholars Maurice C. Daniels, Robert A.

Pratt, F. Erik Brooks, B. J. Hollars, and Melissa Kean reveal how specific institutions throughout the South desegregated during the Jim Crow era.[6] Also, Stefan Bradley's works on the effects of the Black Power Movement on campuses across the nation in the 1960s and '70s inform the latter chapters of this edited volume.[7] The University of South Carolina was never separated from the broader battles for racial equality at colleges and universities, north and south of the Mason-Dixon Line.

The early chapters of the book describe the life of African Americans from the opening of South Carolina College in 1801, to the end of a valiant experiment in biracial education in 1877. In chapter one, Graham Duncan explores the world of slavery at South Carolina College during the antebellum era in his chapter, "Slavery on Campus: Examining the Lived Experiences of Enslaved People at South Carolina College." Duncan's chapter is an intriguing look at slavery in not just a university setting, but an explicitly urban one too. As the Head of Collections and Curator of Manuscripts at the Caroliniana Library, the university's on-campus archive, Duncan is the leading authority on slavery and the enslaved people forced to labor at South Carolina College. This chapter continues the work he started as an undergraduate at USC in 2006 when he focused upon slavery at South Carolina College for a term paper. Duncan's twelve-page study was the first, and until this point remained, the most extended study of the enslaved and their presence at this institution.[8] As mentioned earlier, various books have examined the role of the enslaved at a wide range of colleges and universities across the United States, and this chapter will do the same for South Carolina College from the scholar who knows it best.

Next, Tyler D. Parry's chapter on the brief but extraordinary history of Reconstruction at the University of South Carolina in chapter 2, "'Irrespective of Race or Color': Examining Desegregation at the Reconstructed University of South Carolina, 1868–1877," is both a window into a period of South Carolina's history where a biracial democracy seemed possible, and a reminder of the deep well of possibilities tantalizingly glimpsed during the Reconstruction period. The brief experiment with allowing African American students to grace the campus of South Carolina was a radical departure from the status of many African Americans on the campus before 1865—enslaved and without freedom. It marked a radical shift that was both a literal and symbolic manifestation of Reconstruction's goals: educational access that was promoted and sponsored by the state. In 1873, as Reconstruction was approaching its twilight throughout the United States, this campus invited both Black and white Americans to join the integrationist experiment and challenge critics who claimed Black and white people could never live harmoniously alongside each other. Though a monumental achievement, it is one that was deliberately cut too short, and consequently the state and University of South Carolina both continue to struggle with memorializing this period in the school's history. As it represents one of many possibilities opened up during the Reconstruction era, it also marks the state of South Carolina's continued need to fully reckon with what was lost with the "Redemption" of the state in 1877.

Chapter three, "Richard T. Greener at the Reconstruction-Era University: Professor, Librarian, and Student," examines the remarkable life and career of Richard T. Greener, the first and only Black faculty member hired at the University of South Carolina during its Reconstruction era. Christian K. Anderson and Jason C. Darby's chapter on Greener focuses on his time at USC in the 1870s, where he served in a variety of roles. Greener—relating back to Parry's chapter on Reconstruction—is also a stark reminder of what life during and after Reconstruction could have been for more African Americans, if simply allowed to pursue such a life. While Greener today has a statue on campus—the fight for which is part of the subject for the final chapter of this collection—for many years, the university simply wished to forget he ever attended the school. Anderson and Darby work here to make sure he is never forgotten in the larger history of the university.

Another angle by which to look at the history of slavery and freedom at South Carolina is shown in Evan A. Kutzler's chapter, "Laying the Mountains Low: The Life and Education of Simon Peter Smith, 1845–1914." Kutzler's remarkable research into the life of Simon Peter Smith is a product of his tireless efforts in locating Smith's extant papers, which were largely unknown until Kutzler traveled to different archives seeking a more complete picture of Smith's well-documented life. His correspondences remind us that the transition from slavery to freedom was, for some Black South Carolinians, a literal experience on the campus. But chapter four also displays how much Black South Carolinians such as Smith were deeply tied to larger currents of movement and education among African Americans across the nation, as his travels would take him to Howard University and Chicago Theological Seminary. In the process, we see a different viewpoint of the history of African America from a man whose life spans the antebellum, Civil War, Reconstruction, and Jim Crow periods.

In chapter five, Brian A. Robinson provides a bridge to understand the institutional shifts in South Carolina that led to the dismantling of the Reconstruction project and the subsequent inception of Jim Crow segregation. In "Struggle for Educational Access in South Carolina, 1865–1890," Robinson gives necessary context for the early chapters in the book. The history of education in South Carolina is inextricably linked to the story of racism and classism that have long plagued the Palmetto State. Understanding how the state struggled with ideas of public education for all its citizens—white and Black—in the antebellum, Civil War, and postbellum periods, Robinson displays the problems, and contradictions, that would ultimately hinder attempts to expand educational access for all South Carolinians, specifically by redirecting attention to the propaganda surrounding the "mixed-schools" and possibilities of Black progress that were a legacy of the Reconstruction era.

In moving the volume toward the university's second desegregation, chapter six examines the push to desegregate the university's law school during the "Long Civil Rights Movement" era of the 1930s and '40s. In this chapter, titled "Before 1963: Race, Education, and the NAACP Desegregation Campaigns at the University of South Carolina," Robert Greene II argues that the NAACP's mission to gain admittance for Charles Bailey in the mid-1930s and John Wrighten in 1947 were part of a larger, national campaign to test the limits of "separate but equal" in southern society. However, the chapter also shows the close—nearly symbiotic—relationship between South Carolina and various historically Black colleges and universities in South Carolina, including Benedict College in Columbia, South Carolina, and South Carolina State College in Orangeburg, South Carolina. Ultimately, the irony of the "failure" to desegregate the law school at South Carolina led to the creation of a law school at S.C. State—which created the cadre of African American lawyers needed to break the back of segregation in the Palmetto State and, ironically, desegregate USC in 1963.

Marcia G. Synnott's chapter, "The Legacy of Desegregation: USC and Its Changing Campus and Student Body since the 1960s," is a powerful account of how much the university has changed since three African American students— Robert Anderson, James Solomon, and Henrie Monteith Treadwell—registered on the campus for classes on September 11, 1963. Synnott's chapter chronicles not only their initial experience on campus, but how much the campus would change via the influx of African Americans in the 1960s, '70s, '80s, and beyond. After all, the story of the desegregation of any campus does not merely begin and end with the first African Americans on a campus. Instead, Synnott's narrative in chapter seven should push us to think about the long, difficult legacy of desegregation on a southern college campus.

This theme continues with Ramon M. Jackson's chapter on the impact of the Black Campus Movement at the University of South Carolina. "Peace, Love, Education, and Liberation: The Black Campus Movement at the University of South Carolina" is a local examination of a nationwide issue during the Black Power Movement: the influx of not just African American students onto previously all-white or nearly all-white campuses, but the influence of ideas from the

Civil Rights and Black Power movements as well. The rise of such groups as the Association of Afro-American Students, the creation of an African American Studies program, and the installation of classes on Black life and history at USC are all central hallmarks of chapter eight.

Holly Genovese continues our look at life for African American students after 1963 in chapter nine, "'What's Next, Southern Fried Chicken?' Confederate Memory and Racial Violence at the Postintegration University." Here, Genovese crafts a narrative that looks at the long, tiring efforts to overturn a white supremacist ideology that reigned on the campus for generations. By the late 1960s, the need to create a campus welcoming to all clashed with the cultural and political movements of the anti-war and Black Power movements. The effort was not easy—and, in numerous ways, the fight to desegregate the spirit of USC continues today, as evidenced by ongoing campus campaigns to change building titles derived from slave owners, segregationists, and rampant white supremacists.

To end our collection in chapter ten, Katharine Thompson Allen and Lydia Mattice Brandt recall recent efforts to memorialize the university's tense and uncomfortable relationship with race. In "'The Right Time': Performing Public History at the University of South Carolina, 2010–2020," Allen and Brandt push for greater recognition of the difficulty to remember the enslaved students on campus at USC, along with the push to create a statue to honor Richard T. Greener. The fight over the memory of African Americans at the University of South Carolina is both reminiscent of other campus fights over historical memory—but with a unique tinge, as South Carolina's unique history makes the battle urgent.

Collectively the chapters in this volume resemble similar efforts by other institutions to commemorate and/or restore the historical presence of Black people in American higher education. As noted, the University of South Carolina holds a history that both resonates with other institutions, both in the South and elsewhere, while significantly departing from broader historiographies that are periodized as "antebellum," "Jim Crow," or the "Civil Rights era." This volume reflects a continuity in the narrative of Black resistance that suggests that, even during the periods of legal segregation and disenfranchisement, Black South Carolinians continued to fight for equal representation, whether they were on or off the campus grounds.

It is also worth noting that the original inception of this commemorative volume was born through the efforts of Valinda W. Littlefield who, serving as the director of the African American Studies Program, oversaw the 2013 commemorations that highlighted two moments of desegregation: the first in 1873, and the second in 1963. Littlefield's foreword to this volume provides the context through which this volume was initially conceived and the herculean task of organizing such a significant event in the 2013–2014 academic year. Many chapters in this volume were first drafted as part of the 2013 committee, and these published versions are the final products of the original research. Other contributors are those who continue to hold close ties to the university and have generously provided their expertise on other areas that were heretofore not considered in the original 2013 commemorations. Importantly, each of the contributors in this volume holds an affiliation with the University of South Carolina in some capacity, be it as alumni or faculty. In the case of Henrie Monteith Treadwell, who graciously accepted our offer to write this volume's afterword, they even comprise one of the trio of students who desegregated the University in 1963. This collective effort as showcased in the forthcoming chapters reveal the deep connection that many alumni and faculty hold with the institution and the tireless efforts they pursue to ensure the marginalized histories of Black people on campus are brought to the forefront not only in the university's history, but that their presence is imbedded in its very landscape.

The multifaceted experiences of African Americans at USC are stories that have statewide and national implications. No one can dare to separate this story of struggle and perseverance from the larger narrative of the history of South Carolina. It is our hope that future narratives about the history of the University of South Carolina will center these, and many other, experiences of African Americans.

Chapter One

SLAVERY ON CAMPUS

Examining the Lived Experiences of Enslaved People at South Carolina College

Graham Duncan

As the sun rose over the yard of South Carolina College and the school's bell began ringing, the students and faculty arose for another day of recitations, chapel services, and study. But for the enslaved men and women that lived and worked on the campus the day began hours before. Cooks awoke in the darkness to start fires in detached kitchens and bakehouses to prepare breakfast for the students. Women had started fires in the open yard of Steward's Hall under large cauldrons to boil water for washing students' sheets, towels, and clothing. As the students filed into the dining hall for breakfast, enslaved men and women went to their dorm rooms to strip the beds, sweep the floors, tend the fires, and clean the public spaces. After services following breakfast, they would do the same in the college chapel. While the students were in class dishes would be cleaned in preparation for serving dinner, which the enslaved cooks began preparing as breakfast was served. Vegetables for the next day's meal were brought in from the garden adjacent to the kitchen, and a wagon driven by an enslaved man dispatched to the nearby mill to buy flour for the next morning's biscuits. Firewood was in constant demand, and after returning from the mill the wagon would be sent to bring another load to be split and stacked behind Steward's Hall. Repairs, overseen by an enslaved carpenter owned by the college, would continue on the windows of the old library and chemistry building, while other hired enslaved men would repair the fence in the yard and replace worn bricks on the wall surrounding the school. A particularly skilled and trusted enslaved man would enter the chemistry laboratory hours before the professor to set up the apparatus for that day's experiment and gather the correct chemicals from the locked cabinet in the room. He would stay throughout the class to assist with the experiment and longer to clean the apparatus and return the chemicals to the correct place in the cabinet. Their day would end late after cleaning the dining hall and dishes following supper in the evening. Then finally, the enslaved men and women would retire to garrets above detached kitchens and cellars below faculty houses knowing that in a few hours they would awake in the darkness to start again.

The enslaved men and women that performed these vital tasks and others for the college did so in circumstances that were remarkably different from most of the enslaved people in rural South Carolina. They may have enjoyed greater autonomy and freedom of movement than their counterparts on plantations, but the uncertain nature of their bondage to an institutional body meant that they were subject to the whims of competing masters—the school's faculty, officers, and students. It also meant that they were in daily contact with young men and boys from the state's elite families, men and boys who were accustomed to complete mastery within the state's patriarchy and racial hierarchy. Navigating this world was a challenge, to say the least, but the institution that survives today as the University of South Carolina is a testament to both the heartache and determination of the enslaved men and women that lived within its walls.

When the Board of Trustees of the recently chartered South Carolina College met in December 1804 to consider the proposed by-laws for governing the new school, it is not a surprise that the institution of slavery, and how it would operate on the campus, was among the topics under consideration.[1] By the turn of the nineteenth century, slavery was one of the defining characteristics of South Carolina society. Enslaved persons had arrived in the English colony within a year of the founding of Charleston in 1670, and by 1800 South Carolina had the second highest number of enslaved persons in the nation (behind only Virginia) and the highest number of enslaved persons by percentage of its total population. By 1820, a majority of the state's population was Black, the overwhelming number of whom were enslaved, a figure that would last into the twentieth century.[2] Further, the foundational document of the new college, "An Act to Establish a College at Columbia," expressly gave the Board of Trustees the authority to "grant, bargain, sell or assign, any lands, tenements, hereditaments, goods or *chattels . . .* in as ample a manner as any person or body politic or corporate can or may by law" (emphasis added).[3] Of the twenty-six original trustees, only two (Theodore Gaillard and William Johnson) had no enslaved persons listed in their households in the 1800 or 1810 Federal census.[4] Those that did included some of the state's largest slaveholders, namely, Wade Hampton, Charles Cotesworth Pinckney, and

Thomas Taylor. These men, and those like them, would guide South Carolina College through its antebellum years. In consultation with the faculty and officers of the college, they attempted to shape every facet of daily life at institution including the physical spaces, curriculum, library collection, composition of the faculty, student life, and the enslaved workforce. However, neither the trustees, faculty, officers, or students had complete control over the lives of the enslaved— external factors and the actions of those enslaved men and women on the campus would help define the nature of slavery at South Carolina College. This chapter will shed light on the lives and labor of those enslaved men and women who worked on campus to directly support the college from its founding in 1801 until its closure in 1862. Without their forced labor the college could not have operated, and the modern University of South Carolina would undoubtedly be a different institution than the one we know today.

While this chapter will focus on the lives and actions of the enslaved men and women at South Carolina College, it will necessarily do so through the written words of the white college officials who enslaved them. Almost no records are known to survive that were created by those individuals who were forced to labor on campus. This chapter will rely on a fine reading of the college's official laws and policies, the records of meetings of the Board of Trustees and faculty, personal papers of college officials, and church records to reconstruct the lives of the enslaved workers at the college. However, the very nature of these types of records mean that they often reveal only descriptions of the labor performed by enslaved individuals and nothing of the fear, sorrow, and loneliness and the joy and companionship they all certainly experienced on the campus.

South Carolina College must be understood as a publicly funded college located in a growing urban environment with slavery at its core. These factors both shaped the operation of the institution of slavery on the campus and impacted the lives of the enslaved men and women who lived and worked there. Realizing that enslaved individuals at South Carolina College were not a monolithic workforce, tasked with the same labor, is also key to understanding their lived experiences. Therefore, it is necessary to recognize four distinct groups of enslaved persons on the campus: those hired by the steward (renamed the bursar in 1842) to work at the Steward's or Commons Hall, those hired or owned directly by the college or the marshal to work on campus, those privately owned or hired by faculty who lived on the campus, and those owned or hired by individuals not affiliated with the college but contracted to work on the campus (chiefly to construct new buildings). These groups of enslaved individuals experienced the campus and its white occupants in fundamentally different ways, and they also influenced the framework under which the college's officers and Board wished the

The nineteenth-century South Carolina College campus was located
within a growing urban environment. 1872 Bird's Eye view of Columbia.
South Caroliniana Library, University of South Carolina.

institution of slavery to operate on campus in fundamentally different ways. This
chapter will concentrate on the first two of those groups to document as fully
as possible the lives of the men and women most closely associated with South
Carolina College. To provide a complete picture of the institution of slavery on
campus, more work needs to be undertaken on the enslaved individuals not directly associated with the college.

At the Board meeting of December 6, 1804, a month before the first students
would enter the college, the Trustees adopted rules that would govern the institution. Article X represents the first articulation by the college's governing body of
how the institution of slavery was to function on campus. They decided that to
"each tenement there shall be one servant . . . and such servant shall receive no
compensation, but what shall be allowed him by appointment of the faculty, to be
paid by those who think proper to employ him."[5] The tenement system established
by the construction of the first college building (now Rutledge College) mandated
"suites" of three rooms grouped in units of six. Each of these six groupings would
constitute a "tenement," and the building would contain four tenements housing

approximately fifty students total.[6] In the case that all tenements were occupied, and all students chose to pay for their services, one enslaved person could have been tasked with attending to twelve students. Under this rather vague arrangement, the students would apparently directly pay enslaved individuals (or more likely their owners) who had been preapproved by the college president.

By December 1806, enrollment had grown to fifty-six students, up from only nine in January 1805, and the Trustees decided that a more regulated system to govern the institution of slavery was necessary. During their meeting of December 1806, the Trustees adopted a set of provisional laws that changed how enslaved workers were employed on campus. Rather than having students directly pay for enslaved labor, the Trustees decided to officially introduce and regulate slavery on campus by mandating that the steward (the official in charge of feeding students in the "Commons") would "cause all the inhabited rooms in the College, and the entries, to be cleanly swept once every day, and all the beds to be decently made at the same time." Additionally, he would ensure that the chapel was swept weekly and "cleanly washed" every fortnight. To compensate the steward for these services each student would pay "four dollars every year, to be charged in his bill of commons, one half in advance."[7] This law would be amended at the next annual meeting of the Board of Trustees in November 1807 to stipulate that the responsibility to "employ as many servants as . . . necessary" lay with the college faculty rather than the steward. Students would continue to pay four dollars a year for these services, but the money would now go to the college treasury rather than to the Commons.[8] Finally, in June 1808, the trustees officially ended the practice of students hiring enslaved persons directly by adopting a rule that forbid a student to "keep, own, or use a servant" under penalty of suspension or expulsion.[9] Together, these changes put into place the system that governed enslaved individuals that were "employcd," but not owned by the college, for the most of the antebellum era—students would pay a flat fee and the faculty oversaw the hiring and work of an enslaved workforce, usually through one of the nonfaculty college officers. While no reasons are explicitly given for changing this system twice within two and a half years of the beginning of the college, the rapid growth of the student body is surely one cause. However, in light of specific complaints raised in the decades to come about similar arrangements, the practice of students directly owning or hiring enslaved persons—and the subsequent lack of control the Trustees, faculty, and college officers had over these individuals—must also be considered a factor.

In February 1808, shortly after the faculty were put in charge of overseeing the campus's enslaved workforce, they met to put into effect the resolution of the Board of Trustees "relative to the employment of servants for sweeping and doing other duties around the College."[10] It was decided that rather than managing the process directly, the college would enter into a contract with the steward to "send daily a sufficient number of faithful servants to make all the beds, and sweep the rooms, passages, and staircases by 12 o'clock" for two hundred dollars a year.[11] The college steward, the first non-faculty officer of the college authorized by the Board of Trustees, was tasked with "boarding" (feeding) the students, in a compulsory system for a flat rate per student. The unwritten expectation was that the steward was to hire enslaved persons to undertake the work of making student beds and sweeping rooms, passages, and staircases. Additionally, all the duties needed to run the "Commons" would be performed by rented enslaved labor. The practice of hiring an enslaved workforce was familiar to all parties involved in early nineteenth-century Columbia. It allowed those that needed labor for a specified amount of time to rent enslaved individuals at an agreed upon rate. The practice was widespread in the South, with as much as fifteen percent of the region's enslaved workforce being hired out in any given year and been a feature of South Carolina society since the early colonial era.[12]

The original Steward's Hall was located on the north side of campus and stood until 1847 when it was demolished to build present-day Harper College.[13] After its demolition, the Trustees purchased a house at the northeast corner of Greene and Main streets to use as the second Hall.[14] The scattered nature of the antebellum records of the college, the abolishment and reinstatement of the compulsory system at various times throughout the decades, and the changing nature of overseeing cleaning duties on campus makes it difficult to know exactly how the office of the steward functioned at any given time. However, enough documentation does survive to generally understand the lives and actions of enslaved men and women at the Commons. An early account, submitted by the steward to officials in 1815, provides the most detailed listing of the activities of enslaved persons attached to the Commons. During the year, in addition to purchasing foodstuffs, the steward hired "6 able men-servants constantly around the dining room and kitchen," "1 man in the bake house," "4 women servants in the kitchen," "1 Butcher . . . & 1 Waggoner," [and] "2 who cut wood, work in the garden, & go to mill."[15] A report by members of the faculty from the year before complained about the quantity and quality of the food, the dirty tablecloths, and that "the servants are too few to give attendance"—an apparent reference to the six men who worked in the dining room and kitchen.[16] When William Carlisle accepted the position of steward in 1841, he specified that he would bring with him "an able bodied man with his wife [,] an excellent cook,"[17] and by at least 1846 a "washerwoman" named Anna had been added to the staff at the Hall. In his 1849 report to the Board of Trustees, Bursar A. H. Gladden requested that the hall be "enlarged . . . to enable the servants to pass around the tables," and that washrooms be constructed "as the servants have to perform that duty in the open air which is exceedingly disagreeable in cold and wet weather."[18] Both recommendations were adopted by the Board.[19] Taken together all of this provides a picture of Commons Hall as a bustling compound with a main hall big enough to accommodate dozens of students with at least six enslaved men waiting on them. Behind the main hall was a detached kitchen where enslaved women cooked three meals a day, a separate kitchen for baking with an enslaved baker, an enslaved butcher, a vegetable plot tended by enslaved gardeners, and an area for washing clothes and linens (which was open-air before 1849) staffed by enslaved washwomen. The compound also seemingly contained a shed for firewood, a stable for the wagon's team, and a vegetable garden. When fully staffed, over a dozen enslaved individuals would have worked at the Hall.

The 1815 account also makes clear the degree to which these enslaved individuals moved throughout the city of Columbia. The two men who worked in the garden and chopped wood also were tasked with going to the mill, and the wagoner would not only have transported material on campus but was likely tasked with errands into town to pick up meat, grain, vegetables, and other supplies from merchants in the city. Provisions were made for other enslaved people affiliated with the College to live on campus, but none of the documentary evidence states where any of the enslaved individuals hired to work at the Hall lived. There may have been quarters built on the Hall's lot, or it is possible that they boarded with other Black residents of the city. Throughout the antebellum era, Black residents always constituted at least 45 percent of the town's population and were a majority in 1840. While most of those individuals were enslaved, the town did have a small free Black community. By 1860 it is estimated that over three hundred free people of color lived in the city, or 8.5 percent of the Black population. In the 1850s the town rewrote its ordinances and judging by the granularity of some of the new rules it is likely that they were formulated to restrict existing activities. Town authorities specifically banned free persons of color from becoming mechanics, clerks, or salespersons, reselling produce, or operating boarding houses. However, Columbia's free people of color were vital to the town's economy and worked in a variety of occupations including as bakers, barbers, cabinetmakers, carpenters, cobblers, domestics, draymen, dressmakers, gardeners, hostlers, musicians, painters, seamstresses, tailors, and washwomen.[20] Enslaved workers from the college certainly interacted with this free community, which presented a stark contrast to their condition of bondage. The experience of enslaved individuals seeing and interacting with this free community was probably in the front of the minds of the faculty members when they urged town authorities to "remove a certain negro family [most likely a free family] farther from the College" in 1845.[21]

The nature of Commons Hall also meant that it was the place that brought enslaved individuals into contact with the college's faculty and students most often. Most of these interactions resulted in, at best, complaints from the faculty and students, and, at worst, ruthless acts of violence perpetuated against the enslaved workers by the students they served. Complaints registered to the Board and faculty included inattentiveness and dirty tablecloths as described above, unappetizing preparation of certain foods,[22] and that the Commons were "too often left to the care of the Servants, without any white person to direct."[23] Many of these complaints could be attributed to the students' "unpleasant associations connected with the place as a place of compulsory boarding,"[24] but the cruelty from students toward the enslaved individuals in the Hall—and the college officials' feeble responses—reveals more about the culture of white supremacy cultivated and perpetuated by the college. Many of the college's students were drawn from the ranks of the state's elite planter families, and they would have grown up surrounded by enslaved individuals who served and obeyed them. Unsurprisingly at a school that was founded to perpetuate the existing power structure and staffed by an enslaved workforce, these planters' sons viewed themselves as the rightful masters of these enslaved workers and descriptions of their actions and abuses make clear their ideas of mastery.

The school's faculty was tasked with administering discipline to students for all manner of offences, and the first relating to violence toward an enslaved member of the Hall's staff was brought before the body in 1810 when "a servant belonging to the Steward" was "cruelly" beaten by William Gill. The student then aggravated his offense in the eyes of the faculty when he refused to appear when summoned by President Jonathan Maxcy to answer for his actions. This case resulted in a three-month suspension for Gill, after which time he would be readmitted if he would "acknowledge his faults and promise obedience to the laws." This was one of the harshest penalties a student would ever receive for an offense against an enslaved individual on campus, but the faculty made clear that it was not the act of violence that was being punished. Instead, Gill was "particularly informed that the Faculty consider his disobedience to the summons of the President as the most aggravated and criminal part of his conduct."[25] In other words, Gill striking property that was owned by another man and then attempting to usurp the campus hierarchy by failing to appear at a presidential summons was being punished, not the violent act itself. This episode would be followed by dozens of others over the next fifty years at the college. Students were brought before the faculty to answer for beating, chastising, cutting, striking, verbally abusing, and whipping enslaved individuals in the Hall.[26] One of these cases, that of James F. Leckie "severely whipping" a man, resulted in an eight-month suspension. Upon reinstatement, Leckie was again suspended for "swearing at the Servants in Commons," but would eventually return to the college and graduate in 1825. The other students were sent away with censures, admonishments, warnings, and promises of future punishments. Given the frequency of the documented attacks, the unwillingness of the faculty to act, and the repeated abuse and harassment from students like Leckie, there were certainly many more assaults that went unseen or unreported.

At the same February 1808 meeting, during which the faculty put a system in place concerning the hiring of enslaved workers for Commons Hall, they also discussed arrangements for a different group of enslaved persons on campus. They decided to continue "the employment of the servant whom the Faculty hired of Mr. Herbemont on the first of Dec. last," for one hundred dollars per year. This individual was deemed the "proper College servant," though the only duty listed was "scouring the Chapel" twice a week.[27] Men hired directly by the College for work on campus outside of the Commons became a fixture on the antebellum campus, though their number and length of hire would vary each year. During the first three decades of the nineteenth century, information about the lives and work of these men can be taken directly from the minutes of the faculty and Board of Trustees. They were hired for "cleaning the College Yard and scrubbing the entries" of buildings, building repairs, glazing, repairing fences, and attending the Board during their meetings.[28] Additionally, enslaved men were hired specifically to assist the Professors of Chemistry and Mathematics as early as 1815 and 1821, respectively.[29]

Some of these "College servants" became so valuable to the operation of the institution the Board of Trustees used the powers granted them in the charter to purchase them outright. This also reduced annual expenditures for hiring these enslaved individuals, which were a constant source of anxiety for the Trustees. The first, and best documented, of the men purchased by the college was Jack, who was being hired in 1815 when he first appears in the documentary record.[30] In November 1815, the Standing Committee on Treasurer's Expenditures recommended that the college officers be given the authority to purchase Jack as "the peculiar qualities of the servant make it desirable that he should be the property of the College."[31] A year later, in December 1816, the Trustees petitioned the governor to apply to the state legislature for an appropriation to enable them to purchase Jack, and in the subsequent petition, Governor Andrew Pickens Jr. noted that Jack had been hired by the college for five years, and praised him for being "honest, sober & civil." Over those five years, Jack had kept the "Philosophical apparatus in order," and thus aided some of the professors "considerably in the Mechanical part of their duties." The trustees feared that without the appropriation for his purchase they would be forced to employ some other "ignorant person, whose awkwardness may occasion serious damage of the apparatus" and who may be "deficient in the essentials of morality." Financially, Jack's purchase would help alleviate the "extravagant" amount being spent for the hire of enslaved persons, and given that he was "young, healthy, and accustomed to the climate of this place," he could be forced to labor for years to come.[32]

Though Jack's duties or "peculiar qualities" are not explicitly defined, some conclusions can be drawn given his attachment to the chemistry professor. The duties and skills of Simon, hired for the chemistry professor forty years later, provide a clue to Jack's responsibilities on campus. Simon could "read and write very well" and was "humble, orderly, intelligent, and industrious," making him "much more serviceable . . . than an ordinary slave could be." He was employed cleaning scientific instruments, organizing the cabinets where chemicals were stored, and painting "the interior of the laboratory, cabinet and apparatus room including all mineral cases, closets, tables, etc." When not needed by the chemistry professor he worked "whitewashing, glazing, scouring, and improving the Campus."[33]

The governor's petition was received favorably by the state legislature, and after the appropriation was approved the trustees finally concluded the purchase of Jack in December 1816. He was "given up to the Professors who are to have the control of his time and services" under the stipulation that the Trustees were "to incur no expense from his board and clothing."[34] To affect this last consideration, the faculty determined that Jack should "should have the use of his leisure hours for his own benefit."[35] This arrangement, which allowed Jack a considerable amount of autonomy and freedom of movement throughout the campus and town, was reaffirmed in June 1819 when the faculty granted Jack "the use of the time for his own benefit, excepting on such occasions as he may be wanted to do any services in the New Building" during the vacation.[36] However, this relative autonomy and the control of his own time would begin to change the following February when "Dr. Cooper enquired concerning the distribution of Jack's time."[37]

Thomas Cooper was a native of England who arrived in the United States in 1794. After a career in law and medicine, he turned to science and accepted a position teaching chemistry at Carlisle (present-day Dickinson) College in Pennsylvania in 1811. He was elected Professor of Chemistry at South Carolina College in 1819 and became the institution's president in December 1821. By the following year he had begun "to lead a movement to convert South Carolina to states' rights," and in 1825 he introduced a course on political economy at the college. This course instilled in his students his belief in "*laissez-faire,* free trade, slavery, and decentralization." He became recognized as an "important defender of slavery, and many of his opinions on the subject were later repeated" by his students turned politicians.[38]

In April 1821, a year after his inquiry into Jack's time, Cooper, with the faculty's concurrence, submitted a letter to the Board of Trustees proposing among other measures, support for a public school system, a review of the college's by-laws, and a voluntary commons system. The document also includes a three-paragraph personal invective directed toward Jack, or "Jacko" as Cooper derisively termed him. In stark contrast to the petition to the legislature less than five years earlier, he began by labelling Jack "idle, careless, void of veracity, and of honesty," and claimed that "the Faculty are compelled to adopt an anxious caution in employing him at their meetings" due to his "tale bearing propensity." Further, Cooper avowed that Jack thought himself more of the "Servant of the Students than of the Trustees . . . and if the last Insurrection did not succeed, it was not for want of this mans [*sic*] endeavors to aid it." Finally, Cooper took issue with the arrangement the faculty had made with Jack to earn his own money for board and clothing—and undoubtedly the degree of autonomy this afforded—declaring that "The Servant of the Trustees, ought not to be permitted to earn any money in the employ of the students: he should have no motives of action, subject to their control." Combined, these charges made Jack "a dangerous person to be employed in College," in Cooper's mind. To him the only remedy short of banishment from the campus was to ensure that he had "one master . . . the Chemical Professor," which happened to be Cooper himself, "who should be responsible for the performance of all the duties assigned to the Servant." He urged at the very least that he be enabled to "direct reasonable punishment when I think it would be of service," as "[h]itherto, he has received none; and I am persuaded he is the worse for the liberty shewn him."[39] The board approved all of Cooper's suggestions, and just over a week after his letter was presented they decided that the "charge of Jack be entirely committed to Dr. Cooper and that he be authorized to direct proper punishment to be inflicted upon him, whenever he may deem the same expedient." Further, if Cooper deemed it necessary Jack could "be hired out so as to defray the wages of another servant."[40]

Cooper leveled no complaints regarding the performance of Jack's duties in the Chemistry Department. Instead, he directed his ire at Jack's ability to earn money when not busy with college business and his relationship with the students. Despite laws to the contrary, Jack was clearly being employed by the students.

Though the specifics of his employment by the students are not listed it seems likely that Jack was probably using his spare time to undertake personal errands for students in the city. Cooper also strongly insinuated that he was reporting the substance of faculty meetings to students. As already shown, student discipline was frequently a topic of discussion at these meetings, and advanced notice of the thoughts of faculty members on particular cases was valuable information to those students. Cooper claimed Jack had aided students in an "Insurrection"— most likely a reference to a series of complaints lodged by the students against the steward and Commons Hall in April 1820. It is entirely conceivable that Jack did endeavor to aid the students in these actions. After all, Jack was responsible for boarding, or feeding, himself, and Commons Hall—a location on campus that was already serving the students—would be a likely place for him to eat. If that is the case, then he had every right to be as angry as the students about the badly baked bread, poor quality of meat and vegetables, and lack of cleanliness.[41]

Simultaneously with Cooper's inquiries and complaints to the Board, he was intervening in Jack's off-campus religious life. In April 1820, Jack applied for admission into the membership of the Presbyterian Church in Columbia. Following normal procedure for any "coloured person, not previously a member of any sister Church, who may apply for admission to membership," Jack was placed on probation for three months "in order that any defects in the character or deportment may be made known." After three months, Jack's probation was extended due to a "variety" of unnamed circumstances, and then extended again in April 1821 after the Session was not "satisfied with his conduct." In July 1821, less than two months after Cooper presented his complaints about Jack to the Board of Trustees, church officials appointed one of their members to confer with the "principal officers of the College respecting the moral character and deportment of this person [Jack] and to report accordingly." In October, an unfavorable report was delivered to the Session and the body decided to postpone Jack's admittance indefinitely.[42] Given Cooper's positions as president and professor of chemistry and the spitefulness he exhibited toward Jack over the preceding year, he was undoubtedly one of, if not the only, college officer consulted by the church representative.

Sadly, the Session's entry about postponing Jack's membership was not the last mention of him in the records. The entry was amended with an asterisk to indicated that he "soon after died."[43] Less than a year after Jack's charge was committed to Thomas Cooper, the faculty paid an enslaved man named Peter "for the expenses of Jacko's interment" in an unlisted location.[44] The Trustees settled an account with "Dr. David for an attendance on Jack the college servant," a year after his burial, bringing to an end the College's first experience with slaveholding.[45] In the petition presented to the 1816 legislature Jack is described as young and healthy, so it seems unlikely that he died of old age. While it is impossible to know for certain that Cooper was directly involved in Jack's death, the vehemence that the president exhibited in his letter to the Trustees and his willingness, almost eagerness, to inflict violent punishment cannot be ignored. What is known is that Jack was willing and able to use his intelligence and enterprise to render himself valuable to the college, to earn money that he controlled, and to build a life for himself off campus that allowed some degree of autonomy. In doing so, he caused college officials to rethink the institution's relationship with the institution of slavery—particularly the benefits to the college of owning rather than hiring enslaved men. However, his actions also resulted in increased scrutiny of and eventually aversion to his autonomy. This scrutiny and aversion, combined with harsher measures governing the lives of all the state's enslaved population in the mid-1820s in the aftermath of the Denmark Vesey conspiracy, would help define the lives of other enslaved men on campus after Jack.

In the seven years following Jack's death, the college purchased three more enslaved men: in 1828 Jim from Dr. Thomas Wells, for $450; in 1829 another man named Jim from "J. Barrett," also for the sum of $450; and in 1829 a carpenter named Henry from James Wallace, the Professor of Mathematics at the College. After these initial entries in the Trustees' minutes, the men named Jim would be differentiated as Jim Blue and Jim Ruffin. Again, a desire to limit expenditures, both on hiring enslaved workers and repairing the College buildings, drove College officials' desires to own individuals directly. Like Jack, the man named Jim purchased from Wells was "employed in the College Laboratory," and all three were tasked with "glazing and whitewashing . . . sweeping rooms, making beds, attending on Profs at recitations . . . [and] repairing College buildings." Unlike Jack, these men were not expected to clothe and board themselves. Instead, clothing, usually consisting of boots, cotton, linen, or satinet pants, cotton shirts, vests, linen or tweed coats, wool socks, and fur or plush caps, were supplied by the college yearly. The Steward was required to board "them at the Commons for their services in waiting on tables." This decision, surely endorsed by President Thomas Cooper, effectively eliminated the need for and the ability of these men to use time that they were not laboring for the College in other paid employment.[46]

However, this arrangement did not eliminate the movement of these men around Columbia. One of the most dramatic episodes in the college's history of enslavement—Henry's escape—is a direct result of the necessity and ability of these individuals to leave the campus on college business. It also proves these enslaved men were more than willing to apply their knowledge and abilities to take advantage of this relative freedom of movement and leave the town completely. At the annual meeting of the Trustees in late November 1833, the Board's secretary reported on the extraordinary actions of Henry over the preceding three months. In August, Henry ran away from the college after "forging a pass in the name of the Secretary" and was not captured until he had traveled nearly 150 miles to the outskirts of Savannah, Georgia. After his capture, he was taken to the nearby jail in Coosawhatchie, where, after "a few days confinement, he escaped" again. Next, he was found back in Columbia, at which time he was "immediately committed to jail and there confined." After conferring with the "Trustees residing in Columbia," the secretary sold Henry in November to "Mr. Williamson, a negro trader" for eight hundred dollars. Additional details about Henry's escape are found in a notice from P. J. Besselleu, the jailor in Coosawhatchie, entitled "Broke Jail" that ran in the *Savannah Daily Republican* from October 1 until November 23, 1833. He described Henry, "the property of the Columbia College, South-Carolina," who "assumes the name Henry Crude," as a "large Mulatto Man" around six feet tall and "genteel in appearance." When he escaped from the jail, he was wearing a "blue broad cloth coat and pantaloons . . . [and] a black Beaver Hat." Besselleu assumed, most likely correctly, that Henry Crude was literate and confirmed that he had a forged pass "when committed to this Jail, which he wrote himself." Moreover, Besselleu was also operating under the supposition, again most likely correctly, that Crude had forged another pass upon his escape from jail.[47]

Unfortunately, the brief report of the secretary and newspaper notice do not indicate why exactly Henry Crude ran away from the college. Perhaps it was to visit loved ones from whom he was separated by his 1829 sale, or maybe an attempt at freedom after reaching the coast. Likewise, it is not clear why, after escaping the jail in Coosawhatchie, Crude chose to return to Columbia. Maybe this was only a planned short visit to loved ones in the Lowcountry, or perhaps he thought returning voluntarily would mitigate the consequences of his running away. What is certain is that Henry Crude formulated a detailed plan to leave campus that was predicated on his literacy, bravery, and the knowledge that he could move relatively freely outside of the campus with a pass from the secretary. He, Jim Blue, and Jim Ruffin, like Jack before them, would have been a common enough sight off campus as to not arouse suspicion from white town folk, and Crude used this unique feature of urban enslaved life to make good his temporary escape. However, what is also certain is that upon his capture, the Trustees brooked no opposition to their authority—unlike when dealing with misbehavior by students. In his report, the Board's secretary, seemingly in attempt to deflect from the shock that he and the entire college administration had been fooled and defied by an enslaved man, described Henry Crude as having "for some time previous had behaved so much amiss as to render him of no value to the College." He most certainly would not have described the carpenter this way to

"Mr. Williamson," the man who purchased Crude in the weeks before the report. Moreover, the statement is patently false given the fact that the college sold Henry Crude for a profit when compared to his purchase four years earlier. It is unclear what became of Henry Crude after his sale in 1833, but it is likely that he may have become one of the thousands uprooted and sold as part of a domestic trade that was filling the states of the Old Southwest with enslaved individuals.

Henry Crude's actions affected not only his life and the lives of Jim Blue and Jim Ruffin, who the secretary assured the Board "will be sufficient to perform all the duties required for the ensuing year." His actions also contributed to the creation of a new college official central to the operation of the institution of slavery on the campus. At the same meeting in 1833, during which the Board learned the details of Crude's escape, capture, and sale, they took up a proposal first suggested by the faculty in 1824 to create an office "to take care of and superintend the College Buildings."[48] However, given the events of that year, this request from nine years earlier was amended to also stipulate that this office should be charged with guaranteeing that the "servants employed about the College faithfully discharge the duties required of them."[49] The matter remained unresolved until the December 1835 meeting of the Board of Trustees, at which time the college laws were rewritten and the office of the college marshal was created. This new office was tasked with the strict supervision of the enslaved people hired or owned by the college, but also with restricting other enslaved or free Black people from entering campus. The free movement of Black men and women between the campus and town must have been a common occurrence given the specificity of the marshal's job duties. He was to ensure that no "servant other than the servants of the officers, and College servants, shall be employed in or about the College" by furnishing a badge to "those servants who may have the permission of the Marshall so to work and be employed about the College," and authorized to remove "from within the College enclosure, all such persons not belonging to the College." Additionally, the marshal would monitor the "condition of the buildings, especially as to their want of cleanliness and repairs," and "superintend all the repairs and cleaning" of the same"—tasks that would be carried out by enslaved laborers.[50]

Beginning in 1836, the enslaved men who worked on the campus outside of Commons Hall were generally under the supervision of the marshal, though exceptions were made for individuals that continued to be attached to individual professorships. The marshal was responsible for their hire, and accounts and receipts documenting these arrangements are abundant in the university's records. Although these tell us little of the daily lives of these enslaved individuals, and often not even their names, they do give a listing of the varied tasks that they performed that were vital to the operation of the college. These included building gates and fences, repairing fireplaces, flooring, windows, drains, carts, wells, and the bakery oven, laying brick, plastering, painting and whitewashing, maintaining the cistern, cutting wood, planting trees, cleaning the library, "scouring" buildings, and making beds.[51] These men and women were also assigned irregular tasks deemed necessary by circumstances. In 1836, a "Servant . . . was sent . . . to put out a Bonfire on campus."[52] In 1845, the Faculty decided that a more secure location to store the arms of the cadet company's arms was needed and a carpenter named Toby was hired to fit up the "East Wing of the Commons Hall . . . under the direction of a Committee."[53] In 1851, President William Campbell Preston reported to the Board that during a fire at DeSaussure College, some students took advantage of the confusion and "seized and carried off the Bell with which College exercises are commenced." To remedy this, "the faculty sent a College servant at the prescribed hours to announce them with a handbell."[54]

In addition to the men and women hired by the marshal, Jim Blue and Jim Ruffin continued to live and work on campus throughout the remainder of the 1830s and '40s, but hardly any documentary evidence survives describing their lives. In May 1849, the president reported to the Board that the "two servants owned by the College are sickly; one of them is wholly unable to work, being very old and suffering from a [sic] incurable malady."[55] Jim Blue died the following month and Jim Ruffin in October 1850. Both were buried by Joseph McMillan in unknown locations.[56] After the escape and subsequent sale of Henry Crude and the inability to force labor from Jim Blue and Jim Ruffin in the years before their death, College officials decided to end the practice of purchasing enslaved individuals. Simon was hired to work in the chemistry laboratory in the early 1850s, but despite the urging of Professor Richard T. Brumby to purchase him, it was decided instead to appropriate $600 per year for the hire of a white assistant.[57] From 1849 through the outbreak of the Civil War, men named April, Henry, Jack, and Tom were consistently hired each year to work under the marshal's direction on the campus. Their work was supplemented by "tenement servants," an unknown number of individuals who assumed responsibility for cleaning and supplying student rooms.

Despite not having daily interactions with the students or the fact that they were owned or hired directly by the college, these men were not protected from violent abuse at the hands of the students. Like the instances involving the men and women that were hired to work in Commons Hall, the faculty minutes record numerous disciplinary actions brought against antebellum students for vicious assaults upon the "College servants." Likewise, the punishment meted out to students was minimal and ineffectual. Unlike the violent actions perpetuated upon the men and women in Commons Hall, the abuse of enslaved men attached directly to the college took place across campus and students offered varied justifications for their conduct. In 1814, Frederick Belser beat "one of the College servants under the impression that the servant had made a report . . . of his having card parties in his room."[58] In 1850, Austin Black was reprimanded for "whipping a tenement servant . . . for disobedience of orders."[59] One month later, in the most shocking act of recorded violence, Hiram Alexander Troutman struck an enslaved man in the head with a fragment of a brick after being "provoked," but insisted he had not intended to "injure him as much as the event proved." Though finding it a "very great impropriety," the faculty dismissed Troutman with "2 warnings and 2 admonitions" and a severe lecture from the president.[60] Troutman was again called before the faculty in 1851 for "punishing a servant," and was reminded that he had "no right to punish him" and dismissed. The enslaved man that was tasked with ringing a handbell to announce classes in 1851 following the fire in DeSaussure College described above was attacked by a "crowd of students in disguise," beaten, and "deprived of the Bell." The president and faculty considered this an "outrage," and were mandated to "attend exercise at the legal hours whether a bell was rung or not"—indicating that the outrage was not over the act of violence, but at the challenge to the authority of the college officials.[61] J. R. Anderson struck a "tenement servant . . . 5 or 6 times with the handle of a broom" in 1852 and received "2 warnings with a severe reprimand from the President."[62] The next month three students—Buist, Cain, and Freeman—tied up an enslaved man and "punished him with a hickory." They insisted he had been "negligent in attending to his duties," and each received one warning. A week later J. M. McConnell struck a man "with his open hand," for supposed insolence and was dismissed "without further consideration."[63]

In all these instances a member of the faculty or one of the college officers reported the students for their offenses, but on two occasions enslaved men themselves reported violent actions of the students to the faculty. In 1825 "one of the servants . . . made a complaint against Grayson . . . for having beaten him,"[64] and in 1833 "one of the servants . . . complained of ill treatment from 2 of the students."[65] These complaints became part of an ongoing discussion about whether it was "legitimate to use information derived from servants to put the students upon their exculpation," because "in our country all such questions must be cautiously treated."[66] Ultimately, the college chose not to allow the word of enslaved men abused by the students to carry an weight equal to those accused, an action which would ultimately have challenged the society's racial hierarchy. Instead, they relied on the faculty's judgment in the 1825 incident and resolved that in every "instance of a charge of misconduct towards the Servants in the College, the complaint must be instituted by their masters, who much furnish the

Faculty with the information necessary for conviction."[67] As shown, even when "convicted," students would nearly always receive verbal warning or admonitions, if they were punished at all.

Expenditures for the hire of enslaved workers were a source of constant discussion for the Trustees, and the stated reasons behind purchasing enslaved men outright was partially to save money. At the time of Jack's purchase, the college was spending an "extravagant" amount on rented labor.[68] The secretary to the Board claimed that by purchasing Jim Blue, Henry Crude, and Jim Ruffin in 1828 and 1829, the "amount annually expended by the College for repairs will be greatly diminished."[69] However, during the 1844–45 fiscal year, the first year an annual Treasurer's report was printed, nearly one-third of the college's total expenditures went to the hire of enslaved workers.[70] In an attempt to "enforce economy" in 1853, President James Henley Thornwell restricted the "number of servants to the number of wings—making each servant wait on two tenements." However, Thornwell reported to the Board, rather than accepting a doubling of their workload, "the Negroes all 'Struck.'" No other details about this extraordinary labor stoppage are available, other than Thornwell concluding that he "had a great deal of trouble in getting matters adjusted"—presumably by returning to the prior number of individuals assigned to each tenement.[71] To offset some of these expenses, the Trustees reinstituted a flat quarterly fee to be paid by students for "servant hire" in 1853, with the sums to be disbursed by the treasurer "upon drafts of the President."[72] Beginning in 1854 expenditures for "Servant Hire" are listed separately in the annual printed reports from the treasurer and represent on average around nine percent of the college's total expenditures.

While it is not possible to identify all the slaveholders who rented enslaved individuals to the college, many of those that are named were connected to the institution, either directly or through their families. Thus, in many instances, these private individuals were able to profit from renting surplus enslaved labor to the publicly funded college. The faculty meeting in 1808, which was called to regulate the operation of the institution of slavery on campus, indicated that the one hundred dollars per year that was being paid to hire "proper College servant" went to "Mr. Herbemont."[73] Nicholas Herbemont was born in France in 1771 and immigrated to the United States around 1792. By 1807, he had married the wealthy, widow Carolina Neylor Smythe and settled in Columbia where his wife owned an entire city block just northeast of the College. Herbemont became best known for grape cultivation and beginning in 1809, undoubtedly with enslaved labor, he cultivated an urban garden "inspiring ornamental horticulture throughout Columbia and gaining it the reputation as a garden city."[74] In 1807, he was appointed as the French instructor at South Carolina College, a position he held (with the exception of 1809–1810) until 1817.[75] In the 1850s, the college would once again turn to the Herbemonts (this time Nicholas's son Alexander) to rent enslaved labor, paying twenty dollars a month to hire Simon for the Professor of Chemistry.[76] Throughout the 1830s and '40s, the College repeatedly hired Toby for carpentry work from President Robert Woodward Barnwell for as much as twenty-five dollars a month.[77] In 1846–47, Maximilian LaBorde, from a planting family from northern Richland and Fairfield counties, rented an enslaved man named Titus to "Commons Hall" for fifteen dollars.[78] LaBorde was an 1821 alumni of the college, had joined the faculty in 1841 as Professor of Logic, Rhetoric, and Belles Lettres.[79] He would remain attached to the college until 1873, when he resigned (along with all of the institution's professors) after the school's integration.[80] During his time at the institution he lent "intellectual support to the defense of . . . slavery," and became one of the "ablest defenders of slavery in the nation."[81] LaBorde also authored the first history of the school, *History of the South Carolina College*, in 1859. The Cantey, DeBruhl, DeSaussure, Elmore, Fair, Goodwyn, Haynesworth, Kinsler, Shand, and Taylor families—all prominent Columbia families—also leased enslaved labor to the steward.[82]

Today when one stands on Sumter Street looking east at the heart of the antebellum campus bounded by Pendleton Street to the north, Bull Street to the east, and Greene Street to the south, the horseshoe created by the placement of the nineteenth-century buildings is apparent. However, as recognizable as this area would be to a student from 1860, they would most likely be struck by the absence of a second horseshoe of buildings behind the main structures. In the nineteenth century, these would have included kitchens, carriage houses, ice houses, woodsheds, outhouses, and dwellings that housed enslaved men and women. Individuals that were hired or owned by faculty members and their families would have lived in detached buildings behind the faculty residence. These were generally two stories and contained the residence's kitchen. Sometime before 1833, Thomas Cooper "erected a wooden building of 4 rooms" for the accommodation of the enslaved men owned by the College. Before this time, they were "lodged in rooms in the cellar of the President's house which besides other inconveniences proved unhealthy."[83] Although no direct violence upon Jack is present in the documentary record, an unhealthy living environment and the routine violence that was almost certainly present in his life certainly contributed to his early death. This second horseshoe of support buildings would have been where these enslaved men

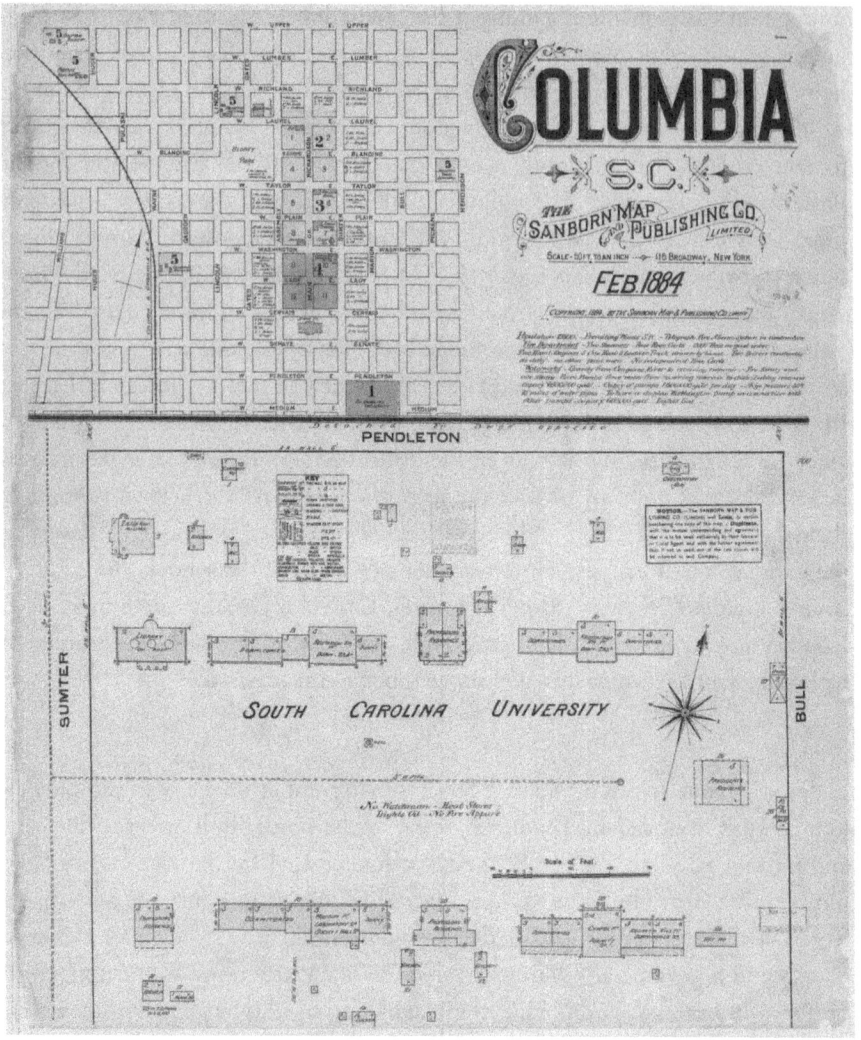

The historic campus, or "Horseshoe," at the University of
South Carolina. Sanborn Fire Insurance Company Map, 1884.
South Caroliniana Library, University of South Carolina.

and women spent nearly all their time on campus—butchering, cooking, washing, chopping wood, tending gardens, sleeping, and in some cases dying. Today, one of these structures remains—a two story dwelling with a kitchen—behind the current president's house.

However, though they may have lived and worked behind the main buildings that survive on today's campus, these men and women should not be thought of as background characters in the story of the antebellum College. At any given time in the mid-nineteenth century, there may have been as many as two dozen enslaved people on campus, as much as ten percent of the entire population, and they were fundamental to the establishment, growth, and operation of the institution. Moreover, the actions they undertook to define their lives—including Jack's financial relationship with the students, Henry Crude's escape, the insistence of the washerwomen on having an enclosed structure in which to work, the willingness of abused individuals to report the violent actions of students, and the extraordinary decision of the enslaved tenement laborers to strike when confronted with unfavorable work conditions, and their activities outside of the campus walls—shaped the very nature of the institution of slavery on the campus and ultimately the institution itself. Without the lives and labor of Abby, Abraham, Anna, Anthony, April, Ceasar, Charles, Cressy, David, Dover, Edward, Ezick, Frank, Harriet, Henry Crude, Henry, Jack and two others with the same name, Jane, Jerry, Jesse, Jim Blue, Jim Ruffin, Jim Sheriff, John Sumter, Keller, Lucy, Paul, two men named Peter, Phebe, Sancho, Sam, Simon, Stono, Titus, Toby, three men named Tom, Walter, and an unknown number of others whose names were not recorded or have not yet been found, South Carolina College could not have functioned and the institution that we know as the University of South Carolina may not exist today.

Chapter Two

"IRRESPECTIVE OF RACE OR COLOR"

Examining Desegregation at the Reconstructed
University of South Carolina, 1868–1877

Tyler D. Parry

n December 1911, a group of Black men convened in Columbia, South Carolina
to celebrate a reunion that linked each of them to the city and the state's flagship
institution of higher education, the University of South Carolina (USC). They
comprised lawyers, diplomats, academics, a former Congressman, and church
leaders, reflecting a standard of Black achievement that both frightened white
South Carolinians and inspired younger African Americans. A reporter from the
New York Age noted that the group's main commonalities lied within two related
experiences: all of them attended USC during Reconstruction in the mid-1870s,
and all of them were denied their degrees when the university was closed to Black
students in 1877.[1] Their gathering was motivated by many factors. First, they
wished to be seen and recognized for their accomplishments, as their mere presence challenged the erasures of Black achievement caused by the toppling of Reconstruction and the subsequent historical revisionism that came at the inception
of Jim Crow governance. Second, their public presence encouraged community
discussions about the state of Black America and ways of uplifting the race. Their
gathering directly confronted the lies of segregationists who claimed Black people
were incapable of intellectual excellence when placed in integrated settings. Indeed, the distinguished alumni of the "mixed school," as it was sometimes called
by opponents, provided a reminder that integrated education had succeeded once
in the state, and it could succeed again if allowed.[2]

The reporter deemed these men the "Class of 1879," stating that this was the year most of them were set to earn their degrees.[3] Each of them was forced to complete their education elsewhere after their expulsion, which added greater weight to the claim that they were deserving of the degrees originally sought. Their inability to finish their education in Columbia was obvious. It was due to "their race" and a lack of "Christian spirit" that forced their removal from campus.[4] By reconvening in Columbia many decades later, they directly confronted the craven nature of the Jim Crow government and challenged white southerners to explain how such accomplished men should be denied the degrees they would have rightfully earned if they were allowed to complete their studies. Their accomplishments preceded their gathering, and their presence symbolized, at the very least, the intellectual and cultural losses wrought by the dismantling of South Carolina's Reconstruction government.

But the reporter also noticed something deeply hypocritical about withholding degrees from men who held no control over their circumstances, especially those legislative measures that were decided outside the university's walls. They noted that some of the "white students" who attended the university prior to the Civil War were allotted honorary degrees, despite the fact that they enlisted in the Confederate Army to fight *against* the Union in order to "perpetuate the institution of human slavery." This reality, they asserted, "has no proper place in the conduct of a people who declare they believe in the Christian religion and philosophy."[5] Using the self-professed Christian principles espoused by Proslavery apologists and segregationists, the journalist highlighted a poignant example of hypocrisy that gripped this section of the Jim Crow South, directly calling out the inconsistencies brought by the illogical nature of racism.

The presence of the "Class of 1879" in South Carolina's capital city provides one example of Reconstruction's enduring legacy in a state that historians suggest changed the most during that era, as Black and white Republicans formed most of the legislators and politicians in the state's government by 1868.[6] Hoping to form a more equitable society, they extended social services without respect to race or class. Instituting a governmentally funded system of public schooling, their efforts completely changed educational access in the postbellum South, specifically remolding the university's structure from one that only served the sons of wealthy slaveholders to opening its doors to people of African descent, both freeborn and the formerly enslaved, and whites from all socioeconomic categories. Though the university's integration was short-lived through the craven betrayals of politicians at the federal level, it's unique standing in the history of Reconstruction demands further attention. Who attended the university? Was there a campus life? Were only men present upon the campus? What were the circumstances under which it closed? In this chapter I do not attempt to provide a comprehensive account of the "Radical" University, as it is often called by historians and contemporary critics, but do use various primary sources to envision student life on the campus, analyze the social relationships that existed both within and outside of it, and examine how the students imprinted a radical legacy that could never be fully expunged from local memory, despite the best efforts made by Jim Crow's revisionist historians.[7]

Previous studies have examined USC's curricular requirements, political atmosphere, and provided many biographical sketches of the student body, and this chapter builds upon their work to emphasize the magnitude of this climactic shift in South Carolina's politics.[8] My objective is to provide readers unfamiliar with this history a reference point for analyzing the men and women who attended and contributed to this campus during this dramatic moment in both the state and national history. It provides biographical material and historical context for public historians and activists seeking to reposition the history of USC from one of antebellum romanticization, to one that reckons with its multifaceted history, in all its triumphs and defeats.

1868: THE YEAR OF WHITE ANXIETY

The passage of the 1868 Constitution changed the politics of South Carolina. Passed by a majority-Black delegation in Charleston, the new constitution was a radical document for its complete reversal of laws implemented under the soft Reconstruction government of 1865. It overturned the "Black codes" designed to subvert African American freedom, abolished debtor's prisons, extended more rights to women, increased funding for public education, allotted Black men the vote, and made "no provision against interracial marriage."[9] Arguably its most significant intervention was the expansion of public funding for state schools, ensuring every South Carolinian, be they white or Black, could gain a formal education without personal expense. Though the law was clear in funding schools for the purposes of educating every resident of the state, it was less clear in its implications surrounding integration. Would Black and white students be compelled to study together, or would they continue to learn in a structure of de facto segregation?

The uncertainty surrounding this issue led to some significant debate, in which a white delegate named B. Odell Duncan of Newberry County raised his own hesitations about adopting the law without more specific language. Duncan played on the supposed antagonisms between poor white populations and newly freed African Americans, maintaining that personal skirmishes amongst Black and white children within the schoolhouse could lead to cross-community resentment and further divide both populations. His primary concern was compulsion, as he worried the law, if not more specific regarding *where* students might attend their primary school, might lead to multiracial classrooms. Duncan invoked classist and racist language, though he masked it by maintaining his stance was of genuine concern for all of South Carolina's children.

Supposedly, the children of poor white people would continue "ignorant, degraded, and prejudiced," while the white families "of means" would simply send their children to private schools.[10] He also cited a "strange condition of affairs," in which the white population might complain they were paying "nine-tenths of the expenses" of institutions they were "shut out from using." Duncan never proved this point, however, as he was assuming a future scenario in which taxpayers would complain about equity, though the only taxpayers he seems concerned in representing are those who are "White" and "of means." He makes additional claims surrounding the status quo between poor white and freed people, attempting to speak on behalf of two communities he was ill-equipped to understand. He cited his belief that both groups already determined themselves to be educated separately: "The freedmen's school are now, if I mistake not, open to all; and yet I believe not one white pupil in the State attends them."[11] Regarding African Americans, Duncan further postulated, "I do not believe they would prefer or even desire to have white children attending the same schools with their own."[12] Invoking the strategy of racial resentment, in which he presupposed that Black and white people were unprepared to intermingle with one another, he argued that racial and class antagonisms were too deeply imbedded within the society, and any attempt to force the measure would lead to violent conflict. "In attempting to enforce mixed schools," Duncan proclaimed, "you bring trouble, quarrelling and wrangling, into every neighborhood."[13] He believed if the children of white people and African Americans were immediately thrust into integrated schools the project of racial harmony would be halted due to the mutual resentment both groups apparently shared about the other. They must be educated *before* they were integrated.

Duncan's opponents expressed surprise that, of all the measures proposed in the convention, he chose to critique the section that ensures every Carolinian obtain a free public education. Seeing through his attempted obfuscations, Jonathan J. Wright, a Black delegate from Beaufort and future South Carolina Supreme Court Justice, attempted to ease Duncan's concerns by stating the section made no claims to forced integration, it simply ensured all people "without regard to race, color, or previous condition" were guaranteed a state-funded education. Wright and many other delegates sympathized with the notion that white and Black children might desire to attend schools in their own areas, enacting a form of de facto segregation that already existed throughout much of the state. Wright confirmed that he was himself against compulsory integration. However, he noted that if the children desired to attend schools together, the law provided the option. Politely dismantling Duncan's attempted fearmongering about compelled integration, Wright asserted such concerns were "only a bugbear, with which some person would frighten you from the performance of your duty" to confirm the proposal.[14] Adding to Wright's critique, his colleague from Charleston, Robert Carlos DeLarge, went further in dismantling the presupposed prejudices existing between Black and white South Carolinians: "While I admit that people have prejudices, I feel confident that my friend from Newberry has greatly exaggerated what he thinks will be the effect of those prejudices."[15] The delegates who favored the proposal would no longer tolerate deflections from its opponents, contending that public education must expand to all residents of the state. Trivial disagreements over language were insincere in their attempts to invent problems. In the end, section 11 obtained overwhelming support, obtaining ninety-eight "ayes" from the multiracial assembly, while eleven were listed as "absent" from the vote. And despite the long-winded opposition, only four people voted "nay," J. M. Runion, Alexander Bryce, L. B. Johnson, and B. Odell Duncan.[16]

Though the measure passed with a significant majority, the anxieties expressed by its opponents in the convention spilled into public discourse, specifically the white press. However, they redirected their focus from primary schools to institutions of higher learning, noting that "Radicalism" had taken over. Consequently, they predicted that the young men of South Carolina would never "sit in classes with negroes," taking the form of a social and economic boycott of the institution.[17] Though the convention's proceedings reveal no discussions surrounding the state university, many commentators prophesied the measure would hold a calamitous impact upon the newly restructured and publicly funded University of South Carolina, claiming unqualified Black students would flood the institution and destroy its once sterling reputation. White anxiety over the sheer possibility of Black enrollment even led to a crisis in 1869, where the university only received "a few applications" for matriculation and "only a handful of young [white] men" enrolled.[18] Of course, these reports blamed the Black population who were "expected" to apply for admission. Despite no applications from Black men, the mere idea that they might apply was used as the reason for the lack of white applicants and the postbellum institution's dwindling enrollment.

White South Carolinians repeatedly vocalized their distrust of the Black population throughout Reconstruction, as they obsessed over protecting the university from an imagined takeover. In 1868, organizations within the university expelled students like Franklin Moses Jr. and Thomas J. Robertson, denouncing them as "two black stains" who proved "false to their race" by uttering "base and subtle falsehoods."[19] Though specificity is lacking, it seems both students advocated for Reconstruction policies, or expressed some support for them, while they attended the university. Moses later became active in Republican party politics and served as Speaker of the South Carolina House of Representatives before being elected governor in 1872.[20] Such sentiments rendered him unpopular within a university and surrounding community that remained largely composed of white secessionists. In 1869, much of the population still asserted that USC was reserved "for whites," proposing a vision of segregated facilities that became a hallmark of the forthcoming Jim Crow period.[21] Their repeated condemnations likely caused Black men who were otherwise qualified for higher education to reconsider enrolling at the state university even after legislation allowed their entry. Most of them either left South Carolina for institutions like Howard University in Washington, DC, or they found employment throughout the state. But by 1873, a Black man applied at the university's medical school, and his acceptance caused a ripple effect throughout the Black community. Within a few years, the institution once reserved for the white antebellum aristocracy became a Black majority campus that expanded its educational vision to the most marginalized populations.

HENRY E. HAYNE, BLACK CHARLESTONIANS, AND
SOUTH CAROLINA'S FREE PEOPLE OF COLOR

Though pressure was building to desegregate the campus after 1868, there were few tangible benefits until Henry E. Hayne took the initial step in October 1873, which for his white critics marked "the beginning of the end" for the institution.[22] Born free in Charleston, South Carolina, Hayne was a known activist both before and after the Civil War, often using his fair-complexion and "passable" European features to disrupt segregated, white-only spaces. Hayne was involved in politics throughout the duration of the Reconstruction period, specifically as the contingents of Radical Republicans were planning to subvert the white conservative politicians throughout South Carolina. His name appears prominently in the 1868 Convention records as a delegate from Marion County, though he was eventually elevated to the state legislature in 1870 and served as South Carolina's secretary of state by 1872. As secretary of state, Hayne held the political and social clout to push for authentic change. On October 11, 1873, Hayne was accepted to the institution's newly formed medical school, becoming the first Black student to enroll at the university. In response, many of the white students left the campus and faculty members resigned. The Board of Trustees resoundingly dismissed them, knowing that Hayne's ancestry was their only motivation to leave. Hayne's actions ushered in a new, albeit brief, era of the university's history: the Reconstruction period of 1873 to 1877.

If Hayne felt alone in this initial phase of desegregation, it did not last long. The population of Black students grew quickly, equaling that of the white population by 1875, and by 1876 Black students were a clear majority on campus. As far as records show, they studied amicably with their white counterparts and the two often engaged with one another in the classroom and in extracurriculars. Hayne's maneuver demonstrated a multigenerational tradition of resistance among Black South Carolinians, but his specific heritage as a "Black Charlestonian" deserves some attention. Historian Bernard E. Powers notes that Black men from Charleston had formed a "cohesive community," as they demonstrated "a keen awareness that equality could only come about if they were willing to act on their own behalf to give theoretical freedom substantive and enduring form."[23] Charleston's free population was especially dynamic in forming schools, churches, and recreational institutions for their children's education, but the enslaved community of this city was also a highly mobile population due to the dynamics of urban slavery. By the time the Civil War ended, Charleston's Black population was uniquely poised to engage in Reconstruction politics and implement legislation that democratized access to educational resources.

Though concentrated in its largest numbers in Charleston, men of free birth existed in each county of the state and they would come to numerically dominate the institution from 1874–1877. Though only around 2 percent of South Carolina's Black population was listed as free in the antebellum period, those born free comprised around 50 percent of the Reconstructed university's student population. Though its measures were designed to equalize and redress the wrongs of chattel slavery and anti-Black racism, the stark overrepresentation of those never enslaved upon the university roster suggests that their familial pedigree and decades of schooling certainly allowed them a head start over the formerly enslaved in South Carolina's new era of educational attainment. As one student recollected, Black Charlestonians were among the earliest to enter the newly desegregated university from 1873–1874, as all of the nonwhite students who obtained a scholarship for entry hailed from Charleston and many of them were free prior to the Civil War.[24] However, such discrepancies should not distract from the reality that these men also helped institute a change in the racial and class hierarchies of the state and provided a prototype for envisioning a better society.

THE FORMERLY ENSLAVED

The entry of formerly enslaved people was a flashpoint for southern white critics, as it embodied the societal shifts they most feared during Reconstruction. Oftentimes, white critics never considered a distinction between those Black men born free and those born enslaved, as they claimed that people of "that race," when outside any other "condition than that of servitude and dependence" were prone to misery and wretchedness when left to their own devices.[25] Only eight years removed from the abolition of slavery in 1865, the possibility of the formerly enslaved overtaking elite whites, who now complained of disenfranchisement, initiated propaganda campaigns that sought to misrepresent the Reconstructed university. Instead of recognizing that it was instituting a revolutionary approach to societal improvement and racial harmony, opponents preyed upon white anxieties surrounding Black leadership and racial conflict.

To ensure no man was barred from entry due to his station or heritage, the Board of Trustees established a "preparatory" department, which provided a "maximum of four years of fundamental grammar, mathematics, and reading" and a "sub-Freshman" class for applicants who showed potential for a university education, but needed additional time to prepare for its advanced curricular challenges.[26] The additional training surely benefitted the formally enslaved, many of whom were less likely to have any previous access to formal education. But in reviewing the biographies of a few formerly enslaved students, we find that they pursued an independent path toward education that proved crucial for their ability to enter the university.

Among the formerly enslaved alumni, few provided as much background detail as William Henry Heard. Born enslaved in Elbert County, Georgia in 1850, Heard's parents lived on separate plantations, though his father, George W. Heard, visited two nights a week by walking the three miles from the plantation to which he was attached. At nine years old, his mother, Pathenia Galloway, and his oldest sister died from a typhoid fever epidemic, leaving Heard and his three siblings "orphans."[27] Throughout slavery Heard labored in plowing fields, recalling the surprising moment in 1865 when he approached the "Yankees" who came to his plantation: "Freedom had come, and I came to meet it."[28]

He knew that education was the way forward, despite being trapped in a society that continued to confine Black people to plantation labor and devalue their intellectual pursuits. The legacy of educational suppression was deep throughout the South and especially severe in this area of Georgia. Heard noted that enslaved people could have their forefinger cut from their right hand if they were caught writing, and when freedom came to his area "there were no teachers in . . . the county . . . and no schools for Negroes."[29] But during the eight years between 1865 and 1873, Heard found a way to educate himself while simultaneously performing the agrarian labor that remained ubiquitous for most newly freed Black southerners. Heard seems to have moved to different plantations by agreeing to various seasonal contracts. Initially, he used his earnings to pay a "poor white boy" for lessons in a spelling book, noting this began his pursuit in basic "spelling, reading, and arithmetic."[30] However, he did not limit himself to paying a fee for external instruction, as he hired himself to a farmer who paid him five dollars per month and provided him a "recitation each night" to continue his education.[31] Thus, Heard placed a stipulation in his contract that noted his desire to include educational advancements alongside any monetary acquisitions. Even during his hourly breaks for food and rest during the day, in which he notes most people understandably used the time to sleep, he spent it in preparation for his nightly lessons. He continued these contracts for a few years, though he was known to break them if the contractor failed to deliver the evening lessons.

His intellectual pursuits eventually bore financial fruit, as he passed the examination to certify as a teacher for the three-month "regular school" established in his area. He continued to acquire private lessons and used the additional income he acquired through teaching to finance them. Eventually, he noticed an "intellectual horizon [of] things I never dreamed of," taking him to Mt. Carmel, South Carolina in 1873 to teach at a 6-month school.[32] On a salary of forty dollars per month he pursued his dream of educating Black children and adults, and he eventually matriculated into the University of South Carolina following Henry Hayne's desegregation efforts. He specifically benefitted from a scholarship program instituted by the Reconstruction government and the university's multiracial Board of Trustees, in which they recognized that many of the state's most talented students could not always afford to leave their livelihoods to pursue a higher education, to say nothing of the familial obligations they held. As Heard describes it, he competed for a scholarship through a test and entered the tuition-free University with a stipend of twenty dollars per month, with which he supported himself and his family. Before he was forced to leave through the governmental change of 1877, he noted he was a "sophomore in the classical department."[33] His story provides a window into the caliber of students who entered the Reconstructed university and the possibilities for formerly enslaved people who were similarly pursuing knowledge in the interim years between 1865 and 1873.

William H. Heard, ca. 1910.
From *The Missionary Fields of
West Africa* (Philadelphia: AME
Book Concern, 1910)

Heard's story is no doubt remarkable, though one can certainly argue it is reflective of many of his formerly enslaved peers, even if they all took different educational trajectories before entering the University of South Carolina. In another example, a person like Owen L. W. Smith, born enslaved in North Carolina in 1851, literally followed Sherman's army to gain his freedom during the Civil War. He enlisted in the Union campaign and fought in various battles in North Carolina and Virginia. Upon the war's conclusion, he returned to North Carolina to find his mother in the town of Newbern. Between 1865 and 1873, it is difficult to reconstruct his intellectual life, though his tenacity for liberty and learning was noticed by his peers. According to one biographical sketch, he spent his earliest postwar days working for a farmer from the North, and in-between his job requirements, he devoted "every spare moment at this disposal . . . to study" and eventually obtained his teaching certificate.[34] He came to South Carolina in 1873 through the invitation of Governor Franklin J. Moses, who appointed him as a magistrate for Aiken County, South Carolina. In this new position he became acquainted with Samuel J. Lee, the first Black Speaker of the House in South Carolina, who noticed Smith's interest and aptitude for studying the law. The two men engaged in an independent study before Smith matriculated into the reconstructed university's law school in 1874 and received his degree before the school was closed to African Americans.[35]

As researchers uncover more information about the university's formerly enslaved alumni, they will find it reflects the remarkable achievements of those who dedicated themselves to self-improvement through education. But one could argue the university's truest virtues were realized by the programs it implemented to ensure it did not replicate the elitism of years' past. By making the university tuition-free and expanding its admissions to all male applicants who qualified, regardless of race, class, or heritage, alongside establishing the aforementioned preparatory programs and scholarships, state legislators broadened institutional access to a degree unknown throughout much of the US South, and arguably the entire United States. Such maneuvers were significant in their ability to block the multigenerational elitism that permeated American society. Theoretically, the free-born Black populations of South Carolina could have structured the postbellum institution in their own favor and retained its benefits to a small percentage of Black people, but they chose an inclusive path. Though they were disproportionately represented in the university's student body, their radical policies established a standard that ensured a William Heard or an Owen Smith could also compete at the highest levels. According to historian Pamela Mercedes White, this was the university's most uniquely radical feature, in that it "involved the reorganization of the state University to permit entrance of ex-slaves to the institution."[36] One can only imagine that, if allowed to succeed, how many more generations of Black southerners could have enriched, and been enriched by, this more egalitarian vision of public education after the Civil War.

BLACK WOMEN AND THE STATE NORMAL SCHOOL

Though obtaining a degree from the University of South Carolina was officially limited to men, it is incorrect to claim the campus excluded women. As Black men gained representation upon USC's Board of Trustees it became evident that they intended to position the university as the primary institutional space that would elevate populations of South Carolinians, even those who could not formally attend the university. By February 1873, eight months before Henry Hayne enrolled in the medical school, it was reported that the legislature had "elected colored Trustees . . . with the avowed purpose to make it a Normal School for colored persons."[37] Thus, the establishment of the state "normal school" upon university grounds served two purposes. First, it established a precedent for desegregating the campus space by encouraging Black and white teachers to study on the same grounds that, just ten years prior, was reserved for white slaveholders. Second, by training people to serve as schoolteachers throughout South Carolina

Graduates of the State Normal School for Teachers pose on the
steps of Rutledge College, ca. 1874. Image courtesy of University
Archives, South Caroliniana Library, University of South Carolina.

many Black women walked the university grounds and attended lectures given by
the faculty, and they subsequently disseminated this knowledge to their pupils.
Though not officially recognized as enrolled students, it was, according to many,
a "*de facto* part of the University," and the educational training these women received was among the finest in the state, if not the entire South.[38]

Multiple sources note that the Principal of the Normal School, Mortimer A.
Warren, secured an extended collaboration between the Normal School and
the university's faculty, in which throughout the duration of their education
the students "received lectures from the faculty of this venerable institution."[39]
Warren's maneuvers were nurtured by his pedagogical philosophy, in which he
"emphasized a rigorous traditional academic curriculum" and "insisted on a training that was in no way inferior to that provided to white children in northern
schools."[40] At one point the students of the Normal School actually "pursued
some of their studies in conjunction with the junior class of this institution."[41] In
many respects, the Black women who comprised the majority of students at the
State Normal School of South Carolina decenter the typically masculine representations of higher education in the Reconstruction South, and their experiences
provide a way to understand how they contributed to the campus's intellectual
life. Given that each woman took a pledge to "teach in South Carolina's public

schools" after their graduation, we can imagine how the university education not only impacted those on its campus, but how the normal school's graduates influenced the men, women, and children they taught throughout South Carolina both during Reconstruction and decades after it ended.[42]

At least two of the Normal School's graduates, Clarissa Minnie Thompson Allen and Celia Dial Saxon, went on to have well-documented and publicly celebrated careers as educators. Clarissa Allen was the eldest daughter of nine children born to Eliza Henrietta Montgomery and Samuel B. Thompson. Little is known of her mother, as most biographical sketches simply note she possessed "amiability and good sense," was a "worthy helpmeet," and "well fitted for the position of mother."[43] It seems likely that her mother's ability and willingness to raise so many children allowed Allen's father to obtain significant accomplishments in politics, as he served as a delegate in the pivotal South Carolina Constitutional Convention of 1868, and went on to serve as an alderman, justice of the peace, coroner, member of the State Legislature, and as colonel of the staff of the governor of South Carolina. So admired by his peers, T. McCants Stewart once wrote to Allen in September 1891 to gush about her father and his legacy: "I shall never forget your honored father, Judge Thompson, who contributed intelligence, humanity, and justice, to the problem of law which he helped to solve in our native State, dear old Carolina."[44] As the child of a progressive politician, Allen held a keen interest in interweaving politics and education for social change.

Though Thompson identified as a Black woman, her parents held documented genealogical ties to European, African, and Indigenous people. She crafted fictional writing that was semi-autobiographical, exploring themes of romantic love alongside the problem of elitism and classism within Black America and the need for racial loyalty. Her most famous work *Treading the Winepress; or, A Mountain of Misfortune* explored these questions in a fictional town she called "Capitolia," which represented her hometown of Columbia. Though *Treading the Winepress* is now considered a novel, it was actually serialized in the *Boston Advocate* and never published as a single, bound piece of writing.[45] Had it been published as single volume, however, Allen would have been the "second African American woman to publish a novel."[46] Her essays and poems engaged many themes throughout the late nineteenth century, from memorializing heroes like Frederick Douglass, discussing the horrors of lynching, and even making an appeal for the humane treatment of animals.

Though an accomplished writer, education remained her top priority. One commentator even noted in 1895 that Allen had not "written much" lately, as she regarded her duties "in the profession" as her life's work, and her efforts demanded "so much of her time and attention that she has very little to give to composition."[47] Allen's teaching pedigree was expansive. After completing her education at the State Normal School, she remained in South Carolina for many years, obtaining many high-ranking positions. She was appointed as "first assistant" at Howard School in Columbia; assumed charge of "Poplar Grove School" in Abbeville, South Carolina; and became a full-time lecturer at Allen University, a Historically Black college/university in Columbia, where she taught classes in "Latin, Algebra, Physical Geography, and Ancient and Modern History." She eventually left Allen to further her career in Texas, and one writer notes that upon her departure from her home state there was a "general expression of sorrow" from "students and teachers alike."[48]

Celia Dial Saxon held a similar commitment to educating Black southerners, though she would stay in South Carolina (specifically in Columbia) and educate its population up to her death in 1935. Saxon graduated from the State Normal School in May 1877 and spread educational excellence throughout her community for fifty-seven years. Like Clarissa Allen, her biographers noted that her degree was effectively the same as that from the University of South Carolina, since the two schools were physically and educationally attached.[49] She was known as one of the finest educators in the United States, celebrated by northerners and southerners who observed her command of the classroom, first in the "Howard School" and then in Booker T. Washington High School, both in Columbia. A contemporary biographer noted that, in addition to her skilled teaching, she was "a scholar of no mean mark," having completed many advanced certificates after her graduation and gaining teaching accolades as a Sunday School teacher in the local Bethel A.M.E. church.[50] Her scholarly accolades were also recognized by the South Carolina State College of Orangeburg, in which she was awarded an honorary Master of Arts degree in 1926.[51]

But it was her commitment to academic excellence, her high expectations for her students, and her community service that made her such an influential and celebrated figure. In addition to her work in the classroom, she served as the chairperson to Columbia's Phyllis Wheatley Club for Girls and Women, which was organized to "establish a home for working girls" in the city and an eventual hope to establish a center for destitute young women of color. Saxon knew that the city already financed homes for white women, motivating her to find ways to secure protection for Black women who needed to reside in the city.[52] Her local impact was publicly recognized by 1931, in which an elementary school was named in her honor. Saxon's obituary reveals a legacy of broad community impact, in which "thousands of her former pupils and friends" paid their respects. The building could not even contain everyone in attendance, as it was noted that many were forced to remain outside during the service. She was eulogized by

Celia Dial Saxon. Image courtesy of the Richard Samuel Roberts Collection, South Caroliniana Library, University of South Carolina.

church leaders and professors throughout the Columbia community, specifically Josiah Morse, a Jewish faculty member at USC who advocated for interracial collaboration in the early twentieth century.[53]

In producing educators like Allen and Saxon, one can certainly argue the State Normal School fostered excellence among the best and brightest of the State's educators for the brief period in which it was attached to the university. The notion that they felt an affiliation with the university community and benefitted from its academic instruction, shows how the Reconstruction project charted a progressive path toward expanding educational opportunities to all Black South Carolinians, even if the formal structures between men and women were not yet equal. But it is clear that Saxon and Allen were well respected by their community, and their early entries into public education, scholarship, and activism was nurtured by the Normal School's links to USC. Indeed, when placed in historical context, their efforts toward public education saved generations of Black youth. As historian Katherine Mellen Charron argues, "In an era when the State Board of Education approved history textbooks that championed the Lost Cause, Columbia's African American teachers labored to convey a more accurate portrait of the state's past."[54] One can certainly imagine that, if it was allowed to succeed, the Radical University was on a course to eventually adopt an admissions process that guaranteed opportunities to the men *and* women seeking to matriculate into the institution and use their skills for the public good.

WHITE STUDENTS AND WHITE ALLIES

The university's white student population is much harder to calibrate during the Reconstruction years, which marks a shift from the typical narratives of Black erasure that factor into much of African American history when told through the Eurocentric paradigm. But white students did attend the university and their names appear in the narratives written by their Black colleagues. From the available documents, the Black students viewed the white students as allies for social change who broke social barriers of masculine intimacy and friendship. It was not uncommon to see Black and white students traveling into the city together or conversing with one another as their arms draped over the other's shoulders, in turn demonstrating an intimate proximity that would violate the standards of Jim Crow laws passed after the dismantling of Reconstruction governments in 1877.[55]

Between the years 1873 and 1877, white students were a small percentage of the campus population, comprising only 10 percent, according to one estimate. But their presence was important for producing a necessary defense of the institution. As white detractors prophesied that the university was doomed when overtaken by Black students, and claimed "the young men of South Carolina will not sit in classes with negroes," multiracial coalitions contested the narrative by showing how the multiracial student population interacted within one another, neither population feeling superior nor inferior to the other.[56] Though it is possible this claim is overly romanticized, no administrative documents, disciplinary reports, or student recollections reveal instances of racial conflict between those who lived on campus. The only moment a parent withdrew a white child from the university was upon learning that his son would be taught by Richard Greener, the university's Black faculty member, arguing it was inappropriate for a Black man to have a dominant position over a white student, even if he was a professor.[57] However, this event is an outlier when viewing how Black students viewed their white counterparts at the Radical institution.

But who were the white students? And where did they come from? According to Jesse Kess, a current USC faculty member who has collected biographical information on many of the Reconstruction-era students, the white students came from both the North and the South in relatively equal percentages.[58] Though it is difficult to determine their financial circumstances from the brief records we have available, many of the southern white students hailed from farming families and were multigenerational southerners. The northern students were often the children of ministers, abolitionists, or faculty members, likely venturing to the South to help move forward the Reconstruction project. By attending a multiracial school only a few years removed from the Civil War, one can assume that, for them, this moment embodied the possibilities of creating a more equitable society in the postbellum era.

Though many of these students continued their lives after the university, it is not always clear from the documents how they viewed the university, nor did many of them leave behind substantial testimonials recounting their experiences. In fact, much of what we know about many of the white students come from the statements of their Black counterparts decades after the university's forcible closure. The statements reveal the mutual respect the men continued to hold for one another long after they attended the integrated USC. In 1886, T. McCants Stewart was asked to testify on behalf of his former schoolmate Edgar Caypless, who was being considered for a country judgeship in Denver, Colorado. One report mentioned that Denver's Black community was vigorously campaigning in his favor, which caused local officials to investigate his background before his confirmation. Stewart knew Caypless well, as both men had graduated from the university's law school in 1874 and 1875, respectively. After listing Caypless's intellectual pedigree, he enthusiastically proclaimed that his colleague and friend was, beyond his many professional accolades, a gentleman free of racial prejudice: "He . . . was an exceedingly popular fellow with both white and colored people. He was uniformly kind, courteous, and gentlemanly in his demeanor to all, irrespective of race or color, and was always regarded as a man above prejudice, and of a warm friendship for our race. He commanded the friendship, confidence and esteem of the colored people, and deserved it."[59]

Stewart's emphasis on friendship and Caypless's fraternal bonds with Black people verified not only the latter's qualifications for a judgeship, but the general atmosphere of the integrated university. In many ways, this was a living refutation of those who viewed integration as a path toward chaos. It is impossible to know if any pieces of this biography were embellished, but Stewart had no reason to lie for personal gain, as he and Caypless were over one decade removed from their collegiate years. The fact that he responded to the inquiry suggests a firm belief that Caypless and his other white classmates were living proof that racism was not a birthright for the white population and that they could amicably occupy the same space with their Black counterparts and work with them to build a better society.

For their part, some of the white professors publicly defended the student body and the university from spurious and unfounded attacks.[60] By 1874, the university held new faculty members from the North that departed from the philosophical ideas of the antebellum era, and they collectively mounted an ardent defense of multiracial education and Black excellence. Faculty members like Fisk P. Brewer hailed from staunch abolitionists in New England. Prior to entering USC in 1873, he served as librarian and taught Greek at the newly "Radical" University of North Carolina at Chapel Hill (UNC). However, his public advocation for integrated education at UNC and openly entertaining Black people at his home garnered him significant notoriety among white southerners who rejected his integrationist meddling. The combination of local harassment and the boycotts that caused UNC's closure required Brewer to look elsewhere for employment. He briefly served as a Consul in Greece under the federal government, but eventually found the 1873 University of South Carolina a perfect vessel for realizing his vision of multiracial education. In 1876, Brewer penned a public response to the critics of the integrated university, noting that many of its Black students, once enslaved and forbidden to read, were now studying arithmetic, Greek, and Latin, and, most of all, they were engaging in an educational setting that appeared truly integrated. Though noting that students were still housed according to their race, they were keenly aware that if a white man and a Black man could share the same seats in a railroad car or wagon "for the sake of convenience or economy without any impropriety," then surely they could sit in the same seat in a classroom to "hear about medicine and law and science and literature."[61] Brewer's assertion of fraternal bonding is bolstered by similar testimonials from others who noted that Black and white students engaged in sports, embraced one another as they spoke, and even walked into town together.[62] The university not only disproved racist generalizations of Black intellectual inferiority but also rebuked the belief that the races could not amicably coexist in the same space. It completely subverted the fearmongering promoted by the opponents of racial progress.

But Brewer was not alone in mounting a defense in the public arena. In 1875, Henry J. Fox, Professor of Rhetoric, Criticism, English Language, and Literature, wrote a lengthy essay in the *Methodist Quarterly Review* challenging the claim that African-descended people were inherently inferior to people of European descent. Fox's tract was a defense of the Reconstruction government against Christian ministers who claimed that southern governments were debased by Black political leaders. Though the essay is a broad, sweeping defense of African Americans' intellectual capabilities and a condemnation of the "bitter" commentaries promulgated by self-proclaimed Christians, Fox uses his own observations of the university's student body to prove a valuable point: cooperation and collaboration between the races was possible if it was allowed to organically develop, and that Black students were as capable, if not more so, than their white counterparts. He provides one telling example from the university as it stood in 1875: "The students are nearly half and half, the colored student does not fall below his more highly-favored white associate in the higher departments of mathematics or languages. In fact, the first, probably, that will graduate with honors under the new *regime* is a Negro 'black as the ace of spades.' These are the people we are asked to exterminate or, at least, cast out."[63]

A few points from this section deserve further attention. First, Fox noted that the representation of students was roughly equal, as Black students did not yet outnumber white students at this point. The reference suggested that any scholastic attainments individual Black students accomplished could not be dismissed as simply due to their numerical dominance within the university. Any accolades they obtained were competitively earned. Second, he makes note of the complexion of the honors graduate, which was meant to contest the theory that intellectual advancement was only possible for those who were mixed, in whatever percentage, with European ancestry. A few paragraphs before this assertion he noted the many accomplishments of Benjamin Banneker, whom he described as "a Negro of un-mixed blood." Using his own observations as a professor and societal critic, he maintained that each Black student accepted into American institutions of higher learning demonstrated excellence: "[T]here has not been one who has failed to plant the banner of his race's capacity as high as that carried by the more favored castes."[64] Ultimately, he condemned those so blinded by their incoherent racism and paranoia that they could not see the benefits of promoting education among Black Americans.

COMMUNITY IMPACT AND A RADICAL LEGACY

As Wade Hampton settled into the governorship of South Carolina in 1877, many predicted his intent to destroy the Reconstruction government and its achievements. There were few more prominent targets than the state's flagship institution. But Hampton did not accomplish his destructive goals by using law enforcement or physically assaulting the students. Instead, he intended to "starve out the University . . . and reopen it as a school for white youth exclusively."[65] By hemorrhaging funds, dismissing the faculty "of Northern birth," and squeezing out the Board of Trustees, the "Redeemers" easily retook state governmental positions under the contention that the taxpayers now held the reins of government.[66] Of course, "tax-payers" were only visualized as white southerners who promoted segregation. To distract any potential critics from this stark example of inequality and governmental tyranny, South Carolina's citizens were ensured in May 1877, "some equitable arrangement will be made for the education of the colored people."[67] It is a misnomer to declare any public institution in this early march toward segregation as "equitable," but African Americans did create a number of dynamic institutions throughout South Carolina and beyond, and the alumni of the Reconstructed university drove many of these efforts.[68]

After 1877, the men and women who studied on the campus carried their skills to various institutions throughout the city and state. But they left a specific imprint upon the developing Historically Black colleges and universities organized throughout South Carolina in the nineteenth century. Thomas E. Miller, who pursued a law degree at the Reconstructed university of South Carolina, became the first president of South Carolina State College in 1896, an institution located in the city of Orangeburg, South Carolina, that was created to educate the state's Black population after segregation was legally instituted in 1895. Joseph W. Morris, also a former USC law student, became President of Allen University in 1885.[69] Clarissa Thompson also joined Allen's faculty for fifteen months, teaching a wide variety of courses in "Latin, algebra, physical geography, and ancient and modern History."[70] Additionally, G. A. Townsend, a prominent South Carolina minister who graduated from the Reconstructed university in 1876, spent six years teaching at Claflin University, the "first institution of collegiate rank to be established in this State for Negroes."[71]

The alumni's contributions to education, however, were not limited to higher education. As noted, Celia Saxon taught and influenced thousands of students in her multidecade career in South Carolina's schools. William Dart, a Black Charlestonian who graduated from USC in 1876, and Clarissa Thompson were lauded for their contributions to the "Howard School," Columbia's first, and for many decades, only, public school available for the educating Black South Carolinians. Dart served as its principal in the late 1870s, while Thompson served as "first assistant."[72] Those who left the state used the skills they acquired at USC to impact their societies in both the United States and abroad. Richard Greener, who obtained his law degree at USC while also serving as the institution's librarian and first Black faculty member, was appointed Dean of Howard University's Law School from 1877 to 1880.[73] Others went into politics and government service. In 1910, Whitefield McKinley was appointed a customs collector by the federal government, becoming the first African American to supervise the Georgetown port of entry. George Washington Murray served as "the sole black congressman," and the only Republican elected from the state of South Carolina, in the 53rd and 54th Houses of Representatives (1893–1897).[74] Regarding their work overseas, the reconstructed institution is arguably most notable for producing three consuls general to Liberia, including Henry H. Heard (1895–1898), Owen L. W. Smith (1898–1902), and William D. Crum (1910–1912).[75] Richard T. Greener also served as US consul in Vladivostok, Russia, becoming the "first black consul in what was considered a white country."[76] In the late 1890s, both Edgar Caypless and T. McCants Stewart became involved in regional politics in Hawaii during the conflicts over annexation and colonial rule. Caypless, in particular, supported and represented native Hawaiians who sought to restore the royal family to power, and in 1904 he was elected mayor of Honolulu.[77]

In returning to the 1911 gathering that began this chapter, it is evident that the presence of the reconstructed institution could never be fully hidden from USC, the city of Columbia, or the state more broadly. In this case, the alumni directly challenged the attempted erasure by Jim Crow historians who would deny or viciously misrepresent the achievements of Reconstruction. For even when these former students were not present on the campus grounds, the Reconstruction era's impact was extensive locally, nationally, and internationally long after the university's closure. Simultaneously, the lack of representation these former students have historically received, until quite recently, in public commemorations, memorials, and scholarship reveals the power of Jim Crow governments to not only violently intimidate and eradicate their social and political opposition, but erase the very accomplishments of the Black body politic, even though their efforts benefitted a much larger share of the citizenry without regard to race, class, and, in many respects, gender.[78] Fortunately, the alumni secured their own legacy by never retreating into the background. Through their work in various communities and institutions, the respect garnered from peers and associates, and their willingness to eulogize, praise, and even testify on behalf of one another reveals the myriad possibilities through which they could have further enriched USC, if only they could do so. It is high time this era of the University of South Carolina receives its due attention.

Chapter Three

RICHARD T. GREENER AT THE RECONSTRUCTION-ERA UNIVERSITY

Professor, Librarian, and Student

Christian K. Anderson & Jason C. Darby

Three years after graduating from Harvard College as that institution's first Black student in 1870, Richard Theodore Greener became professor of mental and moral philosophy at the University of South Carolina (USC). That same fall of 1873, Henry E. Hayne enrolled as the institution's first Black student and soon the majority of the students were African American. This was an extraordinary and unique moment not just in the history of the university but in the entire South (and indeed country). Prior to Reconstruction, only one African American had earned a bachelor's degree from a state university.[1]

While at USC, Greener was more than just a teacher, though that would have been extraordinary enough. He also took over the library when the librarian left without notice. He brought America's first free-standing academic library (founded in 1840) back to life from the disorganization wrought by the Civil War and a prior librarian apparently ill-equipped for the job. He successfully lobbied the General Assembly for money to make repairs and hire student assistants. He created a modern catalog, based in part on his experience at Harvard and aided by his knowledge of Latin, Greek, and French. Concurrently, he enrolled in the Law School, graduating in 1876. He would teach law classes at USC and later at Howard University where he also became dean of the Law School.

The University of South Carolina closed in the spring of 1877 as the era of Reconstruction in the South was ushered to a halt as a result of the Hayes-Tilden Compromise of 1877, the rise in racial terrorism and intimidation at the polls, and the repeal of the South Carolina (S.C.) State Scholarship Act, which eliminated financial aid support for Black students at the university.[2] Greener, along with all other faculty and students, were subsequently forced out[3] and the university would not reopen until 1880, this time for whites only. It would not desegregate again until 1963.

For more than a century Richard T. Greener was a man mostly forgotten at USC. Edwin L. Green devoted only a few paragraphs to the Reconstruction-era university in his 1916 history, derisively lamenting that the "pride of the State should be brought to the infamy of the negro."[4] He relegates additional details about the Reconstruction-era university to the appendix (pp. 409–15), where one finds not a more detailed history but a racist screed. The section of Green's appendix devoted to the era is titled, "The Negro In Possession, 1873–1877." As if the title of the section isn't obvious enough, Green's words make clear that he does not regard those four years as properly part of the university's history, but rather as an occupation by unwelcome outsiders. Surely, this is the kind of history W. E. B. Du Bois was lamenting when he wrote, "The whole history of Reconstruction has with few exceptions been written by passionate believers in the inferiority of the Negro."[5] In fact, Green and contemporaries like southern educational historian Edgar Wallace Knight[6] wrote about the Reconstruction era in a manner aligned with the Dunning School of thought, a historiographical viewpoint of the era that maligned those seeking to change the laws and social mores of the time to benefit all races.[7]

Daniel Walker Hollis gives the Reconstruction-era university a more even-handed assessment, acknowledging Greener's contributions in his 1956 institutional history.[8] Twenty years later, Pamela Mercedes White came to a similar conclusion in her 1975 master's thesis chronicling the "Radical University" of the Reconstruction era.[9] By comparison to his uneven treatment in the histories of the University of South Carolina, Greener's pioneering role at Harvard has been mostly ignored in that institution's histories with the exception of the 1993 collection, *Blacks at Harvard: A Documentary History of African-American Experience at Harvard and Radcliffe*.[10]

Outside of the university, Greener periodically appeared in histories by African American, educational, and southern historians. Alrutheus Ambush Taylor discussed Greener's accomplishments in *The Negro in South Carolina During Reconstruction* (1929) and his protégé, John Hope Franklin, Duke University professor and preeminent African American historian, discussed Greener's role at the university and a later debate with abolitionist Fredrick Douglass in his seminal historical text *From Slavery to Freedom* (1947).[11] University of North Carolina professor and southern historian George Brown Tindall examined the

Reconstruction-era university in *South Carolina Negroes, 1877–1900* (1952). Greener appears intermittently elsewhere, including in a 1994 motion picture that drama-tizes what may have been the most prominent trial of his legal career, the defense of his former student who had been accused of misconduct at West Point.[12]

As the university approached its two hundredth anniversary in 2001, Greener was rediscovered at the Columbia institution: he was mentioned in a book about the history of the student experience at Carolina[13] and was the subject of a play, *The White Problem* (using the title of one of Greener's more famous essays) by Jon Tuttle, commissioned specifically for the bicentennial.[14] Michael Mounter defended his dissertation, "Richard Theodore Greener: The Idealist, Statesman, Scholar and South Carolinian" in 2002 and Professor Katherine Chaddock pub-lished *Uncompromising Activist: Richard Greener, First Black Graduate of Harvard College* in 2017. Greener's Harvard and University of South Carolina diplomas and his S.C. law license were discovered in 2012 in Chicago, bringing him into the national media spotlight.[15] And, in 2018, a nine-foot statue of Greener was unveiled on campus after a seven-year effort to recognize him.[16] While previous mentions of Greener had audiences limited by interest and circumstance (the play only ran during 2001, for example), the statue stands prominently next to the Thomas Cooper Library, where it is impossible to miss.[17]

This chapter focuses on Greener's time at the University of South Carolina as professor, librarian, and student. Integrated into this discussion is his political and racial activism throughout the state. Mounter's and Chaddock's biographies give the larger scope of his life and the titles of those two works allude to a fourth category that could be added to this chapter's title: that of activist. Instead of treating this as a separate role, we discuss his activism as it relates to his work as professor, librarian, and student.[18]

Institutions of higher education in southern states adapted to the new realities of Reconstruction, admitting students who had previously been excluded from participation, including women and those from poorer white families. A few made modest attempts at integration. But nowhere was the change so radical as it was at the University of South Carolina. As Michael David Cohen explains: "South Carolina took the steepest route of all. There the poor, women, and even formerly enslaved African Americans won the opportunity for a higher educa-tion."[19] The path that made this possible was the passage of the Reconstruction Amendments and the requirement that the former Confederate states adopt new constitutions that incorporate the abolishment of slavery, full (male) suffrage re-gardless of race, and the protection of civil rights. South Carolina, in rewriting its constitution in 1868 with a Black-majority delegation, went even further, codify-ing a strong educational system for all.[20] Soon the General Assembly was majority

African American, a first in American history. Trustees of the state schools in South Carolina have always been elected by the legislature; by 1873, four of the seven University of South Carolina trustees were Black.[21]

The state institution had been founded in Columbia, proposed by Governor John Drayton in 1801 and opened in 1805, so that it would be situated in the state capital, able to train future leaders for a young state in a new republic. The first building, now known as Rutledge College, was built just blocks from the State House. This close relationship between the institution and state would become even closer after the Civil War as the legislature could not meet in the State House, which was devastated by General Sherman's troops in 1865. The state's House of Representatives met in the chapel in Rutledge College and the Senate in the reading room of the Library. Other state offices were temporarily located on campus.[22]

The trustees made good on the promise of the new state constitution, opening the university to all. Henry E. Hayne, South Carolina's secretary of state, enrolled in the medical school on October 7, 1873, and a week later Walter Raleigh Jones enrolled in the law school.[23] These Black men did what a decade earlier would have been unthinkable: They enrolled in the same institution of higher education that had trained scions of wealthy plantation owners and emboldened the defenders of slavery. They attended classes in buildings named for slaveholders. A normal school to train teachers, most of them Black women, was created and housed on the campus.[24]

Sixteen bachelor's degree students[25] and eleven law degree students[26] graduated from the University of South Carolina during this period, though nearly two hundred students[27] matriculated through the preparatory school and college. The alumni of the Reconstruction-era institution earned a quality education, high school equivalency diplomas, teacher certificates, bachelor's degrees, and law degrees. Most of the students were Black. And many of those Black alumni, even with a limited timeframe to matriculate at the University of South Carolina were able to make a distinct mark on their communities and nation(s) and achieve prominence in various fields of human endeavor once they left the institution. The university's Black alumni who emerged from the era found success in politics, higher education, law, religion, business, and many other areas. For a growing number of Black men and women in the United States to achieve these types of successes in the nineteenth century, the conditions for African Americans had to be changed via federal edict and constitutional change.[28]

Anticipating the looming reality that Black people would one day seek admission to the University, white Democratic lawmakers proposed an 1867 bill that would have transformed The Citadel military college in Charleston into a college exclusively for Black students as a compromise for keeping the

Columbia institution exclusive to white students; however, the proposal did not pass.[29] A plan, five years later, to exclusively push for Black students to attend an agricultural and mechanical institute beside Claflin University in Orangeburg also had not worked out as some white legislators had intended.[30]

White student enrollment at the university steadily declined through the 1872 academic year at the prospect of the admission of Black students. The seven-member board elected by the legislature in 1872 had a total of four Black trustees, including S.C. House Speaker Samuel J. Lee,[31] legislator James A. Browley, S. A. Swails,[32] and W. R. Jervey, a Charleston County Methodist minister. While there is a small gap in trustees' records during the era, it is likely that the decision to integrate the university ultimately occurred in the summer of 1873 after Black S.C. Supreme Court Justice Jonathan Jasper Wright was offended by segregated facilities while attending a lecture on campus.[33]

In November 1873, Richard T. Greener arrived on campus as the institution's first Black professor.

PROFESSOR OF MENTAL AND MORAL PHILOSOPHY

South Carolina College was closed during the Civil War, owing to the enlistment of its students in the Confederate war effort, and reopened as the University of South Carolina in 1866. In its new form it took on a more modern organization with greater flexibility in the curriculum, similar to Jefferson's University of Virginia.[34] However, it also had a more tuition-driven model because of decreasing state support, which ultimately did not work because students and their families did not have the means to pay in postwar South Carolina.[35] The more elective curriculum still included the Classics but was also divided into specialized schools and departments, which was a departure from the fixed antebellum classical curriculum and mirrored reforms developing around the country. This revived institution aimed not only to educate young men broadly, especially as future leaders, but also to train them in ways to be productive in the struggling state economy. However, the continued strength of interest in classical studies indicates that interest among students extended beyond just vocational training.[36]

As the legislature and trustees moved the institution toward integration after the Constitutional Convention of 1868, they had to remove financial barriers as poor whites and especially Black students, many of whom were recently emancipated, did not have the means to pay tuition. Conservative Democrats pushed back against moves to make higher education more affordable even though it would benefit poor whites.[37]

These reforms set the stage for the university that Greener joined in 1873 as a newly appointed professor. In October of that year, Greener received a letter from the University of South Carolina Board of Trustees indicating that he had been nominated for a position on the faculty by one of the board's new members, James Alfred Bowley, a former slave who had been elected to the state legislature. While he was still weighing his options—and being encouraged by US Senator Charles Sumner and others to accept—another letter arrived indicating that he had been appointed as "professor of moral and mental philosophy, sacred literature, and evidences of Christianity."[38] The opportunity to teach in a newly integrated institution was in line with his views about mixed-race education and could not be passed up. Given his recent experiences, it was understandable that he would take the position.

While at Harvard, Greener had hoped to continue his studies in law, but recognized this would not be financially feasible at the time.[39] Instead, he took a job teaching at the Institute for Colored Youth (ICY), founded by Quakers in 1837, in Philadelphia, owing his job to having met its principal while at Oberlin College. By the end of 1870, Greener was head of the English department at the ICY.[40] Greener witnessed the racial violence that plagued Philadelphia's postwar elections firsthand.[41] On election day in 1871, there was widespread voter intimidation and violence against Black voters. Just a few blocks from ICY's Shippen Street building, school principal Octavius Catto was assassinated for his involvement in registering Blacks to vote in the spring 1871 elections. Greener was one of the first on the scene. After Catto's murder, Greener was quickly appointed as temporary principal of the Boys Department at the school.[42]

The incident fueled Greener's interest in promoting racial justice, which continued and grew once he arrived in his mentor Catto's native South Carolina, where Greener became a frequent speaker around the state, often putting himself in great danger. In Philadelphia, he spoke out for racial and gender equality, declaring in one speech that intellect was "independent of sex."[43] He became a correspondent—and later an editor—for Frederick Douglass's *New National Era* and became an active and vocal advocate for the passage of the Civil Rights Bill, traveling to Washington, DC, to lobby members of Congress and President Ulysses S. Grant for its passage.[44] In 1872, he became principal of the Preparatory High School for Colored Youth[45] in Washington, DC, and while there he further developed his public advocacy and speaking skills, delivering the keynote speech at a tenth-anniversary celebration of the signing of the Emancipation Proclamation. His advocacy for mixed-race schools drew the ire of the school board and its trustees removed him in the spring of 1873.[46]

Upon arriving in Columbia, Greener soon discovered that "integration" was very much a work in progress. Despite having elected officials at the local and state levels and a growing number of Black-owned businesses throughout the city,

Portrait of Richard T. Greener by Larry Lebby, 1984. Image courtesy of McKissick Museum, University of South Carolina.

there were rules and social mores that impeded progress. Public spaces were not uniformly available to Black residents with some places integrated (e.g., ice cream parlors and some bars) with other spaces still catering to whites only (e.g., certain hotels).[47]

Racism was still very much on display. One newspaper reported on Greener's arrival, making special note of his race as a "colored man, or in other words a negro" and explaining that, "As a consequence thereof, metaphysics will now be made as clear as mud."[48]

Greener moved into campus faculty housing in Lieber House (now known as Lieber College), a Georgian-style duplex that sits directly across from the Library (now known as the South Caroliniana Library).[49] The other half of the duplex was occupied by chemistry professor William Main Jr., who was also from Philadelphia and also new to the faculty.[50] Francis (originally Franz in his native Germany) Lieber was professor of political science from 1835 to 1856, when he left for Columbia University in New York.[51] Lieber was a complicated figure: he expressed sympathies for the North and for abolition but feared integration was doomed to fail. He spoke out against slavery and yet owned slaves.[52] In 1863, he wrote the first modern codifications of the rules of warfare for the Union Army, which would later influence the language used in the provisions of the Geneva Convention.[53]

Neighbors Greener and Main were not the only new faculty on campus. When the integrated Board of Trustees integrated the student body, many faculty members fled and others were fired. Many white students also left. Main took photographs of the campus in 1874 and Greener sent a set of prints to Harvard University as a gift.

Prior to his arrival, Lieber House was used by Robert W. Barnwell, a fellow Harvard alumnus (class of 1821). Until just before Greener's arrival Barnwell had served as professor of history, philosophy, and political economy. He opposed the trustees' move toward integration and was dismissed in October.[54] A month later, Greener would live in his now-former home.

The last of the antebellum faculty was Maximilian LaBorde, who had written the college's first comprehensive history, published in 1859.[55] He had served as chairman of the faculty during the Civil War and was again elected chairman on October 6, 1873, prior to the fall term opening with a mere six students. The next day Henry E. Hayne enrolled in the medical school. Student R. Gourdin Sloan struck his own name from the medical school register, defacing it in the process. The new environment was too much for LaBorde and he resigned on October 10.[56] The trustees adopted a resolution, penned by Daniel H. Chamberlain, making clear that LaBorde's and other professors' resignations were

> caused by the admission, as a student of the Medical department of the University, of Hon. Henry E. Hayne, Secretary of State, a gentleman of irreproachable character, against whom the said Professors can suggest no objection except,—in their opinion,—his race; and recognizing this as the cause of these resignations, this Board cannot regret that a spirit so hostile to the welfare of our State, as well as to the dictates of justice and claims of our common humanity, will no longer be represented in a University which is the common property of all our citizens without distinction of race.[57]

This was the environment that Greener entered in the fall of 1873. There would be no standing faculty to lean on and to learn from, no mentoring from colleagues who knew the landscape of the university. Some had more experience at teaching than he did, but they were all in this new journey and adventure together at the University of South Carolina. Some of his new colleagues were ministers who had helped establish churches in the post-war South.

Fisk P. Brewer, though as new to campus as Greener, would eventually serve as something of a mentor, having previously taught at the University of North Carolina.[58] Brewer had graduated from Yale and had studied Greek in Athens and had previously acted as a consular officer in Greece. Brewer wrote in 1876 about his experiences at the university. He explained that while the admission of Black students for the first time in 1873 "was too important a change to be overlooked in the development of the University" that despite the indignation shown by many, "most persons of intelligence will admit, and did admit, that sooner or later such an arrangement, or concession as some would call it, would be proper if not necessary."[59] He wrote of the difficulties the university faced in obtaining legislative appropriations despite strong support from the African American community. He explained how studying everything from arithmetic to Cicero equalizes opportunity. "Education makes a gentleman," he declared.

Greener had little time for adjustment to his new job and life in Columbia. In early 1874, he was already called upon by his fellow faculty members to help lobby legislators on the needs of the University.[60] He pushed for scholarships to be awarded to several students from each of the (then) thirty-four counties, which eventually resulted in 124 full scholarships. However, these awards would go to students who were not at all prepared for the rigors of university study. Greener proposed a "sub-freshman" class, surely inspired by his own experience of repeating his freshman year at Harvard, to help prepare them. This allowed them to be counted among the university's numbers while still giving them the remedial help they needed. Otherwise, they would have to return to their homes where there would be little to no educational opportunities. He took on the extra burden of teaching these students Greek and Latin.[61] In addition, to college faculty like Greener, college students like T. McCants Stewart and Cornelius Chapman Scott also lectured "sub-freshmen" preparatory students and the future teachers trained at the State Normal School.[62] The trustees discontinued the sub-freshman class in 1875 and faculty seemed to have relaxed admission afterward to account for this.[63]

Examinations that Greener gave to his students in 1875 serve as a marker of the level of instruction that they received. The freshman class received a Latin examination on the "Odes of Horace[64]; the junior class was tested on the works of logician William Stanley Jevons[65] and the work of metaphysician Sir William Hamilton,[66] and seniors were tested in history.[67] Students reached out to him for guidance as they sought to advance in their studies.[68] Greener thought highly of the academic talents of students like T. McCants Stewart and C. J. Babbitt and consequently shared their academic accomplishments with the faculty chairman.[69] These two were selected to provide the welcome speech and valedictory address, respectively, at the winter 1875 commencement exercise.[70]

Greener looked beyond South Carolina to help build up the university's enrollment. Many Black men had ventured to the North to seek educational opportunities. Greener and state treasurer (and future law student) Francis L. Cardozo traveled to Washington to recruit South Carolinians from Howard University to return home to study.[71] Six agreed and entered the University of South Carolina in their corresponding classes in 1874; several of these students were graduates of the elite Avery Normal Institute in Charleston, South Carolina, and heeded the call of their former principal Cardozo.[72] A number of students who attended USC were graduates of the Howard Academy in Columbia, the first Black public high school in South Carolina.[73] One of the students, Avery alumnus Cornelius Chapman Scott, recalled in 1911 that, "When the University of South Carolina threw open its doors to colored students, I was a freshman at Howard University" when Cardozo and Greener came to visit him and others and "advised our returning to the State immediately and entering the University. He [Cardozo] gave me $100 to defray the traveling and incidental expenses of William M. Dart, John M. Morris, Paul J. Mishow and myself. And we obtained honorable dismissal from Howard and left immediately. Each of us subsequently repaid Mr. Cardozo his loan."[74] Chapman later became head teacher at the Avery Institute in Charleston, a principal in Greenville, and later a minister and newspaper editor and publisher.[75] Students came to the university from all corners of the state, sometimes leaving jobs and family for the opportunity presented by a university education to create a brighter future for families and friends back home. One such student, H. R. Pinckney left a teaching career in the Lowcountry in early 1875 to pursue a university degree in Columbia.[76]

A reporter from the *Christian Recorder* visited the campus and Greener's classroom in 1874 and reported that, "It was composed of white and colored boys. Their seats were arranged alternately . . . They were neatly dressed, very gentlemanly in their manner and were equally good scholars. I saw not the slightest evidence that the contact was 'degrading' to either."[77] C. C. Scott recalled of his time at the university and of his only professor of his own race: "I do not believe the curriculum was in any particular inferior to that of the University of South Carolina before the admission of colored students or since. Prof. Richard T. Greener was the only colored professor, a brilliant man and polished speaker."[78]

Greener's colleagues, recognizing his oratorical skills, unanimously voted for him to deliver the annual commencement "Public Day" address on June 29, 1874. He used the occasion to eulogize his friend and mentor, US senator Charles Sumner of Massachusetts. Sumner had died March 11, 1874, and his name was draped across the stage of the Rutledge Chapel, the same stage where Preston Brooks, Sumner's attacker on the floor of the US Senate in 1856, had declaimed as a South Carolina College student.

Greener delivered what must have been at least an hourlong speech on June 29, 1874, later published (as a forty-one-page booklet) as "Charles Sumner: Idealist, Statesman and Scholar."[79] More than just a eulogy, the speech was a tour of ideas from ancient times to the Enlightenment to the present day. Greener spoke both in defense of Sumner's abolitionist idealism and in praise of his statesmanship. He marveled at how he was delivering such an address at the university of a state where his name "until within a few years, was uttered only with scorn throughout the State of South Carolina, and in terms of reproach even within these walls, consecrated to learning."[80]

Greener introduced the ways Sumner thought of abolition—that to abolish slavery was to make America live up to the promise its founding documents, the Declaration of Independence and the Constitution, making them applicable to all—and then masterfully concluded with how these apply to the university, comparing the founding documents of the country to the founding charter of the university:

> But Senator Sumner holds a peculiar, fitting and appropriate relation to our University. If, as Professor Huxley has lately said at Aberdeen, the ideal University should be a place where thought is free from all fetters "and in which all sources of knowledge and all aids to learning should be accessible *to all comers, without distinction of creed or country, riches or poverty;*" if that able Federalist, the friend of Josiah Quincy, Chancellor DeSaussure; if Colonels Mitchell, May and Kershaw and others, did not use language in a double sense or without any meaning at all when they reported against such opposition "an Act to establish a college at Columbia" saying in impressive and prophetic language:
>
> Whereas *the proper education of youth* contributes greatly to the prosperity of Society, and ought always to be an object of legislative attention; and
>
> Whereas the establishment of a College in the central part of the State, *where all its youth may be educated,* will highly promote the instruction, the good order and *the harmony of the whole community,*" then, at last, for the first time in the history of the college, has the Honored Board of Trustees brought the University back to the original design of the founders, in harmony with the theory of education abroad and the foremost institutions of our country.[81]

He highlighted this last point, remarking: "After seventy years of exclusiveness, and the development of a royal-priesthood of learning, the state opens wide the doors of the University to "ALL ITS YOUTH," ennobling in this way her own proud record."[82] Sumner had argued for equality before the law in the courts and in the US Senate and here, in Rutledge Chapel, named for the founding fathers Sumner had invoked, Greener argued for equality in education.[83]

Greener extended this advocacy for civil rights and racial equality beyond the campus walls, as a writer and speaker. In 1875, he wrote that, "The fifteenth amendment gave back to us the rights which always belonged to us, and had been only withheld through force and fraud."[84] He was not satisfied with the weak civil rights bill before Congress: "This emasculated bill does not give us what we ask, nor what we have a right to demand." Nonetheless, President Grant later signed it into law.[85]

Professor Greener's public speaking often put him at grave risk and yet he seems to have never let up. Historians of Reconstruction have documented just how tumultuous the period was and that white supremacists and mobs committed murder, intimidated voters, and threatened Black citizens and white allies generally, to "redeem" the South. Outright fraud was widespread in the 1876 election.[86] In this racially fraught environment Greener ventured to speak on behalf of Republican candidates around the state and beyond. Often, he was shouted down to the point that audiences could not hear him and in more than one instance armed mobs threatened him.

The 1876 fall term was delayed until November, which gave Greener more time to campaign. In October he gave speeches in Columbia and nearby Lexington. He also toured Newberry, Abbeville, Anderson, Walhalla, Greenville, Pickens, and Laurens, where he was regularly hounded by "Red Shirts" who would show up at the publicized rallies to harass and intimidate Republican candidates, speakers, and supporters. In Newberry two of his students dragged him off the stage "amid the jeers of the men on horseback."[87] In Abbeville, people were only able to hold their rally safely because it was moved to the "colored fair-ground" and were protected by federal troops.[88] To arrive at an event at the Pickens County Courthouse Greener had to ride through columns of "about twelve-hundred red-shirts" lined up on both side of the road. He was interrupted almost as soon as he started speaking and a man drew his revolver on Greener but was deterred by a Democratic state senator in attendance (even though he also was a member of the Red Shirts).[89]

When Greener spoke, he was regularly greeted with cheers for Wade Hampton or Jefferson Davis and insults and racial insults directed at him. At one event in Laurens the scene was nearly like that from a war where at least two thousand were waiting for Greener and others upon their arrival. Greener testified in Congressional hearings about this violence in December 1876, explaining that these white mobs were waving "banners, mottoes and flags—various flags—the American flag, and in one instance the confederate flag."[90] He volunteered as an election supervisor and was twice assaulted on election day. That he was never injured or shot is, in retrospect, astounding.

These experiences surely must have informed Greener's arguments that racial inequality was not a problem for his race to resolve but was rather a "white problem." In one of his most famous essays, written nearly twenty years after leaving South Carolina, "The White Problem" lays bare that racial inequality is rooted in the fear and racism of the white man. He wrote in 1894 that, "Slavery has been abolished in America; the trail of the serpent, however, yet marks the ground."[91] Greener was to witness this trail on his many travels throughout South Carolina and beyond.

Back on campus, the battle for resources was constant. In a letter to Governor Chamberlain, Greener lamented that "the want of advertising, catalogs, and general printing is crippling to a certain extent the efficiency, both of instruction and discipline."[92] Mortimer A. Warren added "We have had no books, maps, charts or aids of any kind. The State is pledged to assist us to all of these and has done nothing for us."[93] Katherine Chaddock details just how busy Greener was as a professor: "Already one of the busiest faculty members, as well as a law student, Greener embraced even more overload. He was a frequent public speaker in South Carolina and beyond, he served on the Columbia Board of Health, and he was appointed to a commission to revise the state school system. He joined the Union League of America, a nationwide organization promoting equal opportunity across the races, and represented South Carolina on its national executive council. In 1875, he became the first black scholar elected to the American Philological Association, and he was determined to be an active member."[94]

On top of this, Greener also served as college librarian from May 1875 until the end of that year.

LIBRARIAN

Richard T. Greener's time as librarian was short-lived but significant. He organized the library, lobbied the General Assembly for money for repairs, and hired Black students to help him.

Erastus Everson was elected librarian the same season as when Greener joined the faculty. The trustees had not been able to decide on a suitable candidate and finally settled for Everson after four rounds of voting. They had been right to doubt their choice of Everson; he soon proved himself ill-prepared for the job of taking care of a library in disrepair after the war. He limited the library's hours to a mere four hours per day (9 A.M. to 1 P.M.).[95] And he further confirmed that he may not be fit for the job when he simply disappeared from campus in May 1875 without explanation.

It is no wonder that Greener would take over when Everson absented himself from campus. His time at Harvard had given him experience at one of the best academic libraries in the country and he was fluent in Latin, Greek, and French, enabling him to properly handle the collection of books (something Everson had not been capable of doing). Soon the faculty formalized the role that he had taken upon himself, officially appointing him librarian.

Greener inherited a library in disarray. A trustees' report noted that the library had "scores of books, pamphlets and records now in confusion."[96] The new librarian noted in a letter to the trustees the "disorder" in which the library's holdings had been left: "most of the books were upon the floor."[97] To make matters worse, the building itself was crumbling, suffering from years of neglect of its maintenance needs during and after the Civil War, compounded by vandalism from those angry at the state of the "Radical University."

In his short tenure as librarian Greener took up three main tasks: (1) modernizing the cataloging system, creating a modern card catalog system from scratch instead of a mere list of materials (something he had helped Everson do before he left campus); (2) instituting a system for circulating books owing to the fact that many books were in offices and homes around Columbia, unaccounted for; and (3) repairing and improving the infrastructure, including falling plaster and molding shelves.[98] Creating the catalog itself was, "no slight task," he noted, owing to the condition of the library.[99] To help retrieve the books he placed announcements in local newspapers. He hired two Black student assistants to help him and lobbied the legislature personally for the funds to make the necessary repairs. Greener even worked with others to develop an official library card.[100]

By November 1875, the changes were already noticeable. The *Charleston News and Courier* reported that there was a "marked change from the dust, [and] chaos of books and confusion."[101] Greener hung portraits belonging to the Euphradian Society (not just for adornment but for their preservation) and placed busts of prominent men. He also wrote a detailed forty-page report for the federal Bureau of Education, which was later used as part of a book by the Bureau of Libraries.[102] A *News and Courier* reporter noted the careful placement of the portraits and busts:

> Here on one side may be consulted all the catalogues of books in possession of the library, and all the treasures of bibliomaniacs, on the other all the lexicons of various languages. A new alcove has been made up of the books relating to America. On one side of this alcove the books relating to the colonial and revolutionary confederation and constitutional periods are collected, with the speeches of Calhoun, Webster and Clay, and the works of Jefferson, Madison and Hamilton near at hand for easy reference. In each side of every alcove are now arranged busts of statesmen, poets, and patriots, national and State . . . I noticed for example that Cicero and Demonsthenes guarded the classical books; Calhoun,

University of South Carolina Library in 1875. Photograph by
William Main, professor of chemistry and Greener's neighbor in
Lieber House. Courtesy of South Caroliniana Library.

jurisprudence, State-craft and political economy; Martin Luther and Mil-
ton the theological quarter; Washington and Cheves and Hammon, the
American alcove; Kant and Socrates, the metaphysical side; and so on.[103]

Greener had taken on these duties as librarian without extra compensation. When
a permanent replacement was announced by the trustees he reminded them that
he had not been paid for his duties as librarian, including during the summer
months.[104] They reimbursed him for his services.[105] It is worth remembering that
Greener did all this while still maintaining his duties as professor, secretary pro
tempore of the faculty, and treasurer of corporation of the University.[106] His wife
Genevieve, gave birth to their first child, a son, Horace Kempton Greener, in
September 1875. Tragically, he died nine months later. His daughter, Belle (born
1879), became a librarian for Princeton University and then served as inaugural
librarian for the John Pierpont Morgan Library. She was known at that time as
Belle da Costa Greene. Greener's wife had separated from Greener in 1897 and
changed the family's name to Greene and began passing as white.[107]

Greener carried out his duties until his replacement, Louis G. Smith, arrived
on campus. He corresponded with the Boston Public Library, ordering materials

from them, and continued to plead with patrons, including Governor Chamberlain, to return books to the library.[108] In some instances, patrons like the governor would request for others to have access to have permission to keep books from the library that were already in their possession.[109]

Smith, Greener's successor, was less than complimentary of Greener's achievements, claiming that he found the library in the same kind of disarray that Greener had inherited and claimed that he had to create a new catalog.[110] The reporter from Charleston and other accounts seem to dispute Smith's dim view.

Cornelius Chapman Scott, in his recollection of his time at the Reconstruction-era university, wrote in 1911 that, "My impression was that the college library suffered from acts of vandalism committed by persons who were not in sympathy with the new regime, and that Professor Greener, more than any other member of the faculty, rendered valuable service in rearranging the books and restoring the library to its early condition."[111]

In 1907, while touring South Carolina, he visited and gave speeches at Allen University and Benedict College. He took advantage to see his former campus, stopping briefly to look upon his former home, Lieber College, and then to the Library. Upon entry he was not questioned about his race by the attendant, a young woman, but was asked, "Have you been a professor; you look like one?" Greener replied: "yes, a long time ago." Greener then recounted that, "While we were talking, a black man, up on a ladder replacing books spied me, and hastened down to shake my hand. Before he could speak, I greeted him cordially, turned him away from the young lady [and] whispered, 'no names!' Glad to see you; remember you very well." The man, Robert, was the same who had helped Greener in the library three decades earlier. The woman asked him if he knew Robert. "Yes, I met him when I visited the library years ago. He evidently has a good memory!"[112]

LAW STUDENT

As an undergraduate student Greener had hoped to start his legal studies at Harvard under the newly organized law school but decided he could not afford it at the time.[113] Greener explained to Senator Charles Sumner that he was interested in pursuing a legal career and got something of a head-start on his legal studies in Philadelphia, apprenticing when he could with Edward Hopper, and later in Washington at the Office of the US Attorney for the District of Columbia.[114]

The University of South Carolina School of Law was a fairly new entity, having opened in 1867 in the wake of the Civil War; however, many historians of the early twentieth century would claim that the law school actually opened in 1883 as an attempt to delegitimize the achievements of Black students who matriculated between 1873 and 1877.[115] The Law School graduated thirty-nine students between 1868 and 1876, including eleven African Americans.

Greener's entrance into the law school came at a time of transformation in the study of law in the United States. Instead of "reading law" as an apprentice under a practicing attorney, students were increasingly required to hold a bachelor's degree as a prerequisite for admission to a law school, now separate from the undergraduate college at an institution, and pedagogy became focused around the study of cases. The pioneer of these reforms was Harvard Law School's Christopher Columbus Langdell, "arguably the most influential figure in the history of legal education in the United States," who served as dean from 1870 to 1895.[116] The reforms introduced by Langdell and others made their way to law schools around the country.

Law students at South Carolina studied with Cyrus D. Melton in a two-year curriculum (that some students completed in one year). Melton was an 1840 graduate of the college and had practiced law since 1844 when he was admitted to the bar. He was appointed professor in the newly formed law school in 1869.[117] He died in the summer of 1875, and Franklin J. Moses Jr., chief justice of the South Carolina Supreme Court (a Jew and former slaveholder), took over teaching duties, holding class in his chambers on Mondays, Wednesdays, and Fridays at 5 P.M. He revised the curriculum to place more emphasis on Blackstone's *Commentaries* and Kent's *Lectures*, held moot courts, and required students to write essays on legal topics.[118]

The eleven Black students to graduate from the Law School included Walter Raleigh Jones, Henry Barton Johnson, T. McCants Stewart, Joseph Henry Stuart, Lawrence Cain, Francis Lewis Cardozo, Styless Linton Hutchins, Theophilus J. Minton, Joseph White Morris, and Paris Simkins.[119] And, of course, Richard Theodore Greener in 1876.

Walter Raleigh Jones, the first Black student admitted to the University of South Carolina Law School, was also the first Black student to enroll in any state-supported law school in the United States. An 1874 law school graduate, he was considered the "most brilliant young colored man" in the state.[120] He tragically died of meningitis in 1876, shortly after his appointment as a Richland County probate judge.

Legal scholar W. Lewis Burke details the lives and accomplishments of these African American law graduates in *All for Civil Rights: African American Lawyers in South Carolina, 1868–1968*[121] and in his book with James Lowell Underwood, *At Freedom's Door: African American Founding Fathers and Lawyers in Reconstruction South Carolina*.[122] In summary, these eleven graduates were remarkable in the scope and range of their accomplishments. In addition to their work as lawyers, they served in elected and appointed positions, as educators, pastors, and diplomats. As Allen University's second (and fourth) president, Morris established the first law school at a Black college in the South, which awarded more than thirty law degrees during his eleven-year tenure.[123] Morris succeeded another former USC law student, James C. Waters, who served as Allen University's first president.[124] Thomas E. Miller briefly attended the law school, before leaving to read law and being admitted to the state bar. He was later elected to Congress and, post-Reconstruction, became the first president of South Carolina State, the state's only public four-year university for Black students.[125] He was also a founder and second president of the all-Black South Carolina State Teachers Association.[126]

All were Republicans except T. McCants Stewart, an "anomaly" for the time, though he eventually "returned to the Grand Old Party, after being 'frozen out' of a political appointment by objecting white Democrats."[127] He was a practicing attorney in South Carolina and New York, and in the territories of Hawai'i and the US Virgin Islands. He served as an African Methodist Episcopal Church pastor, a professor at Claflin University and Liberia College, a journalist, a civil rights leader, and deputy attorney general and Supreme Court justice in Liberia.[128]

Mortimer Alanson Warren, who was white, also served as principal of the Normal School at the University of South Carolina and was an 1875 law school graduate.[129] Warren and Greener were the only students who were also on the faculty.[130]

Greener enrolled as a student in the Law School in the fall of 1874, a year after he had arrived on campus.[131] He graduated in December 1876 along with nine other law graduates that year (two white, seven Black).[132] His Law School diploma (see Image 3) was discovered in 2012 in Chicago, where Greener had lived his last years, by a construction worker before a house was demolished.[133] Also in the recovered steamer trunk with Greener's law diploma were his law license and Harvard diploma.[134]

Graduating from the Law School fulfilled his ambition to study the law, and Greener found immediate use for his legal credentials and pedigree. After leaving the university in 1877, he returned to Washington, DC. After a stint with the US Treasury Department, he served as dean of the Howard University Law School and opened his own law practice in the District. As an attorney, Greener might be best known for his defense of West Point cadet Johnson C. Whittaker, his former USC student whom he had recommended for the United States Military Academy appointment.[135] His cocounsel was former SC Governor Daniel Chamberlain. Though they lost the case, the conviction was overturned on appeal.

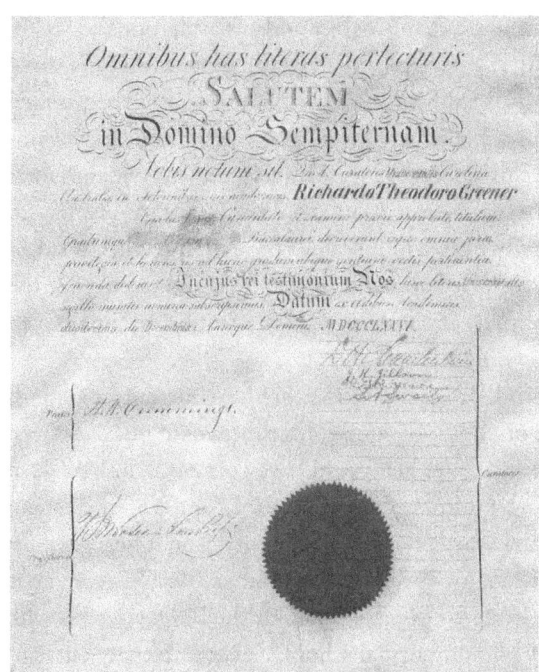

Richard T. Greener's 1876 Law School Diploma, discovered in 2012 in Chicago. Courtesy of South Caroliniana Library.

During the four years the university was integrated, thirty-six students, including Richard T. Greener, studied in the Law School and nineteen graduated. Of that number, nineteen Black students matriculated with eleven graduating and seventeen white students enrolled with eight graduating.[136]

"RICHARD THEODORE GREENER: A STORY OF A BUSY MAN"

As we take the full measure of Richard T. Greener's contributions during his short tenure at the University of South Carolina we see a remarkable career. Should we apply current conceptions of academic productivity—if we created a modern C.V. for Greener, for example—his accomplishments would be seen as nothing short of extraordinary. In less than four years, he left his mark on the campus and state. The Reconstruction-era university was doing too much with too few resources and a disproportionate share of that burden seems to have rested on Greener's shoulders. His time afterward as an activist, scholar, lawyer, administrator, and diplomat all seemed to have been shaped by his time at the University of South Carolina.

We are left to wonder what might have become of Richard T. Greener and the University of South Carolina had it not been forced shut in 1877 and he had been able to carry forward with his academic career and his aspirations to see an integrated education system at the university and across the state within the nineteenth century. Those aspirations for the University of South Carolina's eventual re-integration would be realized some ninety years later when admission of undergraduates Henrie Monteith and Robert Anderson and graduate student James Solomon marked the institution as the last southern flagship state university to desegregate.[137] However, when Greener tendered his resignation to the Board of Trustees in June 1877, he knew that he had done all that he could to advance the cause of integrated higher education at the University of South Carolina, given the growing restrictions of a dawning new era.

In this chapter we have divided Greener's time at the University of South Carolina neatly into three categories but, of course, his time would not have been so neatly divided between 1873 and 1877. He would have constantly moved from role to role, sometimes fulfilling multiple roles at once. In one routine memo detailing expenses related to the library and the preparatory school he signed as, "Librarian & Secretary of the Faculty, Professor."[138] And seeing Greener move nimbly between those roles likely served as inspiration for the Black students who matriculated in the preparatory school, normal school, classic university curriculum, and law school during his four-year tenure with the university.[139]

By the end of the grand experiment of desegregation at the Reconstruction-era university of South Carolina, nearly two hundred students had enrolled in the institution; however, most students were enrolled in the college preparatory department. Graduates of the era were recipients of sixteen bachelor's degrees, eleven law degrees, and a few teaching credentials. Most graduates and former students of the Reconstruction-era university rose to prominence in their own lifetimes after they left the university, producing five college presidents, two congressmen,[140] numerous lawyers, business owners, educators, theologians, journalists, a novelist, an agricultural inventor, foreign diplomats, and a Liberian Supreme Court justice.

In addition to the law alumni already mentioned, there were other former students from the college preparatory department, Normal School, and baccalaureate program that Greener would have taught and worked with. Educator Robert Lloyd Smith embarked upon a political career in Texas.[141] Educator and physician Dr. William A. Sinclair[142] was an integral part of the 1905 Niagara Movement and a founding member of the National Association for the Advancement of Colored People (NAACP).[143] Real estate investor and financier Whitefield McKinlay held great influence behind the scenes in the nation's seat of power, serving as a civil rights adviser to US presidents McKinley, (Theodore) Roosevelt, and Taft.[144] Educator Clarissa Minnie Thompson Allen, a graduate of the Normal School, was one of the earliest Black female novelists in the nation.[145] Her forty-one-chapter serialized novel, *Treading the Winepress*, ran for several months in *The Christian Recorder* and the *Boston Advocate*, a Black-owned newspaper of the era, beginning in 1885.[146]

These are but a few of the people with whom Greener would have associated in the classroom, at the dining hall, in the library, and on the grounds of the university. We cannot help but wonder what those conversations must have been like.

The reforms instituted in the Reconstruction-era USC, including financial assistance for students, stayed in place when the institution reopened for whites only in 1880. The sons of poor white families benefited from the very policies put in place by the Black legislature and trustees.[147] Historian Daniel Walker Hollis notes that, "Interestingly enough, when the second South Carolina College went into operation after Reconstruction, its curriculum was basically much nearer that of the Radical University than that of the ante-bellum College or the University of 1866." This, he concludes, indicates that "the Radical professors were well informed on current trends in higher education."[148]

The end of Reconstruction and the closure of the University of South Carolina "reveals the fragility of some types of change."[149] The university had made enormous changes and long strides toward equality of access to higher education, all made even more remarkable by the fact that this took place in the state that instigated the Civil War. Greener's colleague Fisk Brewer, in his defense of the integrated university in 1876, said of its importance and its imperfections: "It is for the interests of sound learning and for the advantage of all the people that the true condition of the university should be known. Its merits should be acknowledged, its imperfections should not be denied."[150] Modern historian Tyler D. Parry concurs: "The Radical University was not a perfect institution, but it did try to rectify the systemic problems that historically barred large segments of the population from gaining an advanced education."[151]

That the ideology of white supremacy would rear its head and fight back against this progress is not surprising. But the Reconstruction-era USC leaves us with intriguing questions of what could have been had it been able to persist. The original intent behind the founding of South Carolina College in 1801 was to create educated men to lead but this also included creating men equipped to defend and support the institution of chattel slavery.[152] Greener argued for refashioning the institution to harmonize with the principles of equality for all espoused in the Declaration of Independence. What if this trajectory had persisted? What if Greener had seen this idea flourish? The accomplishments of men and women graduates of the short-lived integrated university and normal school give us some sense of the answers to these questions. The antebellum South Carolina College had a significant impact on the state and nation; what greater influence might the Reconstruction-era USC have had?

Greener's life after South Carolina was uneven. He had great accomplishments—serving as dean of the Howard University Law School, as the administrator of the Grant Monument Association, as a lawyer, and as a diplomat to Russia—but also suffered setbacks and disappointments, both personal and professional. His family left him, and he lost his second family in Vladivostok, where he had hoped to return but was never able. Greener vacillated between trying to curry favor with both Booker T. Washington and W. E. B. Du Bois and never quite fully settled in one camp or the other. This may help explain, at least in part, why he was largely forgotten over time.

We consider one final question about Greener and his time at the University of South Carolina: Why did he refer to himself as a South Carolinian after leaving the state? He had lived in Philadelphia, Boston, and Washington, DC, before coming to Columbia and would live in other great American cities afterward, including New York and Chicago. What was it about his time, less than four years in all, in South Carolina that made him feel this kinship to the state? At the University of South Carolina, he contributed greatly and was respected for his contributions. He flourished in a multiracial environment despite having to navigate treacherous terrain. He returned to the state several times, speaking at various Black colleges and universities, but never again on his home campus. He also fondly recalled his days at Harvard so perhaps it his love of academic life that informed his calling himself a South Carolinian.

In 1882, a biographical portrait of Greener was published with the title *Richard Theodore Greener: A Story of a Busy Man*.[153] If anything, that seems to be an understatement.

Chapter Four

LAYING THE MOUNTAINS LOW

The Life and Education of Simon Peter Smith, 1845–1914

Evan A. Kutzler

As US colleges and universities reckon with their historical ties to slavery and white supremacy, there is a keen desire to recover and amplify African American voices. Yet the experiences of enslaved men, women, and children often appear in the historical record, if at all, as fragments. Simon Peter Smith's enslavement at South Carolina College, the antebellum campus of the University of South Carolina, was no exception, but his writings in freedom offer unique details. Born into slavery in the 1840s, Smith's extensive writings began twenty years later in a letter to Edward Franklin Williams, a white minister fifteen years his senior, with themes that echoed in their correspondence until 1914. Smith needed money to travel from Chattanooga to Washington, DC, but his optimism and ambition shined through. "I want to get agood education," Smith wrote in his first preserved letter. "I will try an do what I can now / but I should lik[e] very much to be with your number." He reminded Williams "how sweet the name of Jesus sounds to the believer" and his earnest desire to "over come temtation" and lead a Christian life.[1]

That Smith wrote, Williams kept, and the Amistad Research Center preserved more than one hundred letters between a freedman and a white minister made this unlikely biographical essay possible. Yet the sixty-thousand-word collection has been insufficient to bring sustained attention to his life and voice. It began piecemeal. Scholars first drew attention to Smith's private political thoughts on Reconstruction. In one of the letters, Smith struggled with the decision whether to leave Howard University and finish his education at the University of South Carolina. Going to school in Columbia meant returning to his home state, being near family, and receiving a free education. Smith also had traumatic memories of the school in its antebellum years as South Carolina College. He implied that returning would be a personal and symbolic achievement. "When quite a small boy I use to wait on southern students in that college," Smith recalled. "And I remember once of standing in the door of one of the buildings and cried because I could not go to school. Now thank God there has been a great change, the mountains have been brought low and the vallies are exalted and the way is open for me to go there."[2] Traumatic memories pulled at him to return, but it was an insufficient tug. Smith stayed at Howard University.

The University of South Carolina has taken steps to acknowledge its connections to slavery, including enslaving people and renting human skills, knowledge, and labor from other enslavers. Yet Simon Smith has not been part of the university's commemorative effort. JoAnn Zeise, one of the graduate students who researched and wrote *Slavery at South Carolina College, 1801–1865: The Foundations of the University of South Carolina*, discovered the key excerpt more than one year after graduate students finished the website. Smith's name and words were set to appear in "Revealing slavery's legacy at a public university in the South," a three-part reflective essay on the project in 2014. Unfortunately, the editors of History@Work cut Smith's story and voice to keep the essay focused only on what was written on the website. *Ghosts of the Horseshoe*, a (now-defunct) mobile application that used augmented reality to bring the story of slavery at USC to life, is the only public-facing project to utilize his name and voice.[3]

Belated discoveries, heavy-handed editorial decisions, and short-lived mobile apps have consequences. When the university administration took the admirable step of unveiling two historical markers in December 2017, the panel text included many of the names who appear in college records: "Abraham, Amanda, Anna, Anthony, Charles, Henry, Jack, Jim, Joe, Lucy, Mal., Peter, Sancho and his wife, Simon, and Tom." The marker reminds readers of the importance of calling the names. "Naming these individuals," it reads, "is an effort to remember all of those who made significant and substantial contributions to the University of South Carolina." Unfortunately, just as there is no clear mention of Smith, there is also no indication that enslaved people had lives beyond enslavement. One wonders whether the university would have made the same choice had Smith's life and words been prominently included in earlier interpretive products.[4]

Following Smith's long life offers an opportunity to individualize the experience of someone once enslaved at South Carolina College. Individual lives cross the artificial boundaries of historical periodization and Smith's freedom writings raise an obvious but unexplored point: enslavement did not define him. This has implications for imagining the real people behind those names on USC's new historical marker. Changing "slave" to "enslaved" is a step in the direction of recognizing humanity; however, when writers do not move someone from slavery to freedom in text, it keeps that person enslaved to a warped historical memory. This oversight is no better—and perhaps a great deal worse—than running afoul of the latest rhetorical effort to acknowledge humanity amid inhumanity.[5]

This is more than an essay about slavery and/or freedom. Smith's life touches on themes of African American education, religion, masculinity, systems of patronage, and the American Missionary Association. In an effort not to cast Smith's life too narrowly, this essay follows but does not focus solely on any one of these themes. My aim is to construct a narrative of one person, once enslaved by the University of South Carolina, whose life went far beyond the brick walls of the antebellum campus.

FROM SLAVERY TO FREEDOM TO SCHOOL

Uncertainty shrouds large chunks of Simon Peter Smith's life. In fact, no definite record of his life exists before 1867. After falling out with the American Missionary Association in 1887, his thoughts and movements became shrouded again until he reconnected with Edward Williams a decade later. Smith's parentage—a father from Virginia and a mother from South Carolina—echo the antebellum slave trade between the upper and lower South. His family life also reflected the hurricane of movement of the Civil War era. Whereas Smith ended up in Chattanooga, Tennessee, and then Washington, DC, his mother, father, and sister went to Jacksonville, Florida. They did not communicate again until 1870. "My mother heard through some students traveling over the South that I was here [Howard University,] so she wrote me a letter," Smith wrote. "This caused me to rejoice much and praise God for his goodness and for his wonderful works."[6] That his mother, a literate woman herself, succeeded in finding her son suggests that both mother and child kept the surname of their enslavers.

In the 1850s, a half-dozen slaveholding households with the surname Smith lived in Richland County, South Carolina. George Smith, the only Smith to locally register a will between 1840 and 1864, bequeathed dozens of enslaved people, including a person named Simon, to his wife and sons. By 1860, then, a Simon Smith belonged to John A. Smith, an enslaver of twenty-six men, women, and children. Three enslaved males matched Simon Smith's age range of thirteen to fifteen. In addition to waiting on students, Simon Smith laid bricks. His brother, Harrison, still worked with bricks at the end of the century in Washington, DC.[7]

Amid the mobility of Civil War armies and the flood of refugees, Smith ended up hundreds of miles from Columbia in 1865. Although there is no obvious connection between the white Smith family and Chattanooga, there is value in constructing a *plausible* path to freedom. Several South Carolina regiments fought in north Georgia and eastern Tennessee in the fall of 1863. Tens of thousands of enslaved people experienced the war alongside Confederate armies. Smith may have been a so-called camp slave or body servant to a white Smith. Did he escape to Union lines and seize freedom under the Second Confiscation Act? Was he a refugee in a "contraband camp" for the rest of the war? While the events that led Smith to Chattanooga are unclear, he ended up there alone, poor, and—most importantly—a free man.[8]

Pursuing an education became one of Smith's first acts of freedom. Smith, like many Black men, women, and children in the 1860s, needed no enlightenment to understand the social, religious, economic, and political benefits of literacy and education.[9] It was through his initiative in Chattanooga that Smith began a lifelong relationship with Edward Franklin Williams. Moving to Chattanooga in 1866 to serve as principal of the Lookout Mountain Educational Institutions, Williams oversaw a coeducational, multiracial student body. He left Chattanooga in 1867 when the American Missionary Association appointed him to teach (he stayed only briefly) in the Normal and Preparatory Division of Howard University.[10] Smith reflected on their first encounter twenty years later. Smith addressed his letter to "Dear Friend," but the text played on parental metaphors. Referring to Williams as "my Dear Father," Smith credited Williams as the "one who first extended a helping hand" at the end of the Civil War. "Ah!" he wrote, "I remember with great pleasure the night that you invited me to your room at Lookout Mt. and gave me such encouraging words about study." According to Smith's recollection, after he told Williams good night, "you extended me your hand and I said I will see you in the morning but you still held out your hand and said good night a second time, and took my hand[.] You do not know what tender love it kindled in my heart towards you at that moment." Returning to the metaphor a second time, Smith concluded, "I love you and my mother with parental tenderness."[11]

Effusions of intimacy, what Smith referred to as "out bursts of my soul," require caution, context, and serious consideration. There was an important economic relationship between the two men. From 1867 to 1888, Williams directly or indirectly supported Smith with thousands of dollars. Both men also knew the cultural mores of nineteenth-century America, including the racist paternalism that pervaded organizations like the American Missionary Association. Had Williams or the AMA described the affection, one might rightly discount it as a white fantasy. With care to the power relationships at work, one must consider the possibility that Smith meant it.

Williams arranged Smith's travel from Chattanooga to Washington, DC, and his matriculation into Howard University. Writing to Freedmen's Bureau Commissioner Oliver Otis Howard, Williams described Smith as "exceedingly desirous of obtaining an education but has no means of his own," and asked the bureau to pay his transportation. When the Freedmen's Bureau denied the request, Williams turned to Rev. Lewis F. Clark, pastor of the Whitinsville, Massachusetts, Congregational Church, to cover Smith's tuition and boarding costs. Clark reported to Williams in July 1867 that Whitinsville had raised $187.78 for Smith. He requested that Smith "write to us pretty soon [so] that we may see what he is now & compare it with what he will become after a Washington training. We shall be glad to hear from him as often as you may think best to have him write."[12] Smith received money from the church for years to come. On Thanksgiving Day in 1869, for instance, Clark raised an additional $150.00 for Smith.[13] The relationship to Whitinsville Congregational Church was as essential to Smith's education as his correspondence with, and enduring connection to, Williams. In the fall of 1867, Smith became one of the ninety-four students enrolled at Howard University.[14]

STUDYING AT HOWARD UNIVERSITY

Andrew Johnson signed the legislation chartering Howard University on March 2, 1867, the same day Congress overrode his veto of the First Reconstruction Act. In the late summer, the university became Smith's home for the next nine years. He was among the first twenty-nine students to graduate from the Preparatory Department in 1872. Four years later, he graduated from the College Department.[15] When Smith arrived there were three terms: a fall term from early October until Christmas eve; a winter term from the second of January until late March; and a summer term from early April until late June.

After Williams resigned as principal of Howard and left the city, Smith's letters filled the physical space between the two men and included detailed descriptions of campus life. He watched more advanced students give physiology and theology recitations with keen interest. There were "speeches and compositions" each Friday. "We have music scattered along withe the speaking and we have very good times," Smith recorded. He learned to draw every continent and in the late spring of 1868 he prepared for a grammar examination. He also noted efforts to improve the appearance and health of the campus. The university painted the bedrooms, the recitation rooms, the fences, and even parts of the trees with whitewash. Other landscape improvements included a new gate and a walkway seeded with new grass.[16]

Smith received more than just a classical education at Howard University. In addition to offering Greek, Latin, philosophy, and the sciences, university officials appointed Captain Melville Cary Wilkinson to organize male students into the "Howard University Cadets" in 1869. For the next five years, students purchased uniforms, drilled with "cadet muskets," practiced sword and bayonet exercises, and learned gymnastics. Smith described the rigid schedule: the bell rang at 6:00 A.M.; room inspection took place at 6:25 followed by roll call at 6:30 and a march to breakfast; church exercises began at 9:00 followed by classes until noon when the cadets marched to dinner; drill commenced at 4:30 P.M. until the cadets marched to supper at 5:00. Elected corporal in 1871, Smith often served as officer of the day and led the color guard. The same semester the school added a military component, Smith and nine other students organized the Christian Association of Howard University. Smith served as the president of the student organization.[17]

In addition to military and religious exercises, Smith became an active member of the local Republican party. Although citizens of the District of Columbia did not vote in the 1868 presidential election, Smith attended both of Ulysses S. Grant's inaugurations. "Washington was thronged with people from all parts of the United States," he wrote. "And there was also many glad shouts and sonorous voices going up for their President[.] The night following[,] the Capitol was luminated and also a new house which has been lately build here on the University ground." Smith beamed with hope because he believed "we have a president now who will execute laws to the achievement of our nation." He closely followed legislative debates. Smith observed thousands going to the capital to watch the debates over the Civil Rights Bill in 1875 and "the greates[t] agitation" hung over the city for weeks.[18]

Washington's excitements, dangers, and expenses made for high attrition at Howard University. Students fell sick and Smith frequently complained of ill health. He suffered with a toothache for weeks in 1874 and the pain continued well after its extraction. Student deaths at Howard—like at other nineteenth-century universities—were common. Charles Asbury Harris, who roomed with Smith in 1869 and 1870, died of tuberculosis one week before fall classes commenced in 1871. From October 1873 to March 1874, Smith reported the deaths of six Howard University students from disease. Other students left for financial reasons. Simeon James Reed Nelson added his own note in an outgoing letter from Smith. "I was sorry to leave school," he wrote, "but I am poor as you know and was compelled for this reason to do so. I am now teaching school in Virginia but I do not know how long the Ku Klux will let me remain." This anxiety took a toll on Smith. He worried about having to leave the university without a degree or dying of sickness while pursuing his studies. Seven years after entering Howard, Smith noted that Williams would only recognize three other students: Hugh M. Browne, Ferman G. Shadd, and William "Knox" Brown. "They have scattered and fled some one way and some an other," Smith wrote. "Some are preaching and some are teaching. Some are married and some are dead. And some are loiterers a bout the streets, of Washington."[19]

The financial burden of college tuition, room and board, books, clothing, and washing created constant strain. Teaching night school offered little pay ($.30/ night) and undermined Smith's studies. In 1871 and 1872, he worked as a janitor. Summer teaching sounded promising, but Smith never found steady work in a schoolhouse. For at least two summers, Smith and other Howard students worked as waiters at the Ocean Hotel near President Ulysses S. Grant's house in Long Branch, New Jersey. It may have been the first time Smith saw the ocean. "I was bathing in the Ocean last night with several of the boys and we went so far out in the water that a wave came [and] knocked me down and before I could get up another came and knocked me down again," he wrote, "and it frightened me a little and I soon came out." Another year Smith made his own speaking circuit through Rhode Island and Massachusetts churches and Young Men's Christian Associations. Along the way he visited Martha's Vineyard, Harvard College, Newton Seminary, and nearly accepted an invitation to finish school at Boston University. Expenses always caught up and Smith fell back on Williams and the Whitinsville Church each semester.[20]

Money—and politics—nearly induced Smith to leave Howard University for South Carolina in the winter of 1873–74. The Panic of 1873, combined with the closing of the Freedmen's Bureau one year earlier, made it difficult for Howard University to pay its professors. At the same time, congressional investigations into Oliver O. Howard, who resigned as the university president on November 30, 1873, angered students. At least five of nine South Carolinians in the collegiate department left for South Carolina University: Thomas McCants Stewart, Cornelius C. Scott, William M. Dart, John M. Morris, and Paul J. Mishow. The merits of leaving were obvious to Smith. "I understand that the state gives each student, who enters the institution at Columbia, a scholarship of Two Hundred Dollars per year," he remarked. "They have nothing to pay for rooms, and I understand they have very good instruction there." It is harder to understand why Smith did not follow the other South Carolinians. The memory of enslavement at South Carolina College may not have been the only reason he stayed. None of the South Carolinians who left were officers in the Howard University Cadets. Smith delayed his decision, decided to stay, and graduated from Howard University two years later.[21]

RETURNING TO COLUMBIA

More than a decade after leaving South Carolina, Simon P. Smith returned to Columbia in the late spring of 1877. Many relatives had died in his absence, including his father in 1871, but it was a happy homecoming. Smith wrote, "My mother rejoiced much to see me," and he enjoyed walking through the capital city as a free man with a college education. "Of all the cities that ever I, have visited," Smith confided, "I think Columbia is one of the moss beautiful places that I ever saw. Nearly every street is shaded by large trees; they form almoss an arch across the streets. You may walk the streets here on the hottess Summer day and you need no umbrella to screen you from the rays of the burning sun. The sun cannot smite you by day nor the moon by night." He also remarked on the houses and gardens. Passing the former mansion of John S. Preston on Blanding Street on the way to the South Carolina State House, Smith found himself "compelled to stop and wonder at the beauty." He saw "trees of all kinds [and] flowers of every description; the willow, and the maple, and the magnolias are *very* numerous." It was stunning to both the eyes and nose. "The very streets are perfumed with their fragrance," Smith continued. "This garden is a perfect Eden[.] All it needs is an Adam and Eve to keep it clean." On his walk through the city, Smith also found the city park enchanting, but believed that a northern city would keep it in better repair.[22]

While "Rebels" owned most of the "pleasant homes," Smith found that "many of our people have made themselves some very beautiful homes here." South Carolina State Senator William Beverly and Dorcas Nash owned "one of the most beautiful" houses in the city. "His parlors are decorated with the moss costly furniture, his flower garden is moss enchanting," Smith reported. "I knew this man before the war closed[.] He and his wife were born slaves [and] were not freed until Sherman came here in Feb. 65. Now they are as fine as [anybody] in the city." The Nash home represented to Smith the revolutionary potential of Reconstruction.[23]

The beauty of Columbia only made the political direction of the state more painful. Smith's return to Columbia came in the twilight of Reconstruction between the election of 1876 and the first convening of legislators in the fall of 1877. He saw in the present that arc of nineteenth century history: a revolutionary movement stalled; conservative counterforces poised to prevail. "It grieves me to think that the Ruling powers here at this time are those who are endeavoring to crush the life out of the colored people," Smith admitted, "and I cannot see how the colored people will ever be in power here again." One of the most important issues was education. Smith believed that "those who style themselves as leaders [among] the colored people" did not have the wherewithal "sufficient to cope with white people," and he blamed this on state policy. "They have refused to make an appropriation for the State University," he continued. "Every thing about this Institute now is dead. The Professors are all leaving because they cannot get a support." Visiting the State House, he found Democrats "jubilant" and Republicans "in despondency." He looked to two Black state senators, two state representatives, and recently resigned state treasurer Francis Lewis Cardozo for good news but found them "all [without] hope." While four of the five men still held elected office, their influence had evaporated with the violent, fraudulent, and contested election of former enslaver and Confederate General Wade Hampton III in 1876. "They all seem to think that the colored man is done in this state and he cannot do [anything] more."[24]

The shifting tide in South Carolina also meant that Smith's homecoming would not be a permanent one. His once-powerful friends were unable to help him secure a stable job. When common work paid only twenty-five to thirty cents per day in Columbia, it meant that the African American population could hardly support the salary of a teacher. "Labor is worth nothing and provision [is] higher than I know is to be anywhere else," Smith wrote. "Want sits on many brow! I know not what our people will do here now."[25] The state would not support a Black public school and the starvation wages meant that most Black families could not afford private schools. Smith preached nearly every Sabbath up to three times per day without receiving a cent. "I thought I could get some money that way without fail," he wrote. "Spoke to a preacher of one of the largest churches in this city once or twice, but he says the people are not able." Smith found the same problems miles into the surrounding countryside. "There is no money about here and when the country people bring their produce to the city they hardly get [anything] for what they bring," Smith continued. "Cotton and politics have ruined this state." In the countryside, he had an additional fear. Smith worried about being targeted by "Ku Klux."[26]

Fear of violence, even assassination, kept Smith on edge in the Columbia vicinity that summer, but this caution did not extend to his private observations concerning the class and racial consequences of Hampton's governorship. For Smith, the rise of Hampton represented the reestablishment of the antebellum aristocracy. If Hampton's governorship were oppressive toward African Americans, it was a con on "our poor white trash or sandhill crackers" who thought their lives would improve after Hampton "redeemed" South Carolina from Republican control. "Now they are grumbling," Smith remarked optimistically. "They don't like Hampton." In returning South Carolina to the rule of the antebellum elite, Hampton and other "conservatives" and "bourbons" also represented a return of state-educated white southerners. Most of the new leadership had gone to South Carolina College when the only African Americans on campus were enslaved.[27]

African Americans in the capital city debated that summer about the way forward after the rise of Hampton. On August 20, 1877, Smith attended a meeting about emigrating to Africa led by a Charleston reverend. The speaker argued that conditions would not improve if they stayed in South Carolina another two thousand years. As Smith observed, "Many of them are determined to go and I cannot blame them for they are in bad condition here; they are worse off now than if they were slaves; they once felt that they were protected by the US Government, but since this late experiment they feel that they have been a bandon[ed]." Discussing the changing political situation in South Carolina with Francis Cardozo and a northern white preacher, one of the men suggested that the US government had retreated to a domestic policy of "might makes right." This statement stuck with Smith even if it pained him to believe it. He reflected, "if this statement is not wholly true it is certainly more than half true." By August 1877, after a yearlong educational interlude and a summer making no money in Columbia, Smith asked Williams to help him travel north again to enter the Chicago Theological Seminary.[28]

FIGHTING FOR RESPECTABILITY

Seminary was the pinnacle of Simon P. Smith's educational life. Whereas it took nine years to complete preparatory and collegiate courses at Howard University, the Chicago Theological Seminary took only three years. Smith matriculated into the second or "middle" class in 1877 and, living alone in Keyes Hall for two years, he completed his study in 1879. According to one newspaper, Smith gave "the best graduating speech" at commencement on the subject, "The Effect of Freedom Upon the Freedmen's Religion."[29] During his time in Chicago, the Whitinsville congregation and possibly Williams grew weary of supporting Smith. Enclosing $100 in April 1879, Edward Whitin wrote, "We are glad for your sake as well as Simons that he has now completed his course of study, and hope that in his life work he will be as successful as he seems to have been as a student."[30] Over the next decade, Smith worked for the American Missionary Association in Georgia, Washington, DC, and Tennessee, and he wrote more frequently about race, class, and respectability. His tenure as a missionary also brought to the surface conflict between Smith and the white AMA leadership.

On his way from Chicago to Georgia in 1879, Smith crossed into a segregated transportation system for the first time. After switching trains in Nashville, Smith found himself locked out of white-only cars and trapped in ones with intemperate white men. "Soon after I got in the car a great many white men came into the car where I was and I thought it was all right," Smith wrote, "but I soon found that they were all smokers and I was smoked all the way from Nashville to Chattanooga." Between Chattanooga to Atlanta, white men tried to bait the minister into a confrontation. Smith still held out hope that respectable Black men could expect fair treatment in southern states. In Marietta, Georgia, a year later, Smith described an upcoming trial of three poor white "desperados" who "began prowling [among] the colored people in this town like demons from the lower regions." They made a mistake in harassing Andrew J. Rogers, a prosperous Black barber. Smith believed that "it will cost them more than they are able to pay," and he predicted the men would soon be on a chain gang. What he seemed not to notice was the report in the Marietta newspaper trivializing the case and burying it among sensational articles about Black crime.[31]

As his travel writings allude, class shaped Smith's understanding of the world and featured in his professional life. Taking up his post at the Lincoln Mission, a Sabbath School in Washington, DC, Smith believed that success required support from the Black middle class. According to Smith, "These children that come to the Lincoln Mission S.S. are still from the poorest and some of the lowest classes of colored people in Washington. You can scarcely get any of the so called better class of colored people here to even teach a Bible class in their S.S." He interpreted the divisions in terms of respectability. The Black middle class in Washington, including Smith, held poor Black children in contempt. "I never saw worse children in my life," Smith complained. "They often make so much noise while I am preaching that I have to stop and speak to them." His private view paralleled his public one. Writing for the *American Missionary*, Smith blamed the children's behavior on idle parents who failed to "bring them up as they should." Smith hoped a "lady missionary" would come and "teach the mothers of these children how to make homes happy." He also wanted to evict the "low societies" who used the mission as a dance hall until 3 A.M. The effect of disorderly children and sinful adults gave Lincoln Mission, as Smith put it privately, "a bad name [among] the good colored people."[32]

A bad name was no small concern to Smith. After all, failure at the Lincoln Mission threatened his career. "I am hammering a way and would be glad if I had some thing to hammer on," he remarked. "At times it seems as if I am only striking in the air and hitting nothing." Smith did not shy away from administrative recommendations to render his hammering more effective. He believed Congregationalists should follow the lead of other denominations to build better churches, pay ministers higher salaries, and cultivate integrated congregations. The DC Presbyterians, for example, had recently named a Black minister as the moderator of session. "That is great honor," Smith exclaimed, and he advised Williams that Congregationalists should follow other denominations in "honoring respectable negroes." The Lincoln Mission seemed to symbolize malaise. Smith stopped social gatherings in the Mission, but Black churches continued to use the space without much oversight. "If I were to go and preach every Sunday in a theatre," Smith complained, "I would be dismissed from the A.M.A. and yet I am to preach every Sunday in a place that has been more degraded. Will respectable people come? Let the A.M.A. build a house and take us out of here and we will have a good congregation." The themes of respectability, fears about his mission, and the lack of AMA support reverberated throughout Smith's tenure at the Lincoln Mission.[33]

The appointment of white teachers over African American students also struck Smith as a problem that led Black students to look down on Black teachers. "It is not well to train colored youth too much with white people," Smith feared, because "they soon begin to think that their own people do not know anything, or that they are not competent teachers." His concern also extended to churches. "Every colored pastor that goes to any of our churches in the South that have had white pastors will meet with this prejudice. The A.M.A. ought to put all colored pastors in their pulpits in the South as soon, and as fast as they are qualified to fill them; it will be the means of making them appreciate their own people."[34]

Alongside missionary work, Smith became more vocal about politics and justice. In the late spring of 1880, Smith disagreed with Williams and argued that it set a bad precedent to nominate Grant for a third term. That summer he also became associate editor of the *People's Advocate*, an African American newspaper printed in Alexandria, Virginia. He reported favorably on Garfield's acceptance of the Republican Party's nomination. Despite unfulfilled promises, Smith advised against division. "The success of the republican party in many respects, is the success of the Negro," Smith warned. "The defeat of the republican party, is the defeat of the Negro." Smith signed few articles in the *Advocate*, but as associate editor he shaped its content on national politics, race, and religion over the next two years. On civil rights, Smith became uncompromising. During a national meeting of Congregationalists in Chicago in 1886, restaurateur Robert J. Massop refused to let Smith sit down and eat. Smith successfully took Massop to court and received $125 in damages.[35]

In these peak years of his public life, Smith's satisfaction with missionary work wore off and his relationship with the AMA soured. He resented begging for money and supplies. Smith became defensive when members or AMA officials complained; he longed for a permanent appointment at Howard University. A reassignment from the Lincoln Mission to a church in Knoxville in 1883 created a rift between Smith and the AMA that widened over time. In 1887, amid church grumblings, AMA officials suggested moving the reverend again. Smith accused the organization of abuse: making him build churches in difficult places and, just as the work began to prosper, letting another man "have all the honor while I am buried out of sight." The most insulting charge involved the cleanliness of Smith and his church. One AMA official wrote to Williams, "I am just a little afraid myself that he [Smith] has not escaped the dangers to a certain indolence and negligence which, while constant temptations to us all, are especially temptations to the colored people." The assault against his appearance and work ethic struck at the core of Smith's self-conscious investment in conspicuous respectability. "As to my dress of course I cannot wear clothing like the preacher who is getting three or four thousand dollars a year," Smith told Williams. "But [nevertheless], water is plentiful and I make good use of it." While Smith eventually left congregationalism, he first left the missionary field for churches in Illinois, Mississippi, and North Carolina.[36]

Personal problems compounded professional ones. Smith felt social pressure in Washington, DC, to marry. By the spring of 1881, Martha E. "Mattie" Pryor, the eldest daughter of a middle-class Black family, rejected—or at least deferred—a marriage proposal. Smith inferred the rejection had to do with his small salary. Mattie Pryor was a teacher in public schools and made a salary 30 percent higher than Smith. "I do not care to work and wait for a lady and then after she is married, she is not satisfied," he asserted. "If I must love a lady better than myself, I want her to love me as well as she loves her self. I do not think I shall ever ask this lady for her hand again." Despite his hurt pride, Smith proposed again, and Pryor eventually consented, but Smith's move to Knoxville and money problems prevented them from marrying in April 1885. That fall she asked Smith to give her another year. "I refused to do that and I presume that we will have no further correspondence. She gave me reasons why she desired me to wait another year, but I did not think that they were sufficient reasons, and I thought the best thing that we could do was to break up. She still continues to write but I will break off correspondence."[37]

In the end, Mattie and the Pryor family broke off the engagement. By the fall of 1886, Smith still wanted to marry her; or, at least, he liked the idea of marrying into her family. "I believe if I was married that I would be a much better man every way," he admitted. "It seems to me that a man is not a full man until he is married. But I will never marry just simply to be marrying. The great reason that I have born so patiently with Miss Mattie E. Pryor so long is because I know that she is a woman of worth." Marrying into the Pryor family would increase his social standing. Mattie's father, Charles, worked for the Department of the Interior's Bureau of Education; Ellsworth, her young brother, graduated from Howard University's preparatory department and then from Oberlin College. From their comfortable two-story house on East Capitol Street, neither Mattie nor her mother liked the idea of her moving to Knoxville, Tennessee. After six years, their correspondence ended in the winter of 1887 right as Smith's simmering troubles with the AMA boiled over.[38]

IN AND OUT OF THE ARCTIC NIGHT

Correspondence between Smith and Williams was one of the casualties of the former's falling out with the AMA. Letters became less frequent after 1887; for nine years, the two men may not have corresponded at all. In scattered 1888 letters, Smith asked Williams to help Alexander C. Williams, a young protégé of Smith, attend the Chicago Theological Seminary. Fallout from the AMA feud continued: "The best part of the year, has been darkness to me, but an arctic night does not last all the year." After working at missions for little pay, Smith had accumulated considerable debt, including money he owed on his mother's funeral expenses.[39]

Some things had changed when Smith and Williams began communicating again in 1897. For one thing, Smith had either just left the Congregational Church for the Presbyterian Church or he was about to do so.[40] He had also married and his wife, Katie A. Smith, lived in Fayetteville, North Carolina, while Simon traveled from church to church. The two never had children. Moreover, Katie also never liked North Carolina. When she fell ill, Katie wanted to return to "her old house" in Charlottesville, Virginia. In a rare mention of his wife, Smith wrote that Katie owned "a small real estate left her there and thinks she would like to live on it. It is quite valuable. It is only a half block from Main St." When she moved back to Charlottesville, she lived at 520 Pearl Street with relatives, William E. and Nessine "Nannie" Cox Jackson, part of a middle-class Black family.[41]

Other aspects of Smith's life from the 1870s and '80s also remained the same into the early twentieth century. His traveling work continued into his sixties after Katie Smith's death in 1911. In North Carolina, Smith traveled through the "backwoods country" towns and over dirt roads that burned his feet through his shoes. He continued to witness the transition from Reconstruction to the so-called New South. Smith wrote in 1908 that "it is getting hard for colored people to live in N.C. The prejudice against those who are getting education, and property[,] within the past five years is greater than ever—and they are making times tough for the black man." In 1879, Smith had expected Georgia courts to protect property regardless of race; thirty years later, he expected white plaintiffs, lawyers, and courts to seize African American property. In Smith's last extant letter, written only three months before his death, he still hoped to beat the whole-body pains that afflicted him for months. He worried about his doctor's debts and observed that "the cotton is all in and the black man has no other source to look for money." He also provided two ways to reach him: a post office box and a new street address.[42]

There was something unique about that last address. Smith lived many places in seventy years, but nearly all of them have vanished from the landscape. Howard University and the Chicago Theological Seminary demolished their early brick dormitories last century. Likewise, the historic Lincoln Mission in DC is not the building that Smith knew and the houses he rented in Atlanta and Knoxville are long gone. Even the house where Katie and Simon called home until her death in 1911 is a vacant lot. The only building that tethers Smith's life and letters to a specific spot is the last address in his last letter to Williams: 135 Blount Street in Fayetteville, North Carolina. The two-story Victorian-era building, likely the last place he lived before his death, still stands. Like the fingerprints Smith sometimes left on his letters, the house is a small reminder of Smith's life.

Smith is one of the least known—but also one of the most knowable—African American men who shaped the antebellum campus. His passing reference in 1873, when "the mountains have been brought low and the vallies are exalted," links the steps of one of those historic buildings to Smith's enslavement, his child-hood memories, and his rise out of slavery. In remembering Smith, readers—and researchers—are confronted with a long, complicated, nonlinear journey of which this essay can only scratch the surface. Slavery did not define Smith's life as a tragic waste just as his educational achievements did not guarantee him a comfortable professional life in freedom. Mountains had indeed been brought low by 1873; and yet, as Smith's later life and the long arc of African American history would demonstrate, there were mountains beyond mountains to level and valleys beyond valleys to exalt.

Chapter Five

STRUGGLE FOR EDUCATIONAL ACCESS IN SOUTH CAROLINA, 1865–1890

Brian A. Robinson

African Americans, on the grounds of South Carolina's flagship university as students and faculty members, and African Americans teaching and learning in a state-supported public school system, characterized a victory in the state's history, albeit temporary, for educational growth and access. This chapter attempts to situate the opening and closing of the University of South Carolina to African Americans into a larger struggle between educational access and educational restriction.

This story focuses on educational reconstruction, especially its victories and defeats. The victory, of course, did not last. Victories are characterized as increased educational access, state leadership encouraging and promoting public education [at all levels], and the rising expectations of greater educational infrastructure and opportunity from the South Carolina population. The defeats are characterized by restricting educational access, state leadership discouraging growth in public education, and the stymieing of the rising expectation of greater educational infrastructure and opportunity.

Black students at the state university represented more than a change in the complexion of the students and faculty. They embodied every principle of the Reconstruction project. Educationally, Reconstruction legislation aimed to change the traditions, habits, and values concerning formal education in South

Carolina, a tradition that had for decades limited entry into learning spaces due to complexion, status, and wealth during the antebellum period.

The 1865 state constitution of South Carolina, written after the Civil War, although containing post–Civil War racial adjustments such as "black codes" that heavily policed African American mobility, made no mention of reforming the Free School Act of 1811 or a developing public school system to meet the demands of a post-slavery society. The silent choice not to reform education left intact the restricted educational policy of the antebellum period. Unlike the state convention of 1865, the 1868 state convention, the beginning of congressional Reconstruction, included African Americans who championed state-sponsored greater educational access.

Slightly before, but during Reconstruction, schooling opportunities began to increase rapidly. Reconstruction disrupted the Antebellum tradition. This is evidenced by the enactment of the school law of 1870, the establishment of teaching training school in 1873, an increasing common school enrollment between 1870 and 1895, and establishing the state-sponsored scholarships to attend USC. However, those who desired educational restriction fought to contain and overthrow the changes wrought by Reconstruction. This chapter provides insight into the growth of educational access and examines the movement to restrict educational opportunities during and after Reconstruction.

EDUCATION ALTERING THE SOUTH, 1866–1868

Before and during the Civil War, one of the favored critiques of abolitionists, northern politicians, and friends of education in both the North and the South concerned southern society's lack of educational edifices and educational access. Northern media linked the Civil War to the lack of education in the South and feared that if public schooling was not established in the region, the illiterate masses would again be duped by the same class legislation of the antebellum period that "steadily held the poor white's nose to the grindstone, denied him the common school, practically debarred him from the freehold of land and kept him debased, stupid and ignorant."[1] Essentially, they feared the possibility of another civil war if the masses of southerners remained without opportunities for public education.[2] Northerners believed or argued that the slaveholders' power rested on wealth and status, allowing them to nurture the ignorance and political obedience of the white lower class. As northerners saw it, as long as white southerner leadership kept to the southern education tradition, which debased the masses of southerners' minds, the Union remained in jeopardy, and the reigniting of another Civil War remained a possibility.[3]

Be it a critique from inside or outside the South, commentators on the southern region's education conditions regarded it as the home of an unlearned population, principally because southern leaders discouraged the development of public schools. Print media depicted it as a region of "half-wits" who required an educational stimulus and a cultural revolution. In the South, the need for educational reform served northerners as one of the major pillars for justifying Reconstruction. Education, northerners hoped, could reform southern culture and serve as an instrument of measurement to determine the success or failure of Reconstruction.[4]

During the antebellum period, common schools were socially and culturally assigned as poor institutions, and politically, post-1830, they were classified as Yankee institutions intended to subvert the southern way of life. Northerners stereotyped southern whites as a group who despised education and needed to be driven into the schools by force, if necessary. Nevertheless, because of the southern cultural response to common schools, many white South Carolinians perceived the educational goals of Reconstruction as ideas that northerners and African Americans designed to punish the South and replace their traditions-in this, white South Carolinians were not wholly wrong in their assessment.[5]

Since most white southerners were culturally predisposed to resisting public education and politically inclined to resisting Northern incursions, the perception of public education and reconstruction had to be shifted. White South Carolinians needed to perceive it as a dispeller of ignorance, crusher of the plantation elite, a balancer to society, and a friend of the white masses. However, public education would only go as far as white South Carolinians embraced public schools and, by association, Reconstruction. It is not that whites were the majority in South Carolina, but they still wielded the power in the early postwar years to inflict as much violence and intimidation to control activities and institutional outcomes. In addition, the Republican leadership started from a cultural deficit and could ill-afford to throw salt in the wounds of the defeated ex-Confederates, if they wanted any of their new institutions to be successful.[6]

Republican leaders and Northern media learned that critiquing the South often hardened southerner's perception toward the goals of Reconstruction; thus, instead of critiquing southerners for their historic lack of public education or their reliance on mass ignorance as a form of social control. It was better to racialize education to persuade whites to embrace all that Reconstruction offered.[7] Using race as a weapon to vie for the white southern mind, and motivate white behavior towards learning, seemed more effective than critiquing southern habits.[8]

Promoters of education contended that white southerners realized that Black people, with their bottomless desire for education, could possibly outpace their own educational achievements, that would cause them to scurry to the school-houses and embrace the expanding educational opportunities. With a Black majority population, several Black teachers present in the state, and the presence of Blacks, young and aged, taking advantage of any and every opportunity to learn, the strategy of race-baiting fostered within South Carolina's "uncertain" Reconstruction environment made these "threats" seem more creditable.[9] For example, one writer penned, "it would be a singular spectacle at a future day, to see two grandchildren, one a former master, the other of a former slave, when the latter was the better educated of the two, not from natural capacity, but because the ancestors of the former took no care to secure for him that upon which every free-man's superiority and dignity must in a great degree depend."[10] The racialization of education and the fear of Black educational growth sparked racial violence, especially toward Black educational efforts. Despite these consequences, the strategy increased the educational desires of white southerners.[11] Using race as a weapon to vie for the white southern mind, and motivate white behavior toward learning, seemed more effective than critiquing southern habits.[12]

Playing on the idea of racial competition and the sensory changes to South Carolina's post–Civil War landscape, which saw Black educational efforts translated into tremendous growth in public school attendance and Black colleges' development, decreasing illiteracy rates, Black faculty and students at USC, writers continued to use race to provoke whites to jealousy. For instance, a writer of the *New York Times* noted, "there is no subject more worthy of the attention of the people of the north and the south at present than a consideration of the best means for instruction and elevating the poor whites of the southern states."[13] The article continued, "now, while so much is being done for the good of the black race, might we not at the same time bestow some thought upon plans which may be both simple and practical for the elevation of our white brethren in the South."[14] Racializing education attended to the notion of white solidarity, with hopes of helping whites of both regions, regardless of their class or status, to embrace the goals of Reconstruction and see educational access as a way to elevate the common white person over the elevating and attention gaining Black folk.

Nevertheless, Reconstruction leadership's plan had several blunders that failed to completely overcome the doubt that white South Carolinians had concerning public education and Republican leadership. As Reconstruction leaders worked their plan to make educational opportunities available, their promotion of mixed schools capped the progress that Reconstruction leadership would make in South Carolina. In addition, the mistakes made by Reconstruction leadership gave room for those who desired to restrict public education the ammunition to impede the progress of Reconstruction.[15]

THE 1868 CONSTITUTION AND THE PROBLEM OF MIXED SCHOOLS

As the 1868 constitutional convention left no doubt about Republican leadership's plans to reform the educational policy, moving from a method centered on restriction to a policy of access, anchored in an efficient and far-reaching common school system with greater opportunity for higher education. Educational reconstruction was well on its way in South Carolina. However, as public education and its properties were debated in the 1868 Constitutional Convention, a significant dispute over racially mixed schools overshadowed every other educational related topic. The problem of mixed schools created a public clamor beyond the convention halls. As the idea of mixed public schools created lasting anxiety among white and Black South Carolinians, it increased the disdain for Reconstruction among whites, stymied the support of those favoring public education (inside and out the state and region), and gave ground for the opponents of the educational element of Reconstruction to argue against the development of public education and its expanding opportunities on racial grounds.

It is not that Reconstruction officials believed racially mixed schools would dominate the landscape during the Reconstruction era but rather they believed that free schools opened to all would debunk the claims of inferiority, demonstrate the equal intellectual capacity of different races and classes, prevent imbalanced funding, and achieve a level of efficiency. Moreover, it was believed that Black and white children in the same school could help white South Carolinians evolve their overt form of racism to a more "sophisticated" type (as found in Northern states). The mixed-race proposal was advocated with the hope of using public education to reform the white southern mind.[16]

White Republicans believing in the fruit of the potential experiment of mixed schools, rejecting the advice of Black Republicans who suggested they not encourage mixed schools, miscalculated white South Carolinians' attitudes toward race and racially mixed schools. Given the context, particularly the racial violence and outrages that followed the Civil War, mixed schools, as African Americans predicted, were policy nightmares. Education, particularly the argument of mixed-race schools, was no small threat to the social order. Most white South Carolinians still clung to southern nationalism and the newly framed Lost Cause ideology that centered on strict racial hierarchy. Opponents of mixed-race schools knew education was not a neutral institution. Those who had spent decades restricting educational access understood education to be a political activity and believed the future of the state rested on the formal and informal socialization of its citizens—based on a philosophy that placed white above Black, wealth above poverty, and the intelligent above the ignorant. Thus, they who despised

Reconstruction and its goals could not afford to allow their enemy to educate their children. They could not freely accept mixed schools to exist since they challenged South Carolina's racial and social hierarchy. The disagreements surrounding mixed-race schools became one of the main reasons why public education failed to gain the needed momentum to redirect the course of education in South Carolina during Reconstruction and thereafter. Moreover, the mixed-race school controversy frames the white exodus from the USC during the brief period of desegregation and situates the eventual closure of the university during the Redemption period.[17]

Even though neither Black nor white Republicans sought to force any race into mixed schools by compulsion; nevertheless, oppositional forces propagandized mixed schools to stir the imaginations, fears, and fantasies of whites to lead them to resent the changes established by the Reconstruction government. Additionally, as every discernable or developing difference in South Carolina, seen and unseen, real or imagined, during this era was marked in the southern white mind as impure, making it an effortless task for those opposing the vision of Reconstruction to set boundaries between South Carolina's traditional white ideals against the "Yankee" and southern Black ideals.[18]

Following the 1868 state constitution's ratification, the fixation upon racially mixed schools naturally became a focal point for those hoping to trim both the aims of Reconstruction and the state-supported school system in South Carolina. The tactics to fight against expanding educational access during Reconstruction centered arguments based on race and race relations by way of the mixed-school dilemma. For instance, in near successive articles, *The Charleston Daily* discussed what mixed schools represented to "Southerners." It warned that white South Carolinians must reject any design for education, which "looks to debasing the white man for the sake of elevating the negro."[19]

Because of the mixed school controversy, the system of state-sponsored education developed a reputation as being an institution primarily for African Americans, as it was implemented by Black political leaders and those who loved Black people and Black advancement. Republican Governor Scott contended that if separate schools were not provided, mixed schools would "repel the masses of the whites from the education training that they so much need, and virtually to give to our colored population the exclusive benefit of our public schools."[20] This would confirm the none-truth that this system was solely designed to educate the African American population into social, cultural, and educational supremacy at the most and social equality at the least—both were equally bad and unacceptable.

The white exodus from the University of South Carolina in 1873, as Black men were permitted to enter the college, pushed the discussion of mixed schools to the center and served as the greatest example of educational reconstruction seeking create racial equality. Speaking to this, one writer noted, "if the ring government of South Carolina thinks that it can force social equality upon the whites of the state, it is vastly mistaken. The laws of God and Nature cannot be changed or abrogated by the edicts of, a carpet-bag administration [in regard to mixed schools] when the colored men enter, the whites retire . . . wherever they are attempted harm will come of the experiment, the whites will not tolerate, the blacks do not desire them."[21]

South Carolina's leaders who opposed Reconstruction were willing to offer South Carolina's Military Academy, known now as The Citadel, once an all-white military college in Charleston, SC, as a college for the state's Black population to stave off opening USC to African Americans. The need to keep the University of South Carolina as an all-white institution represented its symbolic placement as the state's intellectual light of white leadership. One writer noted, "Let the college be opened for the instruction of the white youth of the State, and let some suitable place be procured for the use of those colored persons who wish to avail themselves of the benefits of education. Co-education of the races can never be affected, and the only way in which both races may receive advantages from the educational system of the State is the establishment of a separate institution for each."

A racially inclusive USC influenced commentators to lament South Carolina's changes during reconstruction and increased the disdain for Reconstruction-related things. *The News and Herald* represented the heartache white South Carolinians placed in the symbol of the college when it noted that South Carolina would not "realize that she is again herself until the old South Carolina College is once more safely in the hands of the whites of the State."[22] Mixed schools drove the perception that Reconstruction further desecrated South Carolina society.

THE PROBLEM OF REPUBLICAN CONTROL AND
THE REDEEMING MESSAGE, 1870–1882

Under Republican control, the public school system of South Carolina suffered from several infrastructural ailments. Superintendent J. K. Jillson's annual education reports admitted to the school system's problems under the republican government. In one report, Jillson noted,

> Our whole state policy, so far as common education is concerned, has
> been, from the beginning, narrow and illiberal. While other enterprises
> and interests have received due attention and proper care, the education

of the people has been a matter of the last and least consideration. The rights of bondholders have been guarded and made secure; railroads have received material encouragement . . . even the birds of the forests, and the fishes in the rivers, have been protected, but the schools have been left to take care of themselves, and the poor school teacher has been constrained to toil and starve, or else to abandon the profession, than which, no nobler or more worthy can be found.[23]

Jillson admitted that the school system suffered from mismanagement, a lack of legislative support, inadequate school funds and monies for qualified teachers, and a normal school.

Although hoping to correct the abuses of the system, Jillson's reports were used by the Democrats to attack public education, which illustrates how Republican leadership and its education system were egregiously inadequate.[24]

Despite the infrastructural issues, Jillson believed the public-school system required more support, particularly in its need for strong advocates, since it appeared the resistance to public education was more than just a disdain for reconstruction. It appeared to Jillson that the resistance to public education was more than just a disdain for Reconstruction. He began to believe that oppositional groups sought to sabotage and remove the current iteration of the public education system and return the system to its former restrictive policies. His fears prompted him to warn those that were the friends of public education to stay vigilant and refrain from yielding to arguments that spoke or alluded to ending the public education system, in favor of another system or no system. He even encouraged them to find a way to disaggregate the issues of Reconstruction from that of the public education. He thought the continued association between the more political side of Reconstruction with educational reconstruction, would be used to upend the public education system.[25] He stated, "let no hostile faction be permitted to prevail. Let no partisan contention, no sectarian prejudice, impede their progress."[26]

Jillson and Reconstruction leaders unknowingly entered a battle over educational access that had raged in South Carolina well before reconstruction. Although not fully aware of the details of the battle over educational opportunities during the antebellum period, Reconstruction leadership became fully aware of this truth as Democratic political movements gained momentum in their pursuit to oust Republican rule, which included plans to dismantle universal education. For example, as Democrats redeemed Georgia during the early 1870s, there was immediate concern for the future of public education in Georgia. Several articles in the *Atlanta Constitution* expressed fear that the public school system was on its way out. One writer, who opposed Reconstruction, yet favored public education, believed that the return of Democratic rule spelled the end of public education in Georgia, expressing "the failure of the legislature, during its late session, to act definitely upon the question of popular education, excited in me a sense of deep regret."[27]

Georgia's superintendent of education echoed this sentiment, remarking that he encountered an opposing force to public education throughout his state. He noted, "there are also those who look with disfavor upon every project not devised or directed by themselves. Prejudice and narrow self-interest . . . lead them to oppose the schools."[28]

Redemption did not occur in South Carolina in the early 1870s. However, superintendent Jillson had illustrated that the tides too were turning against education as redemption gained momentum. He noted, "the public press is one of the strongest influences brought to bear upon the opinions of men. In many instances, the public press of this state has treated our Free Common School system with contempt, injustice, ridicule, and unfairness."[29]

Despite the Redemption movement and message that sought to overthrow the Republican government, it ironically relied upon a message to improve public education for whites as a method to convince the white public to resist Reconstruction and help them to usurp the Republican government, which included ending mixed schools. Their message hinged on nostalgia and myth. Democrats argued that before the "War of Northern Aggression," South Carolina's proposed free school system was well on its way to providing a substantial educational structure for South Carolinians. They argued that a return to the antebellum system would place South Carolina on the path toward creating a perfect system. By arguing that the older system would do more for the state, they contrasted the public education institution founded under the Republican government as one that supported foreign (i.e., northern) interests and uplifted the African Americans denizens, at the cost of "white" South Carolinians. In opposing universal education, Democrats promised that as soon as Reconstruction found its end, the Republican system would be replaced with one that universally benefited whites.[30]

Although universal education was not something that the redeeming leadership desired, the politics and the educational curiosity of the time necessitated that the Democratic party made it a staple of the redemption campaign. Despite the contempt many whites had for the Republican government and its mixed school drama, whites increasingly adapted to and began to expect an expanding presence of public education. And so, universal education became a pillar of the Democratic platform and a promise of 1876.[31]

By making public education a staple of the democratic promises of redemption, Democrats silenced critics who accused them of only supporting education to gain votes.[32] By enacting new taxes, advocating for the development of the public school system in speeches, and promising to correct abuses of the Republican party's design, the Democrats looked to show that they agreed with public education by (1) promising to remove the financial corruption that plagued the system prior to 1877, (2) increasing the number of qualified teachers, (3) appointing better trustees, and (4) increasing the quality of state schools.[33]

The Democrats return to power in 1876 did not force white South Carolinians to immediately put away their curiosity and expectation for a better school system. In fact, the Democrats return to power began with them making good on their promises to return the state to its former ways of white rule and continue the mission before the war, which included creating a better system of education for whites. As they began to undo Reconstruction, including some its educational and political aspects that visibly blighted the state, such as African Americans attending and facilitating at USC. State leadership closed the university and ending its brief period of racial inclusion. Yet, notwithstanding the Democrats return to power and hoping to give only lip service to advancing public education by doing a little where it shows a lot, they underestimated the craving for public education inspired during the Reconstruction period.

This is evinced by several news articles calling for people to continue to embrace the expansion of public education that began during reconstruction. In an article titled "Education of the Masses," the writer urged South Carolina to embrace universal education in order to obtain national power, noting "it is astonishing that governments have been so long putting the cart before the horse, unable to see their error; fostering and encouraging arts and sciences, navigation, agriculture and manufacturing, and carelessly and indifferently fostering the mind, the power that develops and propels them all. Public education is the direct and the shortest road to wealth and power."[34] For South Carolina to grow and achieve power, the author argued all its people needed intellectual impetus, Black and white, men and women. If South Carolina leaders wanted to respond to the coming age, there was a need to invest in public education not disinvest. Moreover, improving the state's standing in the union, old habits that characterized the antebellum system, structure, and customs, such as trickle-down education, parents keeping their children back from available schools, hypocritic promises by leadership, and class and race based prejudicial practices had to come to an end.[35]

Reconstruction's progressive public school system forced southerners to confront their educational situation even after the Republican government was dismantled. This educational Reconstruction caused most South Carolinians, particularly whites, to remain curious about public education's potential even when redemption was won. Their curiosity derived from the continued advocation for a national public school system, intrastate discourse on how to better the state system, and the educational-related advancement and growth of the Black population.

It is without question that the push for greater educational access during the Reconstruction period contributed to the greater desire for education throughout the state. The increased school enrollment exemplifies this truth. In 1870 with the school enrollment for the state was 30,448; in 1871, 66,056; and in 1872, at 72,000. By 1880, the enrollment number swelled to 133,458. The desire for education never truly subsided, even after the educational politics of Reconstruction were diminished. As an example of the growth of such sentiments in South Carolina, one writer noted, "a commendable interest is manifested by all classes of our people in the establishment of schools, and the desire is general that larger facilities than heretofore shall be furnished for this purpose."[36] These forces did not allow redeemers to immediately return to their antebellum precedent, despite the strong desire for redeemers to do away with the goals and expectations of universal education that stemmed from reconstruction. As Reconstruction came to an end, the battle for educational access remained in the post-Reconstruction period.

The Democratic party, in their return to power, sought to quench the growing desire for educational change and develop a plan to move South Carolina back into the policy of restriction. Nevertheless, before they could achieve their goals, they had to regain the influence over the cultural trend toward educational expansion and arrest the expectation of educational opportunity.[37]

Democrats reasserted their commitment to education in their 1882 campaign and boasted how their rule had improved the public education system while vowing to continue their commitment toward perfecting it. They boasted that "the Democratic Party is the only party that can preserve peace and ensures good government in SC . . . the public school system is not now a perfect system, but we have been laying the foundation broad and deep upon which a finished structure may be built."[38]

However, despite the Democrats' celebration of building a superior educational foundation, there existed a clamor surrounding the system's condition and progress that contradicted the Democrats' boast. A writer in the *Orangeburg Democrat* noted the system was so defective that it was not worthy of being called a system, noting that throughout the state schoolhouses were known to be uncomfortable and in need of repairs to the point that occupants shivered from "head to toe with cold, [and] the bleak winds go whistling through the cracks." The author further explained that the system's problems were well known among the public, "yet, how many have ever raised so much as their little finger to correct this evil? We know and acknowledge its existence and baneful consequences, yet we do not seek to remove it."[39]

Others also discussed their displeasure with the system and the fabricated rhetoric of success promoted by the Democrats. A *Newberry Herald* article noted that "the people should not be satisfied with glittering generalities about free education. Fine speeches, high-sounding eulogies count for naught."[40] Even those external to South Carolina recognized that the redemption leadership's true desire was to contain educational growth, as one critic noted, "It is easy to say that the mass of respectable people in South Carolina are hypocrites, pretending to support popular education while laboring secretly for its destruction."[41] As complaints toward the Democratic-led public education system increased, the often hidden and silent opinion that public education was a useless institution gained momentum and began to come to the public light.

For example, at a meeting held in the county of Ninety-Six in the late 1870s, the conservative leadership of South Carolina discussed the future of public education in the state. The leaders deliberated on its utility and the government's right to provide it. The leaders agreed that universal education was not a necessary feature of the state, noting, "We deny that it is either the duty or the privileges of a Democratic government to educate its subjects. We deny that education makes a better field hand or a better woodchopper, the present school system is radically wrong and must be abolished, poor or rich boys should get their education in the same way they get their clothing-by honest toil [because] public education deprives a man of the highest pride of which he can-that of providing for his household."[42] The leaders went a step further; they believed the state should not interfere in the realm of education. Their ideology was obviously centered on nullifying the common school system that expanded educational access.

The sentiments expressed at the Ninety-Six meeting contextualize why the education system's defects continued without recourse under Democrat rule. It also seems like the system's accumulating complaints and associated problems represented a slow and quiet return to the antebellum ideology of restriction. As redemption leaders said one thing and did another, the public school system suffered from carelessness and "criminal indifference."[43]

The end of Reconstruction marked the decline and the eventual choking of the Republican-led objective to expand educational access and develop the system as one of the chief institutional pillars in South Carolina. The closure of the state's flagship university and removing its African American presence was a sequence in the planned realignment of educational goals for the state. And in reopening USC as an all-white institution in the 1880s, it marked the return to the old antebellum approach to educational restriction.

EDUCATION FUNDING, RACE BAITING, AND
DIMINISHING SUPPORT FOR PUBLIC EDUCATION

The mission of returning the state back towards a policy of restriction continued well into the 1890s but the most work was done in the 1880s. This is best illustrated in the rejection of national aid and a challenge to the two-mill tax, the chief funding source for public education. In the 1880s, Massachusetts senator Henry Blair proposed a bill to use the surplus money of the national treasury for national education. The states with the highest rates of illiteracy would receive greater portions.

Several bills advocating for providing federal aid were introduced in the US Congress between the 1870s into the early 1890s. Among the bills that focused on common schools, Henry Blair's 1881 Bill became the most renowned. The Blair Bill was discussed for ten years in different committees within Congress. It passed the Senate three times, received several revisions, and was reintroduced into Congress five times; however, the bill never came up for a full vote. The bill died in 1890 in the 51st Congress.[44]

The goal of the bill was simple, to increase literacy rates in the United States. Educationally, Henry Blair believed that the United States fell behind and would continue to lag behind other industrial nations. His remedy was to commit $105 million toward public education, focusing on the southern region. He desired to appropriate surplus money from the national treasury, distributing $15 million for the first year and diminish the appropriation by one million dollars each year thereafter based on racially equal distribution. States with the highest illiteracy rates would receive the lion's share of the allotment. The South, specifically South Carolina, would receive one of the more generous portions of the appropriation.[45]

Initially, several South Carolina leaders welcomed the Blair Bill, as one writer described the support given in the state legislature, noted, "in 1882 our General Assembly unanimously urged our representatives in Congress to seek national aid for our schools. Nobody raised his voice against the actions of the General Assembly."[46]

However, as it became less important to fake support of public education, or as one writer noted "the time has passed when we need not act falsely to ourselves to gain favor in Northern eyes,"[47] Democrats became more oppose to the Blair

Bill. Couching their opposition to the Blair Bill in regional and racial politics, Democrats refused to accept the bill on the grounds that it promoted Blacks over whites; and depicted the Blair bill as a secret strategy that would reprise Reconstruction and return the state to Black Rule. One writer explained the perspective of South Carolina's approach to national aid, noting, "we can take care of our own people, we are afraid of this federal trojan horse to come in what garb he may." Continuing, he stated, "Radical rule would not run the state again; by robbing the state once again under the 'pretext of educating the negroes."[48] Resistance to national education primarily took on a racial element as public education slowly became synonymous with Black education and Black elevation-reminiscent of the oppositional arguments to mixed race schools during Reconstruction.

Colonel Asbury Coward, South Carolina's Education Superintendent in the 1880s, understood that rejecting Blair Bill had little to do with Black advantage—as it was propagated. It had more to do with generating confusion, reducing the esteem of education, and creating hostility towards the public school system on racial grounds. When asked what he thought would be the effect of those opposing the Blair Bill, Colonel Coward noted, "I fear . . . that the effect is prejudicial, to a certain extent, to the educational interests of the state, because it has reawakened a latent opposition to the public school system which had become almost dormant."[49] Coward comprehended that opposition to the Blair Bill only mirrored the intentions of those who did not desire to make any effort toward the development of the public education system and return the state to the educational policy of restriction.

Race-baiting was a critical weapon in arresting the positive sentiments generated from public education. By framing the system in racial terms, opponents of universal education slowly regained their influence over the debate between educational opportunity and educational restriction. Moreover, by convincing the whites that educational opportunity meant Black advantage and educational restriction meant white advantage-the choice was easy.

As it seemed necessary to close the University of South Carolina to remove the stain of Blackness from the glory of the state's highest institution of learning, it became equally necessary to reverse anything that would maintain the "black" public school system, and resist any reform, including rejecting federal aid, which would potentially place Blacks in the position to return to USC. In doing so, the public "black" education system became associated with putting the state back on the right footing regarding racial hierarchy and racial expectation. Under such logic, if public education continued its growth and positive presence, it had to be perceived as white uncertainty and Black unpredictability-both of which were unsettling realities. If whites desired to secure their spot above Blackness and ensure white rule, they had to let go of their growing aspirations and expectations for public education.[50]

Around the time Democratic leaders began rejecting the Blair Bill on racial grounds, they doubled down on their use of racial rhetoric and ramped up the message of classifying the public system in South Carolina as one that also privileged Blacks to the whites' disadvantage. Determined to show how, some leaders challenged the efficacy of the two-mills tax, the major funding source of public schools. The two-mill tax was an annual tax levied on all taxable property, which replaced the annual appropriation (the system used to fund public schools throughout the antebellum and reconstruction period).[51] These changes were encouraged by the state superintendent, the governor, and friends of education who believe this would increase the funding for schools; however, the taxes collected did not produce the results desired. The school funds often fell short of the amount needed to have a serviceable system. In several ways, the failure of the schools (under democratic rule) led to the questioning of the two-mills tax (by democratic leadership) and reinforce arguments that public education was an impossibility in South Carolina-an argument that harken back to the antebellum days. It was argued that the two-mills tax and public schools were not only out of bounds with South Carolina traditions which, in the antebellum past do not support increased taxes for public education, furthermore, it was argued that never would it have been imagined that white taxes would be used to pay for Black education under the antebellum model.

Although by the mid-1880s, Black schools were receiving less funding than white schools—despite Blacks paying their share of taxes and contributing to the two-mills tax. As one historian writes, "the relative financial treatment of white and negro schools between the school year ending in 1880 and that ending in 1895 is impossible to ascertain. However, in that period, the school expenditures had risen from $2.75 to $3.11 per capita for whites, while dropping from $2.51 to $1.05 for negroes."[52] Nonetheless, the argument that public education was inexpedient to whites and benefited Blacks became the sole justification for challenging the two-mills tax, the most significant funding source for public education.[53]

As whites repeatedly heard about the supposed Black advantage derived from their own wallets (absent any discussion of Black contributions to public education), came a greater acceptance to the idea that the current system had to be rejected and its very existence was a threat to their interests, security, and future. Speaking to this fact, one writer wrote, "any pretense that our people are anxious to educate their enemies is the most hollow mockery."[54] Despite the understanding that whites received some (if not a lot of) benefits from the public education system, it was often argued that whites only received benefits as a by-product.

According to the *Press and Banner*, the two-mills tax for public schools not only confiscated white property to educated Blacks but also went against South Carolina tradition to use the state to educate anyone, even white children. Thus, whites that were educated by the system were irrelevant. One writer penned, "the state of South Carolina never in the days when it was ruled by white men appropriated anything for public schools . . . It is a mere incident that the white children of the state get any of the money . . . we appropriate half a million dollars for negro education, with the understanding that the white children get a part of it. If there were no negroes to educate, South Carolina would not today appropriate one cent for education, except for paupers."[55] Such an illustration was obviously used to trigger the psychological trauma for white South Carolinians that decided to associate property loss and Black gains with the nightmares of "black rule" of "radical" Republican Reconstruction. In some sense, the Banner wanted to show that redemption was not yet complete and would remain incomplete so long as the "negro tax" that supported "black education" continued to stall the return to the antebellum model of education established on wealth, chance, and charity.

Public education, the two-mills tax, and the Black educational advantage played into the fear of Black unpredictability. The fear of a massively educated and a less predictable Black population was often used to frustrate efforts for developing public education in South Carolina since 1740. In the post-reconstruction period, the debate on rather to educate or prevent African Americans education throughout the nineteenth century was often contextualized in the vein of what was best for white security. What was overlooked during the antebellum period, as it was during the post-Reconstruction period, was how the lack of educational opportunity for African Americans, affected white educational development. Opponents hoping to draw a greater portion of whites, never mentioned the effects public education had on the larger majority of the white population. Instead they focused on upcycling the idea that white security and white safety was in jeopardy due to the presence of public education.[56]

Rejecting the Blair Bill and challenging the two-mills tax was less about destroying the public education system than pigeon-holing the expectations of public school among whites. The efforts by the supporters for restricting education changed the tide of expectations by the end of the post-Reconstruction period. By the 1890s, the state was not expected to make leaps and bounds to prepare its future citizens and denizens to make an impact on the state or the nation through their refined intellectual gifts. New agencies and organizations were trying to develop new ways to make South Carolina's educational situation better, but most efforts in the early 20th century did not change the tide.

Although the public education system never returned to its antebellum precedent, the system did lose esteem as it continued its course of being an inadequate
and neglected system of ill repute. By the 1890s, the battle over public educational
access and restriction swung back in favor of those supporting restriction. The
opposition's control is evidenced by the increasing gap in attention and funding
between higher education and public schools. It was recorded in the *Anderson
Intelligencer* that this gap between higher education and public school set the state
on an "unstable foundation," noting,

> The colleges are advancing, while the common schools are almost at
> a standstill . . . We repeat, then, that it is to be feared that the higher
> and the lower components of the system are growing farther and far-
> ther apart, the former keeping abreast with the spirit of the times, the
> latter falling steadily behind. The noble edifice is resting, not on a solid
> foundation, but a precarious framework of rough, decaying timbers. The
> efforts of our educational architects have been devoted to completing one
> part to the neglect of another.[57]

This noticeable difference not only reflected the class differences and racial
attitudes but, more importantly, signified the deliberate neglect of the education
of the majority irrespective of race as the leadership's effort to monopolize knowledge at the top of the class and racial structure as a means of social control over
the entire population.

The Democrats, who once embraced public education and promised to improve it, had in 1892 now boldly opposed it. They noted, "We are opposed to
state interference with parental rights and rights of conscience in the education
of children as an infringement of the fundamental democratic doctrine that the
largest individual liberty consistent with the rights of others insures the highest
type of American citizenship and the best government."[58] Consequently, public
education, including South Carolina colleges, albeit with differences in degree,
failed to improve throughout the 1890s and well into the twentieth century.[59]

As restriction served as the educational policy before and after reconstruction,
it informs us of the vital role that Reconstruction played within the area of public
education. Reconstruction leaders, led by African American educational demands
and ideals, attempt to end the policy of restriction by increasing access to primary,
secondary, and higher education regardless of race or status. This shows how Republican leaders sought to challenge South Carolina traditions.

African Americans teaching and learning at South Carolina's systems of higher
education, and the legislation that created a new public education system for

greater educational access, exemplifies the importance of expanding educational infrastructure and the short-lived victory of those who rejected the idea of greater educational opportunity. To reiterate, the University of South Carolina's closure in 1877 and its reopening as an all-white college, alongside the neutralization of the financial commitment to public schooling, represented a return to a policy of antebellum restriction, though not precisely in the same way. Nonetheless, the social hierarchy in South Carolina would not be challenged by the unpredictability of learning, and the philosophy of restriction (albeit in a more sophisticated form) was carried well into the Jim Crow period.

Despite this fact, the progress made by African Americans in their own private world toward educational growth and Black educational institutional development was nothing short of remarkable. But it is essential to see the larger politics of the era. The brief period African Americans attended USC is a valuable segment within a larger story in South Carolina's educational history. This brief overview hopefully showed how that story fits into a larger context.

Chapter Six

BEFORE 1963

Race, Education, and the NAACP Desegregation
Campaigns at the University of South Carolina

Robert Greene II

In a 2011 article in the *State* newspaper remembering famed South Carolina
civil rights attorney and later chief justice of the South Carolina Supreme
Court, Ernest Finney, note was made of the law school where his career and legal
thinking were shaped: South Carolina State. The school, like Finney himself,
were presented as scrappy underdogs in Jim Crow–era South Carolina. "Finney
remembers developing a habit of drinking coffee without cream or sugar," the
story reported, "because the law school could not afford refrigerator and other
niceties." However, the story also pointed out a historical irony, one that would
change South Carolina and southern history. South Carolina State's law school
was created only to avoid desegregating the law school at the University of South
Carolina immediately after World War II. "Lawmakers had avoided integrating
USC's law school, only to produce a pipeline of black lawyers from S.C. State
who directed their energy against such segregated practices," it said in the pages
of the *State* newspaper.[1]

"Before 1963: Race, Education, and the NAACP Desegregation Campaigns
at the University of South Carolina" argues that the attempts to send African
American students to the University of South Carolina before the school's famed
September 11, 1963, desegregation need to be remembered as part of the larger
context of civil rights in American history. "Failure" in history can be as valuable
a tool—and moment—as victory. "Before 1963" explores that idea as it relates to
the two attempts to desegregate the University of South Carolina: Charles Bailey's
application to the law school in 1938, and John Wrighten's better known attempt
at desegregation of the same school in 1946.

One key facet of both moments in the history of African Americans at the University of South Carolina is how much they were subsumed by larger, national events in the march for freedom and equality. The National Association for the Advancement of Colored People's (NAACP) desegregation campaigns in the early twentieth century were initially attempts to equalize African American institutions with their white counterparts across the American South. But the fight to make real the "equal" in the proposition of "Separate but equal," which defined the South since the *Plessy v. Ferguson* decision of 1896 led to the eventual triumph of the NAACP in the *Brown v. Board of Education* case of 1954. However, the local phase of this national problem in South Carolina led to the creation of a cadre of African American lawyers at South Carolina State who contributed to the statewide variant of the civil rights movement.

Black colleges and universities in South Carolina, such as Benedict and South Carolina State, also have links to the saga of desegregating USC Law and the broader history of the fight for civil rights in South Carolina. Inevitably, the history of African Americans at the University of South Carolina includes African American institutions of higher learning across South Carolina. They, too, play a role in this story.

"Before 1963" also tracks how the lawyers created at South Carolina State Law School made a critical difference in the civil rights campaigns in the Palmetto State in the 1950s and 1960s. Again, this is one of the great ironies of the history of civil rights in South Carolina: the attempt to keep segregation alive, inadvertently, led to the end of segregation at places such as the University of South Carolina. The building of Black-run and operated institutions in the face of segregation was long the story of the Jim Crow segregation era. "Before 1963," however, brings it into sharp focus within the history of South Carolina and its flagship university.

Finally, this chapter ends by analyzing the legacy of the law school at South Carolina State and the memory of the early attempts at desegregation. Too often, history is measured only in success or failure. "Before 1963" poses a different challenge for our understanding of legal history and race in American society, however. Instead of merely looking at the direct victories or defeats for civil rights, we should instead consider how the long movement for African American freedom and equality of opportunity played out despite incredible odds.

CHARLES BAILEY AND THE NAACP CAMPAIGNS OF THE 1930S

Recognizing the early battles for civil rights and social equality in American society before the *Brown v. Board of Education* decision in 1954 is a key part of understanding the importance of the USC Law School cases presented here. In the last fifteen years, historians have debated the usefulness of pushing the civil rights historiographic calendar back into the New Deal era. Jacquelyn Dowd Hall's 2005 essay, "The Long Civil Rights Movement and the Political Uses of the Past" is the most notable example in this historical subgenre. Hall argued that the civil rights movement as we know it has its origins in "the liberal and radical milieu of the late 1930s." By moving away from the classic narrative of the movement being one that only existed in the 1950s and '60s, the early attempts to desegregate the University of South Carolina—not to mention the complicated aftermath of those attempts—is easier to understand.[2]

To be sure, there are cogent critiques of the "long civil rights movement" thesis.[3] However, regardless of how one conceives of the civil rights movement broadly speaking in American history, there was certainly *a* movement for greater civil rights and freedom for African Americans in the 1930s. Works such as Patricia Sullivan's *Days of Hope: Race and Democracy in the New Deal Era* also explore the idea of thinking about the movement before 1954 as integral to understanding the long and often unwieldy road to desegregation across the South. The experience of desegregation campaigns in South Carolina, in particular, are a reminder of how complicated the civil rights movement looks on a local and state level.[4]

The campaign against segregation in American society, by the late 1930s, was one spearheaded by the legal team of the National Association for the Advancement of Colored People (NAACP). Charles Hamilton Houston, serving as Special Counsel for the NAACP, crafted a legal offensive on segregation via the idea of "separate but equal" coined from the Supreme Court's *Plessy v. Ferguson* case of 1896. Then, the Supreme Court in a majority decision ruled that separate facilities for white and Black Americans were allowed under the US Constitution, so long as those facilities were equal in quality. Justice Henry Brown wrote the majority opinion for the court and, in the process, captured the mood of most white Americans a generation after the end of Reconstruction. "If the civil and political rights of both races be equal, one cannot be inferior to the other civilly or politically," he wrote. "If one race be inferior to the other socially, the Constitution of the United States cannot put them upon the same plane."[5]

Although it is often Justice John Harlan's powerful dissent that is mentioned in current civil rights history discourse—"Our constitution is colorblind, and neither knows nor tolerates classes among citizens"—it was the majority opinion that was the reality with which Houston and his colleagues at the NAACP had to struggle against.[6]

Houston promoted to the NAACP leadership in October 1934 a plan to fight segregation within education. He argued that this was their best avenue for a full assault on legalized segregation in the American South. The principal argument Houston was prepared to put forth was that, quite simply, southern states would have to be forced to live up to the "equal" section of "separate but equal." It was true that by the 1930s, most facilities built for African Americans were not equal in any measure to those built for their white counterparts. Therefore, Houston wanted to call southern states on their separate but equal bluff. This would force such states to both build equitable schools for African Americans and create law and other professional schools for African Americans too.[7]

One location for the attack on segregation would become the law school at the University of South Carolina. Charles Bruce Bailey was recruited for the attempt to desegregate the law school in the late 1930s. Already, Bailey had been a cog in the larger story of Black education in South Carolina. A native of Columbia, South Carolina, Bailey attended Benedict College in the 1930s when a student strike there protested problems facing students after graduation. Bailey and other students discovered that Benedict graduates, trying to enter graduate programs at other universities, "had to do from two to four semesters of undergraduate work" and felt that "they were being short-changed." Eventually, he and several other students withdrew from Benedict and transferred to Morehouse College.[8]

Bailey's own family already had a history with the USC Law School. Paris Simkins, Bailey's grandfather, attended the law school in the 1870s, when the university was open to African Americans during the Reconstruction era. Simkins also served as a representative of Edgefield, South Carolina, in the state's general assembly from 1872 to 1876.[9] "From early childhood, my grandfather was my model . . . all my education was aimed in that direction," Bailey said during an oral history interview conducted by African American Studies professor Grace McFadden in 1980. Now, with the NAACP trying to desegregate law schools—or at least force the creation of all-Black law schools—Bailey had his chance to make history and emulate his grandfather.[10]

Bailey first applied to the USC Law School in 1935. He stated, years later, that his only drawback was being "born on the wrong side of the fence . . . that's not bragging, that's just simple fact." Pushed by Charles H. Houston to apply to the law school, the NAACP nonetheless decided to pursue the case to desegregate the University of Missouri Law School in the famous *Gaines v. Canada* case. Eventually, the NAACP focused the bulk of its efforts on that case, doing little more to help Bailey in his application process to the USC Law School. Lloyd Gaines would be admitted to the law school following the 1938 Supreme Court case victory—but Bailey's attempt to desegregate the USC Law School was largely forgotten by an NAACP stretched thin for resources.[11] His law school application stalled for years, until "Cotton" Ed Smith, running for reelection in 1938, used the application as an appeal to white supremacy. By that point, the NAACP's focus on the *Gaines* case meant no support was forthcoming for Bailey's application.[12]

The curious case of Charles Bailey's attempt to desegregate the University of South Carolina law school has become a footnote to the larger struggle of school desegregation in the New Deal and World War II eras. But Bailey's attempt would be followed up by the better-known John Wrighten case. That case would shake up the history of South Carolina and lay the groundwork for the eventual desegregation of the University of South Carolina in 1963.

JOHN WRIGHTEN AND THE ROAD TO DESEGREGATION

The political and cultural environment of 1947—barely a decade after Bailey's attempt at desegregation—explains how the John Wrighten case would, ultimately, have a greater impact on the history of African Americans in South Carolina. The southern politics of race already began to experience tremors due to the growth of the NAACP, the rise of organizations such as the Southern Negro Youth Congress (SNYC), and an overall more militant attitude on ending Jim Crow segregation. The "Double V" campaign of World War II among African Americans—fighting Fascism abroad while destroying Jim Crow segregation at home—also created the atmosphere for a more militant attitude at home. This meant, however, a more militant attitude in *defense* of segregation as well.[13]

This militant spirit could even be felt in otherwise conservative South Carolina. Already, African Americans were pushing for the right to vote in South Carolina's all-white Democratic primary. *Smith v. Allwright*, a 1944 Supreme Court decision, ruled that state Democratic parties could not discriminate against African Americans seeking to participate in their primary elections. Often, such primary elections within the Democratic Party were tantamount to general elections, due to the one-party rule endemic across much of the American South. African Americans in South Carolina would challenge the all-white primary in the Palmetto State via the Negro Citizens Committee, which asked for Black volunteers to register for the Democratic primary in 1946. They did so to challenge new laws passed by the state legislature which were attempts to circumvent the momentous outcome of *Smith v. Allwright*. George Elmore's attempt to register for the primary would lead to *Elmore v. Rice*, which would attract NAACP support.[14]

At the same time, the NAACP and African Americans in South Carolina closely followed the attempt of John Wrighten to desegregate the USC Law School. Wrighten was a graduate of South Carolina State A&M College, one of several institutions of higher learning in South Carolina built specifically for African Americans. The legal team for Wrighten argued that the only barrier to Wrighten's acceptance to the law school was his race. As the state of South Carolina had no law school for African Americans, Wrighten was therefore entitled to entry to the law school since he met the other requirements. Both this case—soon to be known as *Wrighten v. Board of Trustees at University of South Carolina*—and *Elmore v. Rice* were to be decided by US District Court judge J. Waties Waring.[15]

Waring himself would soon come to occupy a critical part of the history—and lore—of South Carolina's civil rights history. Waring was considered part of "Charleston royalty," scion of a family that could trace its Charleston lineage back to the seventeenth century. He was named to the federal bench in 1941 by President Franklin Roosevelt and, it seemed, would simply be another in a long line of well-connected southerners who received a plum federal position.[16]

Soon, however, Waring would earn the ire of some South Carolinians—and the admiration of many others—by issuing rulings that were in favor of civil rights for African Americans in the state. In *Elmore v. Rice*, Waring ruled in favor of Blacks having the right to participate in the South Carolina Democratic Primary. He merely referenced the *Smith v. Allwright* ruling in his decision. His ruling in *Wrigthen*, however, would create a different precedent and set the stage for the creation of a new law school in the state.[17]

Already, USC faced another situation where an African American student was trying to gain entry. Cleveland M. McQueen, an African American native of South Carolina, applied for the graduate program in education at USC in 1946. The state legislature, trying to avoid any attempt to desegregate the university, approved funding for a similar type of graduate program at the State Agricultural and Mechanical College, or South Carolina State, the African American land-grant university founded in 1896. Already, there was a template for what the state government could do in the face of Wrighten's attempt to desegregate the law school.[18]

Wrighten's suit for entry into the law school at the University of South Carolina had already pushed the state legislature to appropriate money for a new law school, built exclusively for the training of African Americans. That the law school was in the process of being created was used by the representatives of USC to argue against needing to admit Wrighten. This was merely using the precedent set by *Gaines v. Canada*—there, the state of Missouri was ordered by the Supreme Court to either build a law school for African Americans, or to allow Lloyd Gaines entry as a student. The idea of "separate but equal" was being challenged by the NAACP as never before, but in South Carolina, it would lead to the creation of a law school at S.C. State.[19]

Thurgood Marshall, by the late 1940s the leading attorney for the NAACP's legal crusade against discrimination, saw the case as another way to break the back of segregation in the South. However, S.C. State's president, Miller Whittaker, saw the case differently. For Whittaker, it was a rare opportunity to draw more funding to S.C. State from the legislature, and a way to further cement the school's reputation among African Americans throughout South Carolina and the entire nation. As Patricia Sullivan argued, a decision in favor of creating a law school at S.C. State would have served several interests, with the most paramount being that it gave them the opportunity "to fill a chronic need in a state that had only five black practicing attorneys, as compared with eleven hundred white lawyers." While Marshall and other NAACP officials insisted that the creation of a law school at S.C. State would merely prolong segregation in South Carolina, for Whittaker the needs of his college—and of African Americans in South Carolina preparing for a long, sustained campaign against Jim Crow segregation—meant that a ruling that favored the founding of a new law school at S.C. State would be a victory.[20]

Waring interpreted the decision by the state legislature to set aside funds for a new law school as sufficient to meet the criteria of "separate but equal" as laid out by both *Plessy* and the later *Gaines* decisions. In his ruling, Waring made clear that he was following precedent set down by both decisions. "As a matter of fact, the right to segregate has been assumed or tacitly acknowledged by many of our courts, including the Supreme Court of the United States," he wrote in his decision. "Segregation in education," Waring continued, "may be considered a necessity or a luxury, according to the geographical situs." While Waring acknowledged a key argument of Marshall's team—that the law school at S.C. State would not have received appropriate funds if it were not for the threat of Wrighten desegregating USC—he nonetheless made it clear the state government had made appropriate moves to satisfy the requirement of separate but equal. Ultimately, Waring gave the government of South Carolina three choices: allow Wrighten into USC's law school, complete the construction of a new law school at S.C. State, or close the USC law school and make the *lack* of access to law school universal.[21]

This decision was made despite the law school in Orangeburg being more an idea than a reality. During testimony for the case, Whittaker acknowledged that the law school was far from completion. S.C. State was given until September 1947 to finish the law school—which, miraculously, they did. The new law school was led by an African American law professor named Benner C. Turner. Previously based at the Durham, North Carolina–based law school of North Carolina College, Turner was now tasked with whipping into shape a brand-new law school in a matter of weeks. Hired to help him were Leo Kerford and Cassandra Maxwell, who also had the distinction as the only African American woman who worked as a lawyer in South Carolina. By the opening of law school in September 1947, eight men and one woman were enrolled. A new stage in the history of education in the state of South Carolina had begun.[22]

The African American community within and outside South Carolina had been bitterly divided over the issue of a law school at S.C. State. Thurgood Marshall and other NAACP leaders, and local South Carolina–based activists such as Modjeska Simkins, regarded it as a defeat for desegregation in the state. Marshall went so far as to repeatedly warn Wrighten against attending the law school. But he would do so in 1949, and graduate in 1952—a testament to his desire to finally finish a law degree. For many African Americans in South Carolina, the question of enrolling in a law school at South Carolina State was one about access, albeit limited, to the weapon of the legal system in the fight against segregation. By no means was the school perfect. Indeed, it often suffered in the shadow of USC's law school. But it served its chief purpose: preparing a generation of Black lawyers for legal battle against Jim Crow segregation.[23]

THE LEGACY OF THE SOUTH CAROLINA STATE LAW SCHOOL

When John Wrighten passed away in 1996, obituaries quickly made mention of his court case against the University of South Carolina Law School. The case was situated as giving rise to the law school at South Carolina State, which was a necessary training ground for the lawyers in South Carolina who would push back against Jim Crow segregation. A law partner with Wrighten, Russell Brown, spoke for many African American lawyers when he said, "When it comes to Black attorneys, he was considered to be the granddaddy of us all."[24]

Judge Waring, Thurgood Marshall, and many of the other players in the *Wrighten v. Board of Trustees at the University of South Carolina* had no reason to expect that the otherwise mundane ruling by Waring would lead to tremendous change within South Carolina. Yet this is what happened. The lawyers needed to push many of the key cases in South Carolina as a front of a broader civil rights Movement were trained at S.C. State. While the school graduated fifty-one lawyers between 1947 and its closing in 1966, so many of them were critical to the state's civil rights history that it is impossible to imagine South Carolina's history without the law school existing.[25]

The graduates of the South Carolina State Law school participated in a variety of legal cases during the civil rights crusade in the Palmetto State. Virtually every important legal case in South Carolina in the 1950s and '60s that involved civil rights and race in the state included lawyers trained at S.C. State's law school. It was the S.C. State Law School graduates who defended the "Friendship Nine" who participated in sit-in campaigns in Rock Hill, South Carolina. S.C. State Law School graduates defended the right to peaceable assembly among African Americans in the *Edward v. South Carolina* case of 1963—one which would set a critical standard for the right to street demonstrations.[26]

The school produced future federal court justice Matthew J. Perry and future chief justice of South Carolina's supreme court Ernest A. Finney.[27] Perhaps the greatest irony arising from the existence of the law school, however, was the participation of S.C. Law School graduates in pushing the desegregation of both Clemson University and USC in 1963. Matthew Perry was asked by Modjeska Simkins to see to representing her niece Henrie Monteith in a potential court case to desegregate USC. This would lead to the entry of Monteith, along with Robert Anderson and James Solomon entering the doors of USC on September 11, 1963.[28]

Interestingly, while considerable focus has been on the desegregation of USC in 1963, it is noteworthy that another HBCU—Allen University—increased pressure on the school to desegregate in the late 1950s. In 1958, eleven students from Allen tried to apply to the school. Their initial attempts to desegregate the school rebuffed by USC officials, they appealed to a local lawyer to defend them and press desegregation—John Wrighten. However, a series of miscommunications between the local, state, and national offices of the NAACP delayed and, ultimately, stopped any attempt to push forward with desegregation in 1958. The NAACP's failure to get involved in the case and press it damaged the group in the eyes of many South Carolina–based activists. Again, like the other cases, it has been overshadowed by the eventual success of desegregation in 1963.[29]

The rapid success of Perry and other lawyers crafted in the intellectual crucible of S.C. State's Law School meant, ironically, that the school's days were virtually numbered. The desegregation of the law school at USC in 1964 would make it difficult for S.C. State to justify keeping its law school doors open. Eventually, by 1966, the law school in Orangeburg would be closed.

Nonetheless, the impact of the law school on the history of South Carolina has not been forgotten. In the decades since, the desegregation efforts that fell short have been commemorated in conjunction with the 1963 desegregation moment. The student newspaper, the *Gamecock*, serving as the chief voice of students at the University of South Carolina, should also be seen as a place of memory creation on campus. In 1973, one of the earliest recollections of Wrighten's attempt to desegregate the law school can be found. Only ten years after the second desegregation of South Carolina, the staff writer Doug Williams wrote, "The issue almost reached a head that year (1946) when John Wrighten applied to the USC law school and was refused." The Wrighten case was framed as one that, while it failed, was just a bump on the road to the eventual desegregation of the school. The Charles Bailey desegregation drama was not even mentioned.[30]

In 2003, the student newspaper at South Carolina, the *Gamecock*, mentioned the attempt to desegregate the law school in 1946. "(John) Wrighten was denied admission," the *Gamecock* noted, "but took the school to court." The article itself only mentions Wrighten as an example of an earlier attempt to desegregate the school but reported that it led "USC to create a black law school in Orangeburg." It would have been more accurate to point out that the state government was satisfied with the decision to create a new law school for African Americans at South Carolina State College. Nonetheless, this is not a surprising rendering of the John Wrighten case—often merely seen as the prelude to the eventual, seemingly inevitable, desegregation of the University of South Carolina.[31]

For the fiftieth anniversary of desegregation, the *Gamecock* pointed out the peaceful desegregation of the university—a contrast to the mayhem of desegregation efforts at the University of Georgia, the University of Mississippi, and the University of Alabama in the years from 1957 through 1963. However, there was no mention of the Wrighten and Bailey cases to desegregate the law school. This creation of the memory of the desegregation of USC in 1963, thus, linked it to the traditional narrative of the civil rights movement, but divorced it from the longer campaigns for equality and human rights in the 1930s and '40s. Memory of the past is always changing, in some ways always in motion. The changing story of the desegregation attempts at USC is a powerful example of this.[32]

Chapter Seven

THE LEGACY OF DESEGREGATION

USC and Its Changing Campus and Student Body since the 1960s

Marcia G. Synnott

African Americans have always been history makers at the University of South Carolina (USC). Today, they are known by their names and academic and extracurricular achievements. During the past sixty years, they have endured long journeys from their admission as student pioneers in desegregating USC to slowly gaining acceptance by white classmates and by white society that they are an integral part of its history. Nevertheless, racial discrimination persists in South Carolina. Prior to the 1960s, students at the segregated USC were so "provincial," President Donald S. Russell (1952–1957) held public forums on current issues to broaden their perspectives. At one forum, Alice N. Spearman, executive director of the South Carolina Council on Human Relations, "got up and told them. I said, you know, 'you think I'm an older woman talking to you, but I said I'm younger than a single one of you in here.' I said, 'I'm with it and I don't know what century to put you in.'" Invited to speak about social issues at one of the campus religious centers, she found student attitudes "pathetic," because "they had lived in communities that they hadn't had a new thought injected" in the community probably "during their entire lives." Eventually, her persistent message and the work of the South Carolina Council began to attract the positive attention of small groups of college students, both African Americans and whites.[1]

Spearman's observations were substantiated by Howard Quint, then a USC history professor, whose *Profile in Black and White: A Frank Portrait of South Carolina* (1958), quoted editorial opinions, letters to the editor, and articles principally from the *Charleston News and Courier*, Columbia *Record*, Anderson *Independent*, and *Florence Morning News* to show that most South Carolinians supported segregation and white supremacy. Under Governors James F. Byrnes and his successor George Bell Timmerman Jr., South Carolina delayed desegregation by legal maneuvering and official repression longer than other Deep South states. But South Carolina avoided bloody incidents because more pragmatic leadership emerged in the 1960s. Such a shift could not have occurred without the courage and protests of Black activists, many of them students, and the support of a small, but influential group of white progressives.[2]

On January 28, 1963, Clemson College preceded USC in peacefully admitting Harvey Bernard Gantt of Charleston, whom segregation had forced to study architecture out of state, at Iowa State University, on a South Carolina tuition grant. While the state of South Carolina continued to fight a legal battle to prevent desegregation, USC's president Thomas F. Jones, Dean of Students Charles H. Witten, and other administrators used Clemson as a model in preparing for the university's peaceful admission of African American students. The University of South Carolina did not want to experience the violence that marred integration at the other southern state universities that tried to desegregate between 1956 and 1962: the University of Alabama in January–February 1956 (Autherine Lucy), the University of Georgia in January 1961 (Charlayne Hunter and Hamilton Holmes), and the University of Mississippi in September–October 1962 (James Meredith).[3]

Applying for admission to USC, Henrie Dobbins Monteith received strong support from her mother, Rebecca Monteith, a teacher, who won a successful salary equalization case, one of three in which South Carolina was defeated, and from her aunt, prominent civil rights activist Modjeska Monteith Simkins. Other models were her grandmother, Rachel Hull Monteith, who founded the Nelson School for African American children in Columbia, and her aunt Martha Monteith, the wife of physician Dr. Henry Monteith. In her November 14, 1980, oral history interview in Atlanta, Dr. Henrie Monteith Turner Treadwell described her upbringing in a supportive family "that just always had thousands of antennae up, politically speaking." She attended NAACP meetings and met civil rights leaders Thurgood Marshall and Walter White. After USC rejected her initial application because she "was a Negro," Monteith entered the College of Notre Dame in Baltimore. She and her mother filed a class action suit in federal district court. Monteith's attorneys included Matthew J. Perry of Columbia and Legal Defense Fund attorneys Constance Baker Motley and Jack Greenberg. At the hearing, President Jones had the dean of admissions confirm that USC did not admit her because of her race. On July 10, 1963, Judge J. Robert Martin Jr., chief judge of the US District Court of South Carolina, ordered that she and "'all others similarly situated'" be admitted on September 11. She became the first Black woman admitted since Reconstruction. Without a specific court order, USC sent an official letter of acceptance, on August 2, 1963, to Robert G. Anderson Jr. of Greenville, South Carolina, represented by attorney Donald Sampson. A transfer student from Clark College in Atlanta, he became the first Black student admitted by letter since the Reconstruction era. James Lewis Solomon Jr., a teacher at Morris College in Sumter, was admitted as the first Black graduate student since Reconstruction, and the first in mathematics.[4]

Their experiences in entering USC had been made easier by an earlier biracial meeting in Columbia between Monteith, Anderson, and Solomon and Harvey Gantt and Lucinda Brawley, the first Black woman to enter Clemson on September 9, and White students from both institutions. Gantt described Henrie Monteith as a "very smart young lady, a lot like Vivian Malone," who integrated the University of Alabama on June 11, 1963, despite Governor George C. Wallace's "Stand in the Schoolhouse Door." Monteith, like Malone, was able to distance herself from the pressures of integration and seemed to Gantt to be "probably a little more cynical about the system than I was."[5]

Recalling their biracial meeting, Solomon said: "'we spent a day together talking about what it was going to be like,'" and received assurances that "'they would be our friends on campus and if things really got rough, they would be friends we could talk with.'" *Gamecock* editor Joan Wolcott stated: "We want no hotheads stirring up trouble at our state university.'" She believed: "'With intelligence, faith and regard for our fellow students, the integration problem can be settled in the spirit of which our Carolina community was founded.'"[6] When Monteith, Solomon, and Anderson came to USC to register, university officials, fearing there might be "some violence," ensured that police escorted them from Matthew Perry's office to the administration building, where "all of us registered very quickly." Another form of protection was a wrought iron fence to keep strangers off the campus, some of whom drove to Columbia in vehicles with Alabama tags. Their peaceful registration reassured other Black students to seek enrollment in the fall of 1964.[7]

In the photograph of Monteith, Anderson, and Solomon walking out of the Osborne Administration Building after registering for classes, they were together as a group. However, their experiences were both similar and different. Monteith's sense of independence and supportive family sustained her at USC. She thought "my entry into the University was something that I knew was significant and important for Black people. But it was also a very personal experience for me in that I felt that I had the right to go." It was for her "the normal thing to do and

Robert G. Anderson (left), Henrie Monteith Treadwell (center), and James L. Solomon (right) walk out of the Osborne Administrative Building at the University of South Carolina after register-ing for classes, September 11, 1963. Image Courtesy of The State Newspaper Photo Archive, Richland County Public Library, Columbia, South Carolina.

probably Alabama's and Mississippi's having preceded the event, made it a little easier for me." Though "there were one or two incidents prior to enrolling"—in August her Uncle Henry and Aunt Martha experienced that explosion of two sticks of dynamite at their residence, Monteith "felt safe," because she "knew that precautions had been taken and it did not enter my mind that something could go wrong really and the event itself was peaceful." She was not concerned whether other students liked her, because "it did not matter to me that this mass of people like me. . . . I didn't know whether I would like them, you know. I would wait and see how we liked each other. . . . I suppose that if anything might be common to those of us who survived these integration activities, it might be that we were not overly concerned about how people felt about us."[8]

Monteith lived for a year in a single room in Sims College before moving off campus. Attending her first class on September 12, in physics, she wore a plaid skirt, white blouse, and white tennis shoes, clothing typical of what white students wore, and she ate with them the evening meal at Russell House. But she like Anderson and Solomon had to socialize off campus. The administration requested that they not attend USC football games, where the band played "Dixie." She occasionally had lunch with Solomon and "tried more to keep in touch with" Anderson, until he "dropped out" because "the male population there at the University was much less kind" and gave him "a lot more trouble." He seemed to pose both a "sexual and economic" threat to whites. Monteith did not mind social isolation on campus, nor did she seek to join an all-White sorority. She could count on "a group of white women at the University who were my friends in that they made themselves known to me before I enrolled."[9]

Entering without a court decree, James L. Solomon Jr. recalled both discussions with other graduate students and going out for coffee with other graduate students. "'We knew we were entering a new era there at USC, so it wasn't routine,'" He also remembered: "'Some of the professors were not as comfortable with my being there as others.'" Robert Anderson had been optimistic that, like Harvey Gantt, he would not experience "'another Alabama or Mississippi,'" because "'South Carolina has good leadership, far better than you'd find in Alabama or Mississippi.'" Although he became a member of USC's Debate Team during the spring semester of 1964, Anderson apparently felt such hostility that he wanted to leave the university. As the only Black male student on campus, in Maxcy, a men's dormitory on Pendleton Street, he was threatened by a white student who pointed a broomstick at him and yelled: "Nigger, we got you now!" White students also bounced basketballs near his dormitory room and pounded on his door. Anderson asked Solomon "'to walk with him to the Russell House for lunch so I could get a taste of what he was going through.'" As they walked by windows, white students yelled obscenities.[10]

Monteith and Anderson received moral support from the South Carolina Council on Human Relations. She thought it was "very effective at that time," particularly remembering the work of its executive director, Alice Spearman, and her assistant for student relations, Libby Ledeen. Both Monteith and Anderson served on the Student Council's public relations committee. At the February 17, 1964, annual meeting of the Columbia Council on Human Relations, held at the Good Shepherd Episcopal Church, Monteith, Anderson, and two White students, Jean Derrick and Mary Carlton O'Neal (USC 1964), participated in a panel discussion on "Education and Integration at Carolina," the problems and the subsequent success of USC's desegregation.[11]

In the spring of 1964, Anderson, who had transferred to USC, was befriended by Ginnie Good, a sophomore from Maryland, then attending Kalamazoo College in Michigan, who came to work as an office intern for Council executive director Alice Spearman. Good described Anderson as this "very sensitive and alone young man" who said, "'Ginnie, you're the only white girl that's ever treated me like I was a human being.'" Yet he would not cross an implicit racial line by letting her share the same couch with him in the Wesley Foundation. Good realized "the tragedy that this nineteen-year-old college junior had never been recognized for his own worth is the tragedy of the South." In her report on "South Carolina-My Burden," Good wrote how she learned "very quickly that another man's bondage directly affected my own freedom." But she was also "continually amazed that Mrs. Spearman, the executive director, and Mrs. Ledeen, the program director, both white southerners, could have turned out so open-minded and alive." After leaving South Carolina, Good was an exchange student to Sierra Leone before returning to Kalamazoo College. Anderson received a B.A. degree in political science in June 1966; he would not return to USC until 1988.[12]

To reach out to Black high school students, Monteith, who also attended biracial meetings at the Penn Center, promoted Operation Search, launched by the South Carolina Student Council on Human Relations, November 12, 1965. Going "[Beyond] tokenism," it interviewed and counseled "Negro high school students throughout the state concerning the possibility of enrolling in college in S.C., including one of the integrated universities." She sent a form letter congratulating Black high school students on their performance on the National Achievement Test and informed them that Student Council's College Counselor, Ulysses Chambers, was available to visit and discuss possibilities with interested Black students. Harvey Gantt chaired its Recruiting Committee, which sent biracial student recruiting teams to hold group conferences for sophomores through seniors in seven communities: Columbia, Florence, Mullins, Sumter, Newberry, Greenville, and Charleston. As a result of their efforts, South Carolina received a higher percentage of Lehman Fund scholarships for Black applicants to desegregated colleges than did other states. USC president Thomas Jones had emphasized several times, said Monteith, that "South Carolina has been exporting many of its best minds, its outstanding scholars for generations." She concluded her form letter by saying that the South Carolina Student Council was at Clemson for Harvey Gantt, with her when she enrolled at USC, and would be there for other Black students when they entered an integrated South Carolina college.[13]

She earned her degree after taking courses for two years and a summer but felt that "in many ways I wasn't challenged enough. I recall just sort of getting somewhat lackadaisical about some courses, something that I might not, would not, could not have done in a more stringent environment." After graduation in August 1965, Treadwell earned a master's degree in biology at Boston University and later a PhD in biochemistry and molecular biology at Atlanta University (1975); she also completed post-doctoral studies in public health at Harvard University. She chaired the biology department at Morris Brown College in Atlanta (1975–1985). Toward the end of her career, she worked as the director of Community Voices and a research professor at the Morehouse School of Medicine.[14]

In her 1980 oral history interview, Dr. Henrie Monteith Turner Treadwell described her camaraderie with Harvey Gantt, with whom she "interacted quite often through meetings or something there in the state and have maintained that friendship until today." She had interactions with President Thomas F. Jones, usually on paper regarding her representing USC at Black institutions. Both Dean of Administration William H. Patterson and Dean of Students Charles Witten were "very supportive individuals." Patterson was initially her academic advisor, while Witten "sought me out, always interested in how I was doing, if there were any problems." President Jones, along with several other South Carolina leaders, among them Ernest F. Hollings, felt that the integration of Clemson and USC marked a historical change.[15]

Treadwell gave "two answers" to the question of why South Carolina delayed integration longer than other Deep South states. First, "segregation was so entrenched." Moreover, "South Carolina started to be forgotten about because many of us were able to go elsewhere at that point." By the 1960s, academically qualified Blacks were gaining more options in higher education, including offers from leading private universities. For his master's degree, Harvey Gantt chose to attend the Massachusetts Institute of Technology (MIT). In Treadwell's view, USC "was not some, you know, place of high academic standards where it would really do something for me," given that "national defense loans and money from the college" supported her at the College of Notre Dame in Baltimore. "Now the irony is, had they just admitted me," she said, "I probably wouldn't have gone because then there would have been no point to have been made." Her rejection by USC "made it something to fight about and so they might have had two or three more years on their own had they left it alone." She found Matthew Perry experienced and interested "in pushing things forward and certainly was competent and up to the task and that was just a more-or-less natural decision.[16]

Synnott asked Dr. Treadwell to comment on attorney Constance Baker Motley's explanation on why Clemson and USC finally desegregated: whites "didn't fear blacks in '63." Blacks, rather than being "passive," Aunt Modjeska Simkins said, "were very much involved in black institutions of higher education and I guess amazingly, not amazingly, blacks from that same era look at me as the strange one because I did not go to a black institution because that's where the action was according to them." Treadwell added: "it's very easy to say from a New York perspective that those people down there are just passive." But African Americans in South Carolina were cautious, because they saw "people across the country being killed," and they had to decide "whether or not you are going to do that, whether or not you want your home burned down this week." But she did not "think that as a group we have ignored anything."[17]

Asked about South Carolina's "aristocratic racism, which in some ways is the upper class, the South of Broad Street type people," Treadwell described it as "a veneer in some respects." Commenting on "the difference of racism in the North and the South," she preferred "the South. I would take it any day." She had "very good feelings about the state and about the people in the state," because "we interact better, more truthfully, you know. There is more honesty in our interaction than there is in the North." She and Harvey Gantt "used to talk about the fact that we did know what we could and couldn't do and quite often now people don't bother you in the South about where you go and what you do." She also agreed with Gantt's comment: "You might not be able to appeal to a South Carolinian's moral principles, but you can appeal to his sense of manners." This quality "separated South Carolina in some respects from Mississippi and other places. I think it was the sense of manners." She experienced racism in Boston in looking for an apartment and "would have loved it if the NAACP or anybody else had been able to let me live where I wanted to in Boston when I had left." Living in Brighton, Cambridge, and then in Roxbury, a city of Boston neighborhood that was home to many Blacks, she was "naïve" and surprised when making "the mistake of crossing the street towards North Boston and being asked are you crazy, is something wrong with you, by a white man who I guess had my interest at heart but—you know." In the South, she knew "where I shouldn't bother about going and that made life simpler for me."[18]

Although pockets of the Ku Klux Klan existed in the South, "racism in the North is more vicious." While Treadwell "would settle for a white southerner almost any day in general," she remained "cautious" about political leaders in the South and could not identify "anyone that I have a great deal of confidence in." As of 1980, South Carolina had not elected an African American to statewide office, although they were about 30 percent of the population. In contrast, Republican Edward William Brooke III was a political trailblazer in Massachusetts as the first African American attorney general. He served two terms (1962–1966), and then became the first African American since the Reconstruction era elected by popular vote to the US Senate (1967–1979). Treadwell recognized "we will have to have a third reconstruction," even though Blacks in the South have "fought some battles that we won't have to fight again."[19]

When she returned to Columbia to give a seminar at Benedict College in the late 1970s, Dr. John H. Dawson (PhD, Stanford University, 1976) invited her to visit USC's Department of Biochemistry and Molecular Biology. In 1980,

Treadwell said she felt no real loyalty to USC and was then "not a contributing alumna." She said that Black students, about six percent at the University of Georgia in Athens, "do not get the fairest of shakes" in terms of advisement. They received much better advisement at Morris Brown and Spelman colleges. Black students, who numbered about 13 percent at USC's Columbia campus in 1980, still experienced limited career opportunities. "You can find with a black student who finishes medical school, they're not going to get the choice residencies in many cases." For Blacks who earned graduate degrees, "the job scene is pretty good," though only a small percentage earn a PhD, a fact that had not substantially changed by 2020 at historically white, now desegregated universities.[20]

James L. Solomon also gave thoughtful and informative answers about his years at USC during his interview. He was then Coordinator of Facilities Planning in the Columbia office of the Commission on Higher Education. After serving two of his six years in the US Air Force in Okinawa, Solomon went to Shaw Air Force Base in Sumter where he met his wife, Helen, a student at Morris College. He emphasized "that we are very proud of the black heritage, our black heritage. We're very proud of our black colleges." During the early 1960s, he and attorney Ernest Finney "were very, very much involved" in the marches and sit-ins in Sumter. Moreover, James G. McCain of the Congress of Racial Equality (CORE) "was a very good friend of mine and we worked all over the state in those days." Solomon also knew James Felder, who attended Clark College, and became vice president of administration with Operation PUSH (People United to Save Humanity), founded by Jesse Jackson.[21]

As a husband with a family, Solomon decided he "was not a crusader" and wanted to become a teacher. Well prepared with a bachelor's degree in chemistry at Morris College and a master's degree in mathematics from Atlanta University, he decided to apply to USC after reading in the newspapers about Henrie Monteith's lawsuit. Coming to USC to take the required GRE examination, he was surprised "that the television cameras and reporters were there waiting for me." On campus, he met Mathematics Department chairman Lionel Williams, Dean of Students Charles Witten, and Graduate School dean Robert H. Wienefeld. Solomon gained "the impression that the university had made a commitment to blacks" and that there would be no "problems with the administration in enrolling."[22]

As an "older" graduate student, he "had very good experiences" at USC and "just did not experience the kinds of things that Robert did." Solomon attributed Anderson's difficulties, in part, to "his own personality": "Robert was a kind of tense person. He didn't joke very much. He might have had a bit of fear of white people. I don't think that blacks tend to admit it but it would have been very silly in those days if you didn't have a little bit of fear towards whites, from the police and from people."

Anderson did not carry outside the gun he had in his room as protection against the beer-drinking "Guys [who]would bang on his door at night. They'd wait until they thought he was asleep. Kick his door and bang on his door and call him names and they'd stick things on his door, nasty notes, you know, sometimes threatening notes." Had Anderson been caught with a gun, Solomon said, he would have been expelled from USC. When his gun fell out of his pocket, Cleveland McDowell, the second Black student admitted to Ole Miss, June 5, 1963, after James Meredith's October 1, 1962, admission, had been expelled from its Law School on September 24, 1963.[23]

Henrie Monteith did not feel harassed, said Solomon, in part because "they probably picked the dormitory that they put her in," after determining whether "the students that lived in that dorm would accept her more or less." At the "news conference" following registration, "a couple of girls from her dorm came up and talked to her and offered to show her around." Indeed, said Solomon, her "Monteith family is a well-known family in South Carolina, two sides," including "a white side," in terms of grandparents.[24]

Commenting on his own academic experiences, Solomon said: "The graduate, the PhD program in mathematics was very young. They'd only had it about a year or so." He did not "think there were more than seven or eight students in the program at that time." Since "everybody was having problems really digging in and trying to make it kind of made us friends," who "studied together" in their "study cubicles." Disappointed "in the math department at the university," which "was in a constant state of change, a constant state of flux," he judged Atlanta University's math department to be "better organized." In USC's math department: "Most of the professors were foreigners with very pronounced accents, either French or German." Yet, in retrospect, he "would have stayed and finished" his doctoral degree. His experiences took a toll on his health: losing "most of my hair, balding," and creating "tensions" within his family. None of his children—two sons and a daughter—stayed at USC long enough to graduate. His daughter transferred after a year and a half to Columbia College to finish her degree. People "took interest in her as an individual and she got to know people that she could talk with when she had problems."[25]

Solomon thought "that blacks by and large have been kind of disillusioned by the results of desegregation." When schools desegregated, there was a movement to eliminate Black schools and dismiss their academic, administrative, and athletic staffs. As chairman of the Sumter District 17 School Board, Solomon, who in 1976 was the first Black elected official in Sumter County since the Reconstruction era, endeavored "to keep our system desegregated." Blacks in higher education resisted attempts to eliminate their colleges, because they realized that historically white universities like USC would "never be more than twenty-five or thirty percent black." Likewise, South Carolina State University "should never be more than twenty-five or thirty percent white."[26]

Given the General Assembly's final determination on who serves on boards of public colleges and universities. Solomon accepted having White trustees at South Carolina State College; its board was "about forty-some percent white." He opposed appointing "a white president," which would make it "a white college" in the eyes of the Black community. The percentage of Blacks who "graduated from graduate and professional schools" in South Carolina "is about 11.9%." Believing "that the American way is to preserve some of the heritage of each of the ethnic groups," he maintained "it will be doing a disservice to the American tradition and the American way to insist that all public higher education institutions become white." Historically Black institutions are important "to black kids," who "have to have somebody to look up to."[27]

At USC, African Americans have slowly created places for themselves. In 1970, less than 2 percent of its student body were African American: only 279. After some federal pressure, USC increased Black enrollment during the 1970s to almost 12 percent: 3,070. African Americans also began to play intercollegiate sports. In 1969, Casey Manning became the first African American to play on USC's basketball team, which finished second in the Atlantic Coast Conference (ACC). USC men's basketball team won the ACC championship over the University of North Carolina but lost to Pennsylvania in the ACC tournament. Through the support of a biracial coalition that included both the Association of Afro-American Students and white student groups, Harry Walker was, in 1971, the first African American elected as president of student government. That year, Harold A. White was hired as a football graduate assistant. He rose to become USC's senior associate athletics director, handling academic support and student services until his retirement in 2007. In 2020, with the goal of raising $100,000, "the Harold A. White Scholarship was established to assist students pursuing graduate degrees in sport and entertainment management."[28]

Even as they achieved successes during the late 1960s and '70s, African Americans still felt socially isolated, even unwelcome on campus. Gail Ransome, elected the first Black homecoming queen in 1973, supported by the Association of Afro-American Students, heard booing from some White students when she entered the USC stadium. The first Black fraternity, Kappa Alpha Psi, chartered in 1970, joined in 1976 with three other Black fraternities and four Black sororities to withdraw from USC's Interfraternity Council (IFC) due to a spending dispute, and form the Panhellenic Council. Charles McMillan, speaking from USC's office of student affairs, said: "Black students are looking for acceptance as students and this takes time.""[29]

Perhaps a decisive turning point for better interracial relations and greater acceptance of African Americans on campus came when football running back George Washington Rogers, from Duluth, Georgia (1977–1980), propelled USC to defeat the University of Michigan, 17 to 14, in Ann Arbor on September 17. After winning the 1980 Heisman Trophy and being "named College Football Player of the Year and a consensus All-America," Rogers was honored by a joint session of the South Carolina General Assembly, during which he praised his USC academic program in the College of General Studies. The NFL's first overall draft pick in 1981, Rogers played for the New Orleans Saints (1981–1984) and the Washington Redskins (1985–1987), which won the XXII Super Bowl. He then retired due to injuries. On September 12, 2015, USC unveiled a statue of George W. Rogers at the north-end of Williams-Brice Stadium.[30]

In November 1988, USC prepared to celebrate the twenty-fifth anniversary of its 1963 desegregation. Henrie Moneith Treadwell, then program director for the W. K. Kellogg Foundation of Battle Creek, Michigan, and Robert Anderson returned to participate as panelists on "The Origins of Contemporary Desegregation at the University of South Carolina, A Twenty-five Year Retrospective 1963–1988." Dr. Treadwell was the keynote speaker. Anderson, who had served in Vietnam after graduating from USC, earned a social work degree from Hunter College and worked in New York's social services, helping Cuban refugees, and then in the Bureau of Child Welfare. Anderson also conducted an alcohol counseling program. After retiring as a social worker, he worked in the Veterans Administration for twelve years. Appreciating what he saw and experienced in 1988, he told James Solomon: "'Jim, I'm so glad I came back. This changes my whole perspective of USC. I feel so much better about this school.'"[31]

In the fall of 2000, the University of South Carolina had "the highest percentage of African Americans at any flagship university in the nation," observed the *Journal of Blacks in Higher Education*. Its 447 Blacks constituted 17.6 percent of the freshmen and 18.7 percent of all students enrolled, though considerably below the state's 30 percent Black population. These percentages continued for several years. In 2003, when Treadwell returned for the fortieth anniversary of USC's integration, its Black enrollment continued to be higher than at any other southern state flagship university. But by the fall of 2007, while USC's total freshman enrollment had increased almost 66 percent, only 301 Black freshmen enrolled, 8 percent, and total Black enrollment fell to 12.5 percent. Recognizing the continuing need to focus on its recruitment and admissions policies, USC increased its Black enrollment to 11 percent by the fall of 2010.[32]

Both Dr. Treadwell and James L. Solomon have also been recognized for their contributions to USC and to South Carolina. Her strong academic record and scholarship in molecular biology earned her South Carolina's Distinguished Service Award in 2006. On March 24, 2010, Dr. Treadwell, Director of Community Voices: Healthcare for the Underserved at Morehouse School of Medicine, again returned to USC to present the keynote address at its Institute for African American Research under a major South Carolina Humanities Council grant. Reflecting on her pioneering role, Dr. Treadwell said in 2012: "'It was not important for *me* to be admitted.'" She believed: "'It was important that *all* African Americans meeting admissions criteria be admitted. Ending discrimination based on color or race was the real issue for me. I was just a "wedge," and I had a supportive family and community. I believe that people need to stand for something that may be greater than they are or would be.'" Now, an enthusiastic and proud alumna, she hoped that many other students will develop the "'freedom to act,'" as they pursue their own path in life.[33]

Robert Anderson had died in April 2009, but he made a lasting impression as an undergraduate and as an alumnus on race relations at the University of South Carolina.[34] His story was illustrated in an exhibit in the USC Museum of Education: *1963–2013: Desegregation—Integration Robert G. Anderson, Jr. (1944–2009)*. Thorne Compton, who has chaired USC's Department of Art, remembered Anderson from their time on the Debate Team. He was "a person who was willing to break barriers," and "took his presence on campus very seriously, but he didn't take himself too seriously." A civil rights activist who knew the Rev. Martin Luther King, Anderson "was strong and tough minded, smart and brash and certainly not subservient." "'Some of my experiences at Carolina,'" he had reflected in 1988, "'were funny, others painful, and some leave bitter memories and scars.'" He recognized that "as individuals, as Southerners, and as Americans, we should cut out this cancer called racism." To Treadwell, Anderson was "the canary in the coalmine for so many black men who are too often marginalized, ostracized, and ultimately shut away or shut out simply because of the color of their skin." Yet Anderson's spirit, defined by his courage, "will guide many young men and women into the future just because you cared enough to take a stand for justice! Bob Anderson . . . GONE TOO SOON!"[35]

LEGACIES

The path that Henrie Monteith Treadwell forged encouraged the recent generations of Black students to develop their talents to the fullest. Football defensive end Jadeveon Clowney described himself as walking "in footsteps of Henrie Monteith" when he participated in a three-day football festival the last weekend in August 2013. Contacted by telephone at her Atlanta home, she said, with pride: "'Those are my children.'" She never attended a USC football game as a student, but so did years later. Kim Jamieson, one of the planners of a year-long celebration of the 1963 desegregation, Columbia, SC 63, observed: "'Henrie wasn't able to attend because of her skin color, but today, the only segregation of color you'll see at South Carolina football games is garnet and black, and orange.'" Admiring the players, having viewed USC football games on television, she would like them to know about her own courage: "'They are able to live their dream simply because I took a walk one day.'"[36]

Treadwell and James Solomon returned to celebrate the 50th anniversary of desegregation in 2013–14. The events highlighted USC's progress in race relations since 1963. On April 11, 2014, they attended the dedication of USC's Desegregation Commemorative Garden. Inscribed on the granite monument in this garden is Nikky Finney's poem, "The Irresistible Ones," which celebrates those who brought "the bright peppermint of change."[37]

A commemorative plaque honoring James L. Solomon's many achievements was unveiled in a ceremony on April 22, 2019. It will be installed in LeConte College, home of USC's Department of Mathematics. At its February 8, Board Meeting, the trustees approved the following text:

James L. Solomon Jr. Recognition Plaque at LeConte College
Honoring
James L. Solomon Jr.

In recognition of his enrollment as a graduate student in mathematics at the University of South Carolina, the University pays tribute to Mr. Solomon as one of three African-American students to desegregate the University in 1963.

Mr. Solomon had a distinguished career in South Carolina state government, and he was an engaged member of many county and city organizations.

For his service to the State of South Carolina, Mr. Solomon was awarded the state's highest civilian honor, the Order of the Palmetto, in 1980 and again in 1992.[38]

But the legacies of racial discrimination persist, as discussed by Chloe Barlow, on February 3, 2020, in "Students who integrated USC experienced racism, isolation," part of *The Gamecock's* Civil Rights series. The "'pushback among some students around the whole issue of race and racism,'" said Henrie Monteith Treadwell, "'needs to stop. And if it does not stop, I have little confidence that any of us in this nation, regardless of color, or gender, will do well.'" She emphasized: "'You may not want to join my hand but join the effort toward human and social justice.'"[39]

On February 4, 2020, Dr. Treadwell, Research Professor of Community Health and Preventive Medicine at Morehouse School of Medicine, returned to USC in celebration of African American Women's History for an evening discussion with Nikky Finney, The John H. Bennett, Jr. Endowed Professor of Creative Writing and Southern Letters. During their conversation, Dr. Treadwell emphasized again the themes that had guided her life: family network, intellectual curiosity, and commitment to racial justice. "We are becoming a more diverse nation," she concluded, "and we must be ready for it." In 2020, Professor Finney and Dr. Treadwell were included among the eight women honored by Columbia's City of Women. By their exemplary lives they continue the ongoing fight for racial justice.[40]

Chapter Eight

PEACE, LOVE, EDUCATION, AND LIBERATION

The Black Campus Movement at the
University of South Carolina

Ramon M. Jackson

On a frigid day in early February 1968, Student Nonviolent Coordinating Committee (SNCC) organizer George Ware burned with righteous anger. "The Ku Klux Klan or its psychological equivalent went to South Carolina State and murdered a group of students. I am not going to suggest anything people should do. It is crystal clear to me that if people do not develop the strength to fight and change society, they will not have the right to exist," he declared before roughly 200 students gathered at an event sponsored by the Afro-American Students Association (AFRO) at the University of South Carolina, the state's predominantly white flagship university. Bitterly frustrated with the state sponsored brutality that left three Black students dead and dozens wounded in Orangeburg days earlier, Ware offered a new prescription to cure the disease of white supremacy that plagued Black lives in the Palmetto State: Black Power. "We can't improve white people. We can't be improved by them. We were never concerned with integration into this society. You ask about Black Power. I say of Black Power we have some to render white people impotent over our lives. When they have power over our lives, it is *genocide*." Focusing intently on the smattering of Black students in the audience, many of whom were children of the state's Black aristocracy or auditioning for it, he roared, "You should recognize that you are black and *stop cringing from it*."

Other students were already on the move. The malicious assault on Black students at South Carolina State College, dubbed the "Orangeburg Massacre," horrified and outraged Black students at Carolina who immediately spoke out against the murders. After an intense bull session in his dormitory room, Carolina student Lewis James and five of his friends staged an impromptu protest on the grounds of the South Carolina State House holding signs which read: "Genocide at South Carolina State," "Bullets are a good substitute for tear gas and fire hoses," and "Orangeburg police have a license to kill."[1] Student leaders within AFRO, many of whom had familial ties to State College, invited their shaken peers to Columbia to share their story the following day. "The police said they were shooting over people's heads. If that's so, why were people hit between the neck and the waist?" one State College co-ed angrily questioned, "Some were shot in the back." While AFRO members listened intently, another victim chimed in: "Maybe it was too windy for tear gas, but what about the hoses? They couldn't use water because they were afraid we would catch cold. They don't want you getting sick. They want to kill you." State College students blasted Governor Robert Evander McNair for his handling of the crisis and his increasingly murky explanation for the violence that chilly February evening in Orangeburg. "He said there were only about 100 students out there. If that were true, then the police knocked off half of them," an unidentified student quipped. Quaking with a mixture of rage, sadness, and hope, State College students regaled their hosts with stories of how the tragedy had unified the student body, which had been divided over questions of student and Black Power in recent months. "All of the student body is behind the situation. If they weren't before, they are now."[2] They were not alone. Carolina students, like others across the country, were awakened by the violence in Orangeburg and set out to demolish racism and white supremacy on campus and in their surrounding communities. As Ware noted at the conclusion of his call to action, rebellions in America were indeed spontaneous explosions caused by festering generational inequities.

Recent scholarship on the Black Campus Movement, a potent addition to the subfield of Black Power Studies, has improved our understanding of the impact of Black Power ideology on the social and intellectual climate at Historically Black Colleges and Universities (HBCU) and Predominantly White Educational Institutions (PWI). Following the lead of Ibram X. Kendi, scholars have documented this unique, loosely connected national movement led by a new generation of Black campus activists and a multiracial coalition of allies and sympathizers to dramatically reform the racial constitution of higher education to provide a more inclusive and relevant learning experience. Between 1965 and 1972, radical and militant moderate Black campus activists and their allies disrupted higher education in every section of the country requesting, demanding, and protesting for an education that provided students with the inclusive social environment, freedom of cultural expression and intellectual tools required to fix a broken society. At historically Black and white colleges and universities, radical and militant moderate Black campus activists formed politically and culturally progressive Black Student Unions (BSU) and assumed control of Student Government Associations (SGA) to pressure administrations to pursue campus reforms including the recruitment of more Black students, increased hiring of Black faculty and administrators, creation of Black studies courses, programs, departments, and the end of paternalism and racism on campus. Pushing the envelope further, Black campus activists at southern HBCUs such as State College and Voorhees called for the restructuring of majority-white faculty and trustee boards, an end to repressive rules from bygone eras, and the revision of outdated curriculum that prepared students to be docile cogs in the capitalist machine rather than provide them with deeper analysis and solutions to the generational poverty and inequality that plagued their communities. Participants in the Black Campus Movement, whether radical or more moderate, ultimately aimed to revolutionize higher education.[3]

Despite Black South Carolinians' tradition of "forceful, sustained, and militant civil rights agitation" in the decades after World War II along with the presence of six public and private HBCUs and numerous PWIs that gradually desegregated during the pivotal 1960s era, historians have rarely associated South Carolina with the Black Power movement or considered it fertile ground for Black campus radicalism in pursuit of student power, intellectual freedom, and racial equality. Studies of the state's civil rights movement either ignore this period or narrowly focus on the Orangeburg Massacre as a singular moment when the state failed to control the anger and ambitions of its Black populace rather than the catalyst for widespread social change. These scholars explain Orangeburg as an aberration, a tragic moment of incivility caused by intransigent Black militants who threatened to forever blemish the state's hard-won reputation for moderation, stability, and racial peace. They contend that South Carolina, this momentary loss of composure aside, managed to avoid the brutality and violence so closely identified with other Deep South states due to careful negotiation between cautious and conservative leaders of both races. Like a powerful, aristocratic family seeking to hide its dark secrets and fatal flaws, those who share this view prefer to "speak softly the victims' names and move on," an act of racial privilege and ageism that marginalizes the stories of tenacious, militant Black student activists across the Palmetto State who honored the fallen by fighting doggedly to transform South Carolina's colleges and universities into politically radical, culturally progressive, and socially responsible "Black universities" or carved open social and intellectual spaces to allow growing numbers of Black students to question their racial identities, think politically, form bonds within and across racial lines, forge Black studies programs, and ultimately achieve a larger freedom and greater heritage for future students at predominantly white institutions such as the University of South Carolina. Change at the University of South Carolina and the state writ large did not come with relative ease but instead was the product of intense conflict, negotiation, struggle, and compromise often inspired by the same Black college students scapegoated as the cause for state violence and militarism displayed in Orangeburg, Denmark, Charleston, and other cities during the late 1960s.[4]

Explicit within studies of the Black Campus Movement is an understanding that the Orangeburg Massacre was neither an aberration nor irrelevant to Black students nationwide. The malice displayed by South Carolina law enforcement officials on that chilly February 1968 evening in Orangeburg fit the pattern of national backlash against efforts by Black students to transform their campuses and communities. Black campus activists nationwide were rebuked, ridiculed, suspended, expelled, beaten, jailed, injured, traumatized and killed—over a dozen students at southern HBCUs were murdered by overzealous law enforcement—for their efforts to change the racial reconstitution of higher education.[5] Viewed within this context, Governor McNair's use of police power to squash campus rebellions at South Carolina State and, one year later, Voorhees College was part of a devastating campaign of surveillance, political repression and militarized state intervention ordered by white politicians nationally in response to the awakening of Black college students to their second-class status as students and American citizens.[6] These scholars note that the Orangeburg Massacre was one of two major turning points—the other being the assassination of Dr. Martin Luther King Jr.—that fueled more strident activism for greater student power, increased Black representation on faculty and among campus leadership, the creation of Black Studies programs, and an end to racism in the nation's colleges and universities. The Orangeburg Massacre struck Black students in the Carolinas, Virginia, and Washington, DC, like a bolt of lightning setting college campuses ablaze with activism. Black campus activists at North Carolina A&T, North Carolina Central College, Johnson C. Smith, Shaw, and Virginia State University planned and executed marches and mock funeral processions to honor the three slain students. Outraged student activists at Howard University voiced their frustration by seizing the administration building for nearly a week to force campus authorities to accede to the "Orangeburg Ultimatum," a list of demands intended to radically transform "the Mecca" into a true Black university.[7]

Inspired by brewing discontent over the Vietnam War, increased desire for greater personal and academic freedom, and rising frustration with the glacial pace and outcomes of desegregation in public and higher education, and intensified by the violence at Orangeburg, Black students across South Carolina began to push for the racial reconstitution of the educational institutions they called home. While most studies of this new phase in the Long Black Student Movement in South Carolina understandably focus on student organizing and protest at its historically Black Colleges and Universities, particularly South Carolina State, Black students at predominantly white colleges and universities did not sit idly and wait for social change. Between 1965 and 1972, a new generation of Black campus activists at the University of South Carolina (USC)—supported by an increasingly broad, multiracial coalition of allies—demanded a more relevant learning experience and dramatic changes to the racial constitution of higher education at the state's flagship institution. Moderate and militant Black student activists organized and protested for relevant educational experiences, increased recruitment of their peers and Black faculty, and the inclusion of African Americans as full members of the Carolina community. The assassination of Rev. Dr. Martin Luther King Jr. and the heinous assault upon students at State College accelerated their push for change on campus and in the surrounding community.

In the aftermath of these tragedies, Black students at USC channeled their anger and rage into the pursuit of greater student power, racial inclusion, and institutional reform. Student leaders within the Association of Afro-American Students (AFRO) fought for an end to the display of racist symbols on campus, organized culturally relevant extracurricular activities, pushed for greater inclusion in university athletic programs, and spearheaded a powerful insurgent campaign to elect Harry Walker as the first African American student body president at a university in the Deep South. Moreover, they represented their peers in negotiations with USC president Thomas F. Jones and other campus administrators to establish an interdisciplinary program in African American Studies, thus forcing to the center historically marginalized ideas and broadening the university curriculum to include the analysis of the social, political, cultural, and historical experience of African Americans and people of African descent around the globe. Despite a lengthy period of institutional neglect and constant financial strain, this program remains an enduring legacy of the Black Campus Movement at Carolina and continues to provide USC students of all backgrounds with knowledge of Black history and culture while also preparing them to model citizenship in an increasingly polarized American society.

BEYOND DESEGREGATION: BLACK CAMPUS LIFE AT USC, 1965–1971

By the fall of 1967, the racial dam finally began to break at USC. Wilkinson High School graduate Luther Battiste was among dozens of Black students who entered South Carolina's flagship university, the last holdout against desegregation among state supported colleges and universities in the Deep South. Growing up in Orangeburg, Battiste was no stranger to the indignities of segregation and the fierce, determined struggle for racial equality raging in his hometown and across the nation. He remembers his sheltered, nurturing upbringing at Wilkinson, where faculty instilled confidence both within the classroom and encouraged him to join the freedom struggle. "Marching and picketing in the Orangeburg civil rights movement made me a politically conscious person," he recalled. Battiste regularly visited South Carolina State College, where both of his parents were employed, and spent much of his teenage years attending mass meetings featuring prominent civil rights organizers and attorneys or buried in the library stacks studying Black history or politics. "It was during that time that I got my exposure to Matthew Perry," Battiste later remembered. "He became sort of my hero, my role model—the iconic person in my life that I aspired to be like."[8]

To Battiste, Carolina was an idyllic yet alien world. "It was like being lost in a sea of whiteness," Battiste recalled decades later. He and other Black students remembered walking around campus for days at a time without encountering another Black student. It was quite a culture shock. Token desegregation had done little to change hearts and minds, as most white students and faculty were largely hostile to the idea of granting Black students full membership within the Carolina community. "Nothing was done to make our adjustment easy," he lamented. "In the beginning, there were no black athletes or black organizations of any kind." Far removed from the insular Black neighborhoods of his youth, Battiste quickly learned that he was not only unwelcome but, even if he were, city life had not changed much in the brief interim since the passage of the 1964 Civil Rights Act. Although he was student at Carolina, Battiste was prohibited from dining at several nearby restaurants. "There was a place across the street called Cogburn's. If you were Black, you could only order from the window. You couldn't go in and sit down and eat. You had to order from the window to get food." His unfamiliarity with the racial boundaries of Columbia's neighborhoods made seemingly simple tasks like getting a haircut perilous. After receiving a "bowl cut" from a Black barber in a barbershop that only served whites, Battiste was advised by locals to visit nearby Washington Street—the city's longtime Black business district—where he was eventually rescued from certain ridicule and social ostracism.[9] Classrooms at Carolina were not oases. "I became an International Studies major because I started out in Political Science and one of the teachers in the department was so racist that a Black student couldn't pass his class. You had to pass two of them to graduate," the Orangeburg native explained. French professors would often assign Black students roles as domestic workers in skits used to improve student proficiency. Rather than suffer such humiliation, Battiste dropped the course.[10]

The shifting social and political climate also offered challenges. Black students often questioned their own racial identities, debated the merits of continued use of nonviolence, and tested new rhetorical and tactical strategies to create change on campus. Was it possible to be culturally "Black" yet also a part of the vibrant intellectual and social community at Carolina? Initially, Battiste focused much of his energies on academics and navigating the sometimes lonely, confusing, and tense social scene. Many Black students, like his first roommate Gordon Granger, left unexpectedly out of frustration, fear, or financial uncertainty. By his sophomore year, Battiste found his footing. He made good grades and his social circle widened to include new friends on both sides of the color line. One of his closest friends was his new roommate Harry Wright, an upperclassman from rural York, South Carolina. Wright tutored the sophomore and convinced him to seek election as a class representative in student government. Often described as a quiet yet brilliant student, Wright, the son of a brick mason and nurse, grew up in a family that valued education and demanded excellence. His grandfather attended the Colored Normal Industrial Agricultural and Mechanical College of South Carolina, known today as South Carolina State University, during the early twentieth century. Later generations followed suit; all his paternal aunts, uncles, and cousins graduated high school and most attended college.[11] A product of segregated schools in York, Wright entered high school just as the seeds laid by the civil rights movement began to bear fruit. White reaction, however, was subdued compared to what his roommate witnessed in Orangeburg. "In York, it was fairly quiet. There were no big demonstrations. Things quietly integrated. It was maybe slower than other places that got publicity but things gradually integrated," Wright recalled. Although the volume of civil rights activity in York did not match what occurred elsewhere in South Carolina, the future doctor did not sit idly by while his peers fought for racial equality. Inspired by national media coverage of civil rights protests, he and several friends desegregated Sunday services at four white churches over the course of a few months. "We showed up when church started and found a seat," Wright recalled with laughter, "I think the church figured that they would be less likely to have an incident in the church if they demonstrated what they supposed to be . . . what they were talking about in the church." Curious and annoyed glances aside, the youths worshipped without incident. Emboldened by their success, they later unsuccessfully tried to dine at a local restaurant but were asked to leave.[12] By the time he graduated from segregated Jefferson High in 1965, the confident, brainy, and courageous teen was no stranger to combating racism through strategic, targeted activism.

Arriving at USC during the fall of 1965, the freshman was struck by the size and beauty of the picturesque campus. Wright knew almost nothing about the experiences of the few Black students who attended the university since Henrie Monteith, James Solomon, and Robert Anderson desegregated the institution two years earlier. There were roughly a dozen Black students living on campus with an equal number of commuter and residential students living in the city. None of the Black students living on campus had white roommates. Wright was paired with Sammy Backman, the son of a Black fisherman who owned a thriving seafood business on James Island. "It was designed. The university matched Black students with black students," Wright recalled. The small group of Black students living on campus became a tight-knit unit. "The Black students used to eat together in the afternoon, evening, and after the day ended at the Russell House for two purposes: To see each other and to make sure nothing happened to anybody," he remembered. Mealtimes provided Wright and his classmates with much needed opportunities for fellowship, levity, and reconnaissance. These gatherings were a welcome respite from long stretches of loneliness, as the students were often the only Black person present in any given situation. Wright, however, was luckier than most of his friends. After deciding to major in Chemistry, the York native was mentored by Earline Houston, one of three Black faculty members at the university. Houston helped Wright develop good study habits, navigate departmental politics, and hired him as a research assistant on several key projects. Unlike Battiste, Wright remembers that most of the senior white professors were helpful and supportive. A few wrote letters on his behalf when he applied to graduate school and maintained close friendships with him throughout his life.[13]

Despite enjoying a more collegial atmosphere than his friends, Wright chafed at the lack of extracurricular offerings for Black students at Carolina. He and his peers initially spent much of their time at events and parties hosted at nearby Benedict College and Allen University, two neighboring historically Black colleges and universities. Carolina social and athletic events often served as cruel reminders that Black students were unwelcome members of the campus community. "We'd go to football games. They had the buses that would go down Assembly Street to the stadium. They were generally crowded but we would find a seat and nobody would sit next to us. So we had perfectly good, uncrowded seats!" Wright joked. He and his friends were peppered with jeers and epithets while seated in the stands. Unable to endure the barrage of insults any longer, one of his more muscular friends leapt to his feet and thundered, "I'm gonna throw you off these stands if you say something else to us!" No one took him up on his offer. Confederate flags waving in the breeze to the tune of "Dixie" at halftime was yet another indignity Black students were forced to endure. "We'd sit down and turn our backs. It was a silent protest. There wasn't much else that we could do. There were 12,000 people there," Wright grimaced. Basketball games were not much different. "We'd go to the basketball games and for the first couple of years there were no Black players on the team. So we'd root for the other team that had Black players. That didn't go over too well. Once they got Black players, we'd root for [Carolina]," he recalled.[14] Experiences like these motivated Wright and his friends to spend their college years fighting to improve race relations, restructure curricular offerings, and create opportunities for Black students to carve out spaces for themselves within the Carolina community.

Shortly after the start of the fall 1967 semester, Wright visited Battiste in his dorm room and tossed him a copy of the latest edition of *Life* magazine, which profiled ongoing Black campus activism at Harvard, Yale, and other colleges and universities nationwide. Mealtimes transformed into bull sessions about the need for a Black student movement at Carolina. "We'd talk about different things," Wright remembered, "At the time, there was a lot going on at other universities . . . building African American organizations, African American Studies and things. *Why not here?*" A political junkie who believed in the power of collective change, Battiste agreed. The roommates convinced roughly a dozen of their peers to establish the Association of Afro-American Students (AFRO), a new student organization devoted to promoting African American heritage while creating a safe space for Black students at Carolina. The organization was to be equal parts social club, study group, and political action committee. AFRO regularly hosted cultural events on campus, organized study groups, maintained "banks" of essays and notes to aid struggling students, and convened town halls where Black students voiced concerns and developed solutions to campus problems. Kenny Price, a soft-spoken, earnest student from Charleston was elected its first president.[15] Despite the worries of administrators and large segments of the Carolina community, Vice President of Student Affairs C. H. Witten permitted the formation of AFRO on the condition that its leaders familiarize themselves with existing rules for student organizations. A racial optimist, Witten genuinely supported and encouraged AFRO leaders to "help the entire Carolina community learn more about the Afro-American heritage."[16]

After the Orangeburg Massacre, AFRO gradually adopted a more militant political posture leaning heavier into an emphasis on Black cultural identity formation, campus activism, and grassroots community service. In October 1968, AFRO hosted its first "Black Week," a series of campus events intended to inspire unity among Black students, raise awareness of Black History and political issues facing Black and marginalized communities, and serve as counter programming against traditional Homecoming festivities. The inaugural slate of programs included study sessions, displays of African art outside the Russell House, and stimulating lectures by prominent scholars and community leaders. "Black Power is the healthiest thing that has hit this country since before the Mayflower," exclaimed political scientist, activist, and self-proclaimed "Black Power advocate" Dr. Charles V. Hamilton during his keynote address at Drayton Hall on October 28, 1968. Describing Black Power as a powerful call for the restructuring of society, Hamilton ably defended against detractors of Stokely Carmichael and H. Rap Brown, reminding his audience that just a few years earlier the duo were teaching Black people in Alabama and Mississippi basic literacy skills and encouraging them to vote. The problem, he claimed, was not their occasionally violent rhetoric but that "institutions copped out on them years ago." He warned whites to avoid courting the violent tendencies of those who had grown discontented with the status quo. The following day, Dr. Hamilton participated in a luncheon hosted by AFRO and several other campus organizations. When asked about the future of Black Power, the scholar reminded listeners that its story was just beginning to be written and fully controlled by its authors. "It has nothing to do with Marx, or Lenin or Trotsky. We are about making a revolution in an indigenous society. How do you make that revolution?" he questioned. Hamilton's visit set the campus aflame with debate over the efficacy of Black Power, the place of Black people in American history, and white defensiveness against the rise of an awakened and vocal Black community arising both on and off campus.[17] AFRO presidents, including Price and Harry Walker, helped the organization navigate the increasingly choppy racial waters at Carolina often wavering between moderation and militancy in their dealings with their fellow students and campus administrators.

White faculty in the College of Arts and Sciences were also discussing ways to revise their curriculum to provide students with a more accurate and racially inclusive analysis of American life and history. History professors John Scott Wilson and Tom Terrill spent nearly a year designing a course on "Negro History," in hopes of challenging the existing Eurocentric narrative and to encourage their mostly white students to think critically about race and its impact on American history and contemporary society. A graduate of the University of Wisconsin, Terrill accepted a teaching position at USC in August 1966 and soon developed a reputation for challenging racial convention during lectures in his exciting yet rigorous courses. Asked about his rationale for developing a course in Negro History, the historian explained that he hoped to reverse the normalization of whiteness within historical scholarship. "In the 1960s, if you made the statement that blacks made a major contribution to the coming of the Civil War and the conduct of the conflict and prompted Abraham Lincoln to not only consider Emancipation but to accept it and push it forward, people would have looked at you like you were crazy. 'Blacks weren't involved,' they'd say," he later recalled. Terrill hoped that the course would expose a new generation of students to classic and cutting-edge

African American scholarship and, hopefully, inspire a few to begin the arduous task of reversing the damage wrought by the spread of lily-white narratives that sustained the culture of segregation in South Carolina and other parts of the Deep South. Citing an "obvious need" and an "abundance of source material" within the university libraries and other archival institutions statewide, Terrill and Wilson presented the idea to the Faculty Senate who approved the course without much resistance. The young professor's background in African history made him the most suitable choice to serve as lead instructor. Terrill also believed that his empathy for the struggles of people of African descent in America would enable him to navigate potential resistance from those who believed that a white man could not objectively teach Black history.

First offered during the fall of 1968, Terrill's course entitled "The Negro in American History" was a timely addition to the Carolina curriculum. During the aftermath of the Orangeburg Massacre, AFRO drafted a thirteen-point plan, which they submitted to the administration; they requested that the university increase the hiring of Black faculty, admit more Black students, and recruit Black athletes. Moreover, they urged Carolina to develop courses in African American history and culture. Terrill's course met the needs of administrators and students alike. Faculty and administrators hoped that Black campus activists at Carolina would consider the course a gesture of good faith that change was on the horizon in hopes that it would prevent the sorts of campus disruptions and violence witnessed at other colleges and universities across the country. A small number of white students registered for the course including future historian Jack Hayes and Henry McMaster, a future governor of South Carolina. Black students considered the Negro History course a welcome addition to a curriculum that was bereft of substantive analysis of the contributions of African Americans to American society. Terrill taught an interpretation of American history that was dramatically different from what was learned by earlier generations of Carolina students. Students read groundbreaking new research on American slavery that relied heavily upon first person testimonies about life on southern plantations collected from the formerly enslaved and their descendants. They studied classical African American literary texts such as James Weldon Johnson's *The Autobiography of an Ex-Colored Man* and novels such as Claude Brown's *Manchild in the Promised Land* to flesh out broader themes in the Black experience during the mid-twentieth century. Only two students dropped the course despite its rigorous reading schedule and the often-difficult racial conversations. Despite Terrill's best efforts, racial tensions sometimes boiled over in the classroom. On one occasion, an anonymous student scribbled a question on the chalkboard: "Can A White Man Teach Black History?" Later in the semester, a shouting match broke out between a Black student whose relative was among the wounded at State College and a white classmate who insisted that law enforcement officers were justified in their use of force. Nearly every discussion of civil rights heightened passions. While these clashes were indicative of broader racial division, they offered Terrill and his students opportunities for debate and introspection that were often unavailable outside the classroom where racial truths were sugarcoated by southern manners and etiquette or prohibited by continued segregation. "It was probably a real challenge. There was probably some question about whether a white teacher was qualified or symbolically could teach it. Dr. Terrill was in a tough position," Battiste remembered. When asked about this inaugural class, Terrill beamed. "The biggest problem in terms of class management was to get through the material because the discussion was so lively! I had to blow the whistle from time to time and say, 'We have to move on a little bit here, kind of take turns more,'" he remembered.

Such enthusiasm was not limited to the classroom. Students were required to complete original research projects utilizing untapped resources in the university libraries. Despite his lack of experience in the field of history, Wright, a biology major, proved to be the star of the class. "Harry went to the South Caroliniana Library before he came to my office to discuss his project. He wanted to compare slavery in the Lowcountry to the slave experience in the Upcountry," Terrill gushed, "Then, he decided to look at the university during Reconstruction. He read board minutes and various other things and he came up with a quite different interpretation than the conventional wisdom. And quite a defensible one." Although this was the only History course that Wright took during his undergraduate career at Carolina, Terrill shared his findings with his colleagues and others in the profession. Later scholars soon reevaluated consensus interpretations about Black life in South Carolina during Reconstruction using approaches and sources that mirrored those developed by the brilliant young scholar. Other students appreciated the course because it served as an oasis from the racial turmoil brewing outside the classroom walls. Claudette Felder, a Black co-ed, felt that the course offered students an opportunity to understand sensitive issues from a variety of scholarly and personal perspectives. "All of us came from all kinds of different experiences," she recalled, "My experience coming from a small southern town in South Carolina was different from someone from an urban area or even someone who grew up in Columbia. I guess it helped in some ways for us to share experiences." Although the course could not possibly resolve racial tensions at Carolina or the state writ large, Terrill's students embraced the opportunity to examine a variety of lingering issues rooted in the haunting legacies of slavery, segregation, and racial capitalism. Impressed with their intellect and commitment to improving race relations, Dr. Terrill enlisted Wright and Battiste to work alongside faculty and other student leaders on the Committee for Curriculum Revision to craft a vision for the creation of a Black Studies program at Carolina.

Working alongside Dean Bruce W. Nelson, Terrill, Battiste, and Wright joined other students and faculty on a subcommittee of the Student Government Committee on Curriculum Revision to explore the possibility of developing a Black Studies program at Carolina. Throughout the summer of 1969, Battiste and Wright drafted a proposal based on recommendations of the "Black Studies Group" and consultation with scholars and administrators at other institutions where such programs had been established such as Yale, Duke and Emory. The duo also joined fellow AFRO members in brainstorming sessions with community members. Members of the Black Studies subcommittee also surveyed Carolina undergraduates about the type of program they wanted. Dean Nelson and other adult leaders on the committee shielded the students from criticism raised by concerned faculty by instructing their colleagues that student leadership was necessary because the "special attitudes and expertise" they brought to the table would ultimately conceive a strong, beneficial program. Echoing student sentiment, supportive faculty believed that the new program would serve as a legitimate symbol of recognition for the culture and achievements of Black people and would play an indispensable role in fostering mutual respect and racial harmony on campus and in the surrounding community. After a series of revisions and compromises, a final proposal was completed and ratified in the summer of 1970.

The Black Studies subcommittee searched for a director with the scholarly and interpersonal skills to strengthen the new program while navigating the choppy racial waters of the university community. Dean Marshall, Battiste, and Wright led the search with input from other members of the committee. They eventually hired Willie Harriford, a graduate of the University of Kansas and former archivist at the Harry S. Truman Presidential Library and, for nearly three years, the Martin Luther King Center in Atlanta, Georgia. Harriford's life and scholarly career prepared him to develop an interdisciplinary, intellectually rigorous, community centered Black Studies program. Throughout his undergraduate and early professional years in Kansas, the budding archivist and historian often questioned the Eurocentric nature of historical scholarship and challenged white colleagues to think critically about the need to collect documents and other materials that reflected Truman's complicated stance on race in America. Disturbed by the tendency among white scholars to marginalize Black history, Harriford envisioned a program that would encourage awareness and appreciation of the

Black perspective, diversify the university's archival holdings, and produce scholars who would directly challenge the prevailing assumption that the rich heritage of African Americans in South Carolina and the broader diaspora was a subject of little importance to broader human knowledge. "Adding Black perspectives to the historical debate doesn't mean that one is right and the other is wrong. Sometimes, if we're going to make judgments we need to hear both sides," Harriford later explained, "I want people to hear it from our perspective, our point of view, and let us tell you the mistakes we made and maybe why you made them." The young, idealistic director considered the creation of a new African American Studies program to be an opportunity to foster interracial dialogue and encourage rigorous, empirical analysis of the Black condition in South Carolina and the broader region. Educating white students at the university about the lives of Black people was an added bonus. Reminiscing about four white students who took one of his earliest courses, Harriford shared that it likely marked the first and only time in their lives that they would experience life as a racial minority. Courses in African American Studies also provided Black students with a safe space to rigorously interrogate how their upbringing shaped their adopted ideologies and strategies for combating racial discrimination and white supremacy. He relished the opportunity to push his students to challenge racial consensus and make informed decisions about how they would respond to their generational struggles. "You don't tell a kid not to be radical," Harriford explained, "You tell them *what it means* to be radical."

Another reason that Harriford accepted the position as director was the caliber of its students and their desire to improve the university for future generations. Battiste and Wright were particularly impressive due to the tenacity and initiative they displayed while starting AFRO on a campus where students burned crosses to protest token desegregation not even a decade earlier. Working alongside talented and committed student organizers improved his odds of successfully building a strong, vibrant, and rigorous African American Studies program at a predominantly white university in the Deep South. Battiste, Wright and Harriford bonded as they shared their experiences as Black students on predominantly white campuses. The new director's empathy and appreciation of their generation's social, cultural, and political condition and intimate knowledge of the modern civil rights movement set him apart from other candidates. Beginning in September 1971, Harriford accepted a dual position as the director of the African American Studies program and an assistant dean and freshmen adviser in the College of Arts and Sciences. Upon accepting the position, Harriford thought deeply about how he could use the wisdom drawn from the difficult racial experiences he endured in Kansas and Georgia to offer guidance and direction to the next generation. "What can I do for them that was done for me? *Show them how to get through this maze.*" Within the classroom, the affable, worldly director provided students with rare, intimate perspectives about the civil rights movement and earlier debates over strategic approaches to abolishing white supremacy that was missing from the existing curriculum, drawn directly from conversations with and documents shared by key movement organizers he met during his time at the King Center. Black and white students flocked to his courses and many agreed to pursue a minor in the discipline. Despite Harriford's best efforts, the road to respectability for the African American Studies Program was fraught with obstacles. Skeptical parents often questioned the validity of the new discipline and worried about their child's future earning potential upon graduating with a degree in the field. The new director often stressed the interdisciplinary nature of the program and emphasized that African American Studies scholars had as many postgraduate opportunities as those in other Humanities disciplines. It was a tough sell, particularly due to racial politics that spawned the program.

Another issue that complicated matters was that students could only pursue a minor in African American Studies, thereby stigmatizing it as a subject unworthy of lifelong study. The Committee of Curriculum Revision's final proposal for the program was ambitious but shortsighted. They intended the program to be not only a major but a truly interdisciplinary experience. Students would take introductory level courses in Political Science or History along with electives in other social sciences that specifically analyzed the "culture and history of Afro-Americans including their antecedents in Africa." To cement its reputation as a community centered discipline, students in the African American Studies program would be required to develop an independent research project or participate in an internship with a local or statewide civic organization focused on solving contemporary racial disparities in education, housing, employment, and other aspects of everyday life in South Carolina. Lastly, they proposed the creation of a wide variety of courses on the Black experience within various departments such as "African Art," "The Politics of Urbanization," and "The Sociology of Minority Groups."[18] The program initially fell short of these lofty expectations. The culture of segregation within academia had produced minimal trained faculty—specifically Black instructors—that were available to teach the requisite number of courses to establish African American Studies as a major. Members of the hiring committee found scant young Black graduates willing to apply or interview due to the state's reputation as a haven for white supremacists and political reactionaries. From its inception through the mid-1990s, the African American Studies program rarely had more than two or three full-time faculty members, hardly enough to provide more than regular introductory courses and a few electives when resources were available.[19]

Fleeting support from university administrators, skeletal budgets, and a minuscule teaching faculty forced Harriford to limit his vision for the program. Later presidents and deans ignored Harriford's pleas for increased funding to support what they perceived was a novelty program. The embittered director surmised that they sustained the program as a racial shield to keep Black students from "acting up" rather than help them become full members of the Carolina community. "They didn't think that it is worth studying. [Some say], 'There isn't a big enough body of work. Where else do you get PhDs in African American Studies? This is just something to make *those people* happy. Now, we're going to do it if it doesn't cost too much."[20] "It was always a struggle," the dean recalled, ". . . And the struggle wasn't always just to get more money, it was to justify what you got." Frequent and dramatic budget cuts severely limited the program's course offerings and public programming. To keep the program afloat, Harriford recruited faculty from other departments to offer cross-listed courses that touched upon key themes in the Black experience. History courses taught by recent arrival Dr. Grace Jordan McFadden, the first African American woman hired at the professorial rank in the College of Arts and Sciences, proved popular with white and Black students alike. Imbued by her parents with a servant's heart and a love of Black history, McFadden was a graduate of Catholic University in Washington, DC, where she immersed herself in a thriving community of Black scholars, artists, and public intellectuals who debated and strategized solutions to the larger problems of miseducation, mass incarceration, police brutality, violence, and widespread poverty that shaped Black life in the nation's capital. A product of the burgeoning Black Campus Movement in the "Chocolate City," she later became an intern with the Teacher Corps, a national program designed to recruit energetic, enthusiastic, talented, and empathetic young people to teach courses in the nation's most impoverished areas—urban cities, rural towns, Native reservations, and Appalachian villages—to provide neglected communities with opportunities to earn their GED and pursue higher education or better paying jobs. Before arriving in Columbia, Dr. McFadden served as Associate Director of the Teacher Corps in Toledo, Ohio, for two years. The national organization's slogan, "Each one teach one," and core tenet that no one was unreachable became pillars of Dr. McFadden's educational philosophy. While serving in a joint position in History and African American Studies, Dr. McFadden and her husband, neuropsychiatrist and educational consultant Dr. Johnnie McFadden, developed an experimental program to train inmates and ex-prisoners to become teachers and forge stronger links between institutions of higher learning and correctional facilities. Coordinated by Teacher Corp interns from Morgan State University and Roger Williams College, groups of inmates and "external" interns—some of whom were ex-prisoners—participated in a variety of activities to build self-confidence, develop leadership skills, improve literacy and technical skills, and strengthen bonds between the prison and surrounding community. Like the Freedom Schools active in Mississippi during "Freedom Summer," successful participants were trained to become teachers themselves. Incarcerated interns creatively mixed knowledge gained on the streets and in prison with lessons gleaned from cutting-edge Black history and literature as classroom instructors, literacy tutors, prison newspaper editors, theater directors, and organizers within the National Prisoners' Reform Association. Wardens and correctional officers often interfered with such activities fearing that ex-inmates would negatively influence those incarcerated. Despite these obstacles, hundreds of inmates experienced a "renewal of faith, hope, purpose and determination" after joining Teacher Corps and earning degrees.[21] A brilliant scholar, Dr. McFadden developed innovative and socially conscious approaches to historical research and instruction as a professor at Carolina. She recognized and challenged silences within the historical literature regarding the Black experience in the United States and the global diaspora.

While serving on the Black Studies Committee, Battiste and Wright searched for other ways to integrate African American students into the larger Carolina community. Emboldened by several near misses by Black students in races for Student Senate and Homecoming Queen and news about the use of bloc voting to break down racial barriers and improve conditions for marginalized students at colleges and universities nationwide, the duo knew it was time for an audacious move. Wright and several older AFRO members who were regularly involved with Student Government realized that prospective candidates for higher office viewed the upcoming election as a popularity contest rather than an opportunity to improve life at the university for all students. They also grasped that racial attitudes had begun to shift. "A Black girl was runner-up for Miss Homecoming and there was a certain excitement among the whites in voting for her," Battiste recalled, "It was as though they thought they were going against tradition and the business of putting the white woman on a pedestal."[22]

Sensing that the winds were changing, the future attorney encouraged AFRO president Harry Walker to run for Student Body president. Born March 19, 1950, in Greenville, South Carolina, Walker was no stranger to the struggle for racial equality in his native state. His cousin, Elaine Means, was one of eight Sterling High School students whose courageous activism toppled barriers in the city's public library system. "Her father and my father were very close. They were aware of it and understood that it was going to happen. They were close by to make sure that things would not get out of hand. Elaine was a maverick." As a youth, Walker often overheard adult conversations about the messy racial situation in Greenville. "Integration was not an easy thing in Greenville," he explained. "City council decided that rather than desegregate the pool at Cleveland Park, they would put seals in it. That was their way of sending a message." Sterling High School, one of the state's oldest Black high schools and a center of student activism in the 1960s civil rights movement, mysteriously burned on September 15, 1967. No one was arrested. A senior at rival school Beck High, Walker questioned whether it was accidental due to the possibility that the school would have served as a potential landing spot for white students after forced desegregation. He remembered many of the Black students who were forced to transfer into white high schools in 1970 were deeply scarred and deprived of the traditional high school experience that provided enough nostalgia to warm their autumn years. Walker, on the other hand, fondly remembers his time at Beck. Built during equalization, Beck High School had a predominantly Black faculty, all-Black student body, quality facilities, and fully funded extracurricular programs. Its young, sharp, politically astute faculty were primarily trained at Black colleges and arrived at Beck with a mission to prepare their students for the "world that was going to be not for the world that had been." One of these teachers, Helen Evans, took a special interest in Walker. "She is the person who encouraged me to start reading books outside of the standard curriculum such as the Ghandi biography. She pushed me to compete," he reflected. Evans encouraged her ambitious pupil to apply to a wide range of colleges because his academic, athletic, and political accomplishments—Walker was elected junior class president—made him an attractive candidate for predominantly white colleges and universities interested in diversifying their student populations. The Greenville native ultimately chose to attend Carolina over Wake Forest, Dayton, and South Carolina State, where his two brothers attended.[23]

"My first impressions were that [Carolina] was large and very white. That was my first experience academically in an integrated environment. I had not had a white instructor before. Never had a white classmate or anything like that," Walker explained. Shortly after arriving on campus, he attended a social at Bell Camp where he met and formed friendships with students of both races including his future wife, Ernestine Sitton, a freshman from Easley, South Carolina. Walker, a Political Science major, was often the only Black student in his classes but his affable manner eased the transition. He also befriended his white suitemates in Maxcy Residence Hall, occasionally joining them for casual conversation or touch football games on the Horseshoe. Like most Black freshmen, however, Walker found a home with AFRO, the center of Black life at Carolina. "If you were a Black freshman on campus you came and introduced yourself. You just got to know each other because you were all you had," he recalled. He and other Black students formed lasting friendships while enjoying dances, socials, study sessions, and other AFRO activities. The Greenville native also joined the inaugural pledge class of Kappa Alpha Psi in 1970, established after national officials threatened to sue the university over attempts by the Inter-Fraternity Council to prevent the Black Greek letter organization from forming a campus chapter.[24] Walker agreed to run for office without Battiste, his future fraternity elder, having to pull rank. "We were sitting on a bench when 'Bat' approached us," remembered Sitton, "I thought it was an excellent idea and that Harry was the perfect candidate. I had a lot of respect for his leadership skills and ability to relate to a wide spectrum of people. I could see clearly that he had the crossover appeal and that if the time was right, he was '*that guy.*'" After talking over the idea with Battiste and several white students connected to Student Government, Walker agreed to enter the race on the conditions that AFRO members gave him their blessing and Battiste agreed to serve as his campaign manager. "I didn't want it to come as a surprise to [AFRO members]. I didn't want it to look like I was trying to use them as a stepping-stone," he explained. After Walker presented the idea during a January meeting of AFRO, they enthusiastically offered their support.

Traditionally, the Student Body presidency was reserved for white male students who coveted the position as a stepping-stone to future statewide political prominence. Walker's opponents Steve Smith and Joe Usry fit the mold, particularly the latter due to his affiliation with one of the larger white fraternities on campus. Smith eagerly defended the status quo describing student government as "not that bad" during one debate. The 1971 campaign, however, marked an important epoch for women at Carolina as well. Jeannine Smith, a junior psychology major from Columbia, ran on her sterling credentials, an ethos of service, and the idea that her candidacy portended the dawning of a new age of love within the Carolina community. "I think that if all students loved each other, then student government could get more things done," she argued. A confident and ideologically moderate candidate, Smith attracted support due to her calls for an end to campus prohibition, the easing of restrictions on campus visitation, improved campus infrastructure, and stronger communication between students and SGA representatives.[25]

Walker cut a striking contrast to his opponents, especially those who behaved as if it was their birthright to wield power on campus. "Harry was like no candidate they had ever had," Battiste gushed, "He had a big Afro, sideburns that connected to his mustache and beard, immaculately dressed, and was in great physical shape."[26] The tenacious, cleverly organized campaign struck a racially inclusive and politely rebellious tone that fit a rising antiestablishment mood on campus. Campaigning under the slogan "Let's Get Things Together," Walker presented himself as a champion for the underdog and protector of student rights from encroachment by the administration. Battiste and campaign organizers designed an idealistic and innovative "Ten Point platform" to appeal to a broad interracial coalition in hopes of securing enough votes to force a runoff, a common occurrence under the existing plurality system. Aside from occasional references to hometown hero Jesse Jackson, Walker avoided explicit references to race and instead focused on presenting solutions to problems that affected the student body. He called for the establishment of a student court, a hotline to permit students to privately seek advice on abortion, and the appointment of a campus Ombudsman to resolve student complaints and investigate improper activity in student government and the university administration. His platform also included requests for experimentation with co-ed dormitories, an end to the prohibition of campus alcohol sales with proceeds used to benefit financially disadvantaged students, increased recruitment and programming for African Americans and other marginalized groups, and the abolition of *in loco parentis* as the defining philosophy of campus life. Ultimately, Walker and his supporters sought to transform student government from a "useless" white male–dominated social club that behaved like controlled opposition to the administration into an inclusive, activist governing body that served the needs of all students. The insurgent campaign literally focused on bread-and-butter issues to attract support from indifferent or apathetic students, pledging to demand that the administration oust Slater Food Service for nearly two decades of "bad food" and "poor service."[27]

The insurgent campaign regularly emphasized that a vote for Walker was a vote against the system. Whereas previous student presidents were sons of state legislators or held roles in either campus or state government, Walker had only served as AFRO president and was not even a member of the state's powerful Black aristocracy. The son of working-class parents, Walker refused to be outworked by his moneyed, well connected opponents. He visited every dorm on campus accompanied by white supporters who assuaged fears of his militant image. "I think he presented himself well once he thought about the issues. He was thorough in thinking about it. He handled questions very well," Wright remembered. Walker's common touch helped him sway even the unlikeliest of voters. "We'd go into some of the houses, some of the rooms and a kid who might have a great big Confederate flag hanging all over his wall would come up to us and offer to do anything to help Harry to win. I supposed some of them felt it would mean they weren't racists anymore," Battiste recalled. As Walker gained

Campaign poster, "Let's Get Things Together" (Harry Walker for President). Luther James Battiste, III Papers, South Carolina Political Collections, University of South Carolina.

momentum, university administrators privately rooted for him. "People began referring to what should be done 'when Harry wins' and more than once I heard them say that 'Harry has a beautiful chance,'" remembered former USC Minority Student Affairs coordinator Charles McMillan. Black Columbia residents also claimed a sense of ownership in the campaign. Wide eyed students at W. A. Perry Middle School clamored to chat with him during a visit to the school where he discussed Black Power, the dangers of drug use and opportunities for study at Carolina. Local civil rights attorney Hemphill Pride met with Walker shortly after he announced his candidacy and pledged his financial support.[28]

It was an unseasonably cold, snowy day when Walker learned that he became the first Black student to ever hold the highest student office at a predominantly white public university in the Deep South. The Greenville native received more votes than his three opponents combined, the widest margin of victory in school history. Although roughly a quarter of the student population voted, twice as many students participated than had done so the previous spring. The bulk of his support came from white students, including sons and daughters of Dixie who resided on fraternity row or toiled in the law school.

Student apathy and tensions along the lines of race and class persisted after the euphoria surrounding Walker's victory faded. Walker was also limited in

Harry Walker elected president. *Gamecock*, 26 March 1971.

his effectiveness due to the role of the presidency which was largely a bully pulpit with restricted powers. His fellow students' desire for greater representation proved a double-edged sword. Nonetheless, it proved to be a momentous event in the history of Black students at USC.

CONCLUSION: THE LEGACY OF THE BLACK CAMPUS MOVEMENT

Protests over race and diversity in higher education swept the nation in November 2015, fueled by concerns that the legacies of the Black Campus Movement had been left to wither on the vine. Inspired by their peers nationwide, an interracial and cross-gendered collection of students at the University of South Carolina clandestinely planned their own protest to demand that administrators do more to promote diversity, tolerance, and inclusion. The campus insurgency, dubbed "USC 2020 Vision" by its leaders, represented both how far the university had come in its transition toward full integration and how much of this project had been left unfinished. Combining tried and true strategies of protest developed a generation ago with modern digital organizing tactics, the dissidents demanded renewed commitment to the creation of academic programs devoted to the study of Black and marginalized communities, increased hiring of minority faculty, and opposition to rising inequality and racism on and off campus.

On Sunday, November 15, 2015, likely to the dismay of protest leaders, an anonymous Twitter user, @DrinkingTicket, prematurely released a petition entitled "Here's No Place Like Home," that outlined their demands. Organizers demanded that the university acknowledge that it was "built on the backs of enslaved Africans" in public tours, especially in areas such as the garden directly behind the president's house where slaves were once quartered. They urged officials to place markers on historic buildings, install and promote plaques devoted to sharing the history of AAAS (formerly AFRO) and other Black alumni, and expand the recruitment and hiring of Blacks and other minorities. Like the campus movement built by Harry Wright, Luther Battiste, Ernestine Sitton and Harry Walker decades earlier, leaders of this new movement sought to attract greater support by offering solutions to problems faced by all minority groups on campus. They demanded the construction of gender-neutral facilities, improved mental and health care for all students, mandatory diversity training for all faculty, staff and health care personnel, and the acknowledgment of gender identity and expression as a protected class under Title IX. To avoid the appearance of being ableist, they urged university officials to rename the Office of Student Disability Services to the Office of Accessibility and Accommodation Services. Organizers also pushed for the creation of a Social Justice minor and cognate. Lastly, they demanded greater transparency and accountability, particularly regarding certain administrators who had failed to effectively respond to student concerns or behaved in ways that were "damaging to the student experience." The students called for the creation of a diverse, representative, knowledgeable Student Board of Trustees to oversee these changes, to be completed by the end of the 2019–20 semester.[29]

Roughly 150 students walked out of class the following day and gathered at Longstreet Theatre, before marching to the Osborne Administration Building. Dramatic footage of the demonstrators, who marched silently in pairs while dressed in black, quickly went viral on social media and elicited swift reaction. Sympathizers and detractors gathered near the administration building as the marchers arrived and presented their demands to three university officials—USC Provost Joan Gabel, Chief Diversity Officer John Dozier, and Vice President of Student Affairs Dennis Pruitt. "The future of USC is in your hands," declared Claire Randall, a biology and psychology major from Greenville as she gave them the list. Gabel informed the demonstrators that the administration would evaluate their demands but offered no timetable. "Change might not happen right away," Dozier explained. After refusing offers for a private meeting, the demonstrators eventually left. Despite the early reveal that the protest was imminent, President Pastides and his fellow administrators were caught off guard. Days earlier, Pastides issued a memorandum to the campus community commemorating the twenty-fifth anniversary of the Carolinian Creed, a document intended to foster a new age of civility and generosity at the institution, and celebrating progress made in a series of recent listening forums with students, faculty, and community liaisons. Carolina had also received four consecutive Higher Education Excellence in Diversity (HEED) Awards and was considered a model institution on questions of diversity and inclusion among Southeastern Conference schools. Plans were also underway to launch the South Carolina Collaborative on Race and Reconciliation, an initiative intended to build bridges between people and institutions to discuss South Carolina's deep history of racism and inequality and develop plans to foster racial equity. The deep racial wounds reopened by the Charleston Massacre and the subsequent political machinations required to remove the Confederate flag from the Statehouse had created an environment that rendered these piecemeal reforms inadequate in the eyes of campus activists. "We've constantly been presenting these things to the administration and told, we're working on it," USC student Jada Parker complained, "And we're tired of just working on it. We're trying to let them know that we are here. We will not be silenced, and we still have things to do." Indeed, the spirit of the Black Campus Movement at Carolina had not died but instead continues to shape the zeitgeist on campus to the present day.[30]

Forged in the fire of the tumultuous racial politics of the late 1960s, the Black Campus Movement dramatically reconstituted higher education at the University of South Carolina. Black student activists within the Association of Afro-American Students, who represented the full spectrum of moderate and militant ideologies, along with key faculty and administrators fought for racial self-determination, student power, and greater inclusiveness within the curriculum and social life of the university demanding full recognition of the history and culture of Blacks in South Carolina and the broader diaspora. Joining their peers at HBCUs and PWIs nationwide, AFRO leadership played pivotal roles in the establishment of an African American Studies program to enrich the university's liberal arts curriculum and end the normalization of whiteness in all aspects of the intellectual community at Carolina. After nearly two decades of struggle for respect, funding, and administrative support, the African American Studies program remains perhaps the most visible legacy of the 1960s Black student movement at the university. Since avoiding termination in the early 1990s, the program has experienced a renaissance that has positioned it to become one of the leading Black Studies programs in the American South, if not the nation. With its newfound base of support and steady integration into the scholarly community at

Carolina, the African American Studies program continues to educate all students and the general public about the Black experience in South Carolina and elsewhere along with critical, informed solutions to contemporary problems caused by white supremacy and systemic racism.

Chapter Nine

"WHAT'S NEXT, SOUTHERN FRIED CHICKEN?"

Confederate Memory and Racial Violence
at the Postintegration University

Holly Genovese

O n the one-year anniversary of the Orangeburg Massacre, students from the Association for African American Students at the University of South Carolina held a memorial service on campus.[1] As part of the service, they asked permission from the university to burn a Confederate flag. University officials denied the request, citing a South Carolina law that makes it illegal to burn the Confederate flag.[2] The law states:

> Any person who in any manner, for exhibition or display, shall publicly
> mutilate, deface, defile, defy, jeer at, trample upon or cast contempt,
> either by word or act, upon any such flag, standard, color or ensign shall
> be guilty of a misdemeanor and shall be punished by a fine not exceeding
> one hundred dollars or by imprisonment for not more than thirty days,
> or both, in the discretion of the court, and shall also forfeit a penalty of
> fifty dollars for each offense, to be recovered with costs in a civil action
> or suit in any court having jurisdiction.[3]

In February 1969, the Association for African American students wrote a letter to the university asking for the flag to come down and for the playing of Dixie at school sanctioned events to end. According to the student group, Dixie was seen as a tribute to enslavement. Though both Dixie and the flying of the Confederate Flag were defended as essential to the experience of white students at USC, the legalities involving the flag made both the protests against its use and the responses legal in nature.

On February 12, 1969, University of South Carolina student Brett Bursey attended an AWARE meeting with rubbing alcohol and a Confederate flag. Fifty to sixty students followed him to the horseshoe in front of President Jones' home where he burned the Confederate flag. He opposed the flag being flown on campus and at the statehouse, as well as the continued use of Dixie at school-sanctioned events. Bursey was arrested and released on a one-hundred-dollar bond. Bursey's actions created controversy and made the discussion more prominent on campus, particularly in the pages of the Gamecock student newspaper.

A conservative white student organization, Young Americans for Freedom, created a petition in concert with law students, against the demands of Bursey and members of AAAS. Many white students insisted that Dixie was an integral part of their heritage. The president of Young Americans for Freedom said, "we feel like this is a symbol of our heritage and we aren't ashamed of our heritage. We feel our forefathers in their time and place did the best they could. We're proud of our heritage."[4] Though the controversy was focused on the playing of Dixie at sporting events, the athletics department attempted to avoid any conflict over the issue. The assistant Director of Athletics at the time said, "I think it's something we have not made a policy on. It's out of our ballpark. We don't tell what cheers to cheer or what songs to sing."[5] Though he was attempting to be neutral, his comments reflect a reification of conservative ideologies by the university and attempts to allow others to make decisions.

In the 1960s, as the first African American students arrived on campus, the traditions, physical landscape, and opportunities available to students of color were entirely conditioned by white supremacist logics. African American students created their own spaces, reminiscent of Fred Moten and Stefano Harney's "hold," where they gained an education and formed a community.[6] For Moten and Harney the only possible relation to the university is subversive. They write, "In the face of these conditions one can only sneak into the university and steal what one can. To abuse its hospitality, to spite its mission, to join its refugee colony, its gypsy encampment, to be in but not of—this is the path of the subversive intellectual in the modern university."[7] For a subversive intellectual disappears, they argue, "She disappears into the underground, the downlow lowdown maroon community of the university, into the undercommons of enlightenment, where the work gets done, where the work gets subverted, where the revolution is still black, still strong."[8] Though they are writing in reference to the twenty-first-century university, conceptions of fugitivity and Marronage can help us understand the experiences of Black students at the University of South Carolina in the '60s and '70s.

For Black students attending USC in the early years of integration, their education was gained despite the university, rather than because of it. Essential to understanding Black students experience at the University of South Carolina in the years post desegregation, is an understanding of the importance of confederate memory, the threat of racial violence (and the haunting/memories of the Orangeburg Massacre), as well as the work of the Office of Minority Student Affairs, an official university committee created to "handle" issues of race.

In this chapter, I consider the controversy over both Dixie and the flying of the Confederate Flag, the work of the office of Minority Student Affairs (an administrative office created to both lesson controversy and support Black students on campus), and the threat of racial violence to explicate the ways in which the integration of the University of South Carolina fomented white supremacy and made explicit institutional barriers to education for people of color in South Carolina.

Many administrators and students celebrated the relatively peaceful desegregation at the University of South Carolina in comparison to the University of Mississippi and other universities across the country, while tacitly accepting the threats of violence against African American students. Though the violence of integration was not as visible as on other college campuses, this was largely a reflection of attempts by university officials to avoid media attention. African American students often feared for their safety and had their spaces on campus violently destroyed.

The Committee of Minority Student Affairs at the University of South Carolina, though billed as a support system for African American students, existed to protect the university from controversy. Avoidance and erasure became the tactic of the university to ensure the physical safety of their African American students, with little acknowledgment of the structures of violence embodied by the institution.

The song "Dixie," in particular, was an integral part of the college of experience for White Gamecocks. A September 1967 article of the Gamecock read:

> Carolina is the breath of twelve thousand students, it is football games at
> night and Saturday classes, fighting crowds in the post office and griping
> about Slater food, trying to make Maxcy monument move, and getting a
> parking ticket if you're lucky enough to get a parking place. It is blanket
> concerts and staying up all night to study, snow fights in the winter and
> fraternity rush, upperclassmen and freshman and victory. It is forget-
> ting how many class cuts you have taken and getting lost in McKissick

Library. It is a hamburger for breakfast, lunch, and supper and Cliff notes and 8:00 classes. It is all the professors and all of the students who listen to them and the ones that don't. It is the energy center and the McMasters. It is hating Clemson and deciding on a major. It is beer. It is Don's and the Four Seasons. It is alumni, buying books with worn out covers, and singing Dixie when Garnto has moved down the field. It is telephones, frat pins, holes in shoes, skinnies, and 70 when that's passing. It is the things that twelve thousand students do.[9]

For many southern white students, the playing of Dixie was as essential to their experience as drinking beer, reading used books, and attending football games. Of course, the Gamecock was clearly written for an audience of middle-class and wealthy white students, ignoring not only the experiences of Black students at Carolina but lower income students as well. Who could not just afford a car, but also a parking ticket? Who could join fraternities? The quintessential college experience as detailed by the Gamecock was not only inherently white, but only accessible to wealthy students, students whose bodies enabled them to take up space at night without risk. At a 1961 football game, historian Dan Carter, then a white college student, was pushed down the stairs by three fraternity brothers for refusing to stand for the playing of Dixie.[10] For African American students, the reactions to protest were far more threatening. These incidents were not limited to football games, but instead shaped the entire experience of Black students at the university.

For university administrators, the possibility of violence against students of color was too great at sporting events. As such, African American students were banned from attending Gamecock football games, ostensibly for their own protection.[11] They were returned their student activity fees, though they certainly could not be compensated for the continued racial segregation of school events and the threats of violence that went unpunished by university administrators. Threats of violence were not limited to the football stadium, however. Though risking physical harm and trauma, African American students protested both the playing of Dixie and the use of the Confederate flag on campus in the years directly following integration.

"DIXIE" IN HISTORY AND MEMORY

The song Dixie first gained popularity throughout the United States during the 1850s, a favorite of many Americans, including President Abraham Lincoln. Though it is primarily remembered as a minstrel song, it was used as an unofficial anthem for the Confederacy. The song was played after each confederate state voted to secede from the Union.[12]

The song, sang from the perspective of a formerly enslaved African American man, portrays slavery as a good and equitable institution. The narrator wants to return to an imagined South in which slavery is a perceived good, a narrative that was only strengthened during the post-Reconstruction era, as organizations like the United Daughters of the Confederacy erected monuments and rewrote textbooks.[13] By playing Dixie at school events, even after formal integration, the University promoted the idea that slavery was a benign, and even beneficial, institution for African Americans. This was a form of violence against Black students. In reviewing the song's lyrics, this sanitization of slavery's violent past is made clear:

> Oh, I wish I was in Dixie, Hooray! Hooray!
> In Dixie land Ill Take my Stand
> To live and die in Dixie
> Away, Away, away down south in Dixie
> Away, away, away down south in Dixie
> Oh, I wish I was in the land of cotton
> Old times there are not forgotten
> Look away! Look away!
> Look away! Dixie land
> In Dixieland where I was born in
> Early on one frosty mornin
> Look away! Look away!
> Look away! Dixie Land
>
> Old Missues marry Will, the weaver
> William was a gay deceiver
> Look away! Look away!
> Look away! Dixie land
> But when he put his arm around her
> He smiled fierce as a forty pounder
> Look away! Look away!
> Look away! Dixie Land
> His face was sharp as butcher's cleaver
> But that did not seem to grieve her
> Look away! Look away!
> Look away! Dixie land
> Old missues acted the foolish part
> And died for a man that broke her heart

Look away! Look away!
Look away! Dixie land

And all the gals that want to kiss us
Look away! Look away!
Look away! Dixie land
But if you want to drive away sorrow
Come and hear this song tomorrow
Look away! Look away!
Look away! Dixie land

Protesting Dixie, alongside other remnants of the confederacy clung to by white students, led to threats of physical violence as well as angry op-eds in the Gamecock.

Tensions heightened on campus at the University of South Carolina after the assassination of Martin Luther King Jr. Two on-campus protests were held and the University merely focused on the $40,000 in damages to Hamilton College and the Field House rather than the emotional well-being and trauma faced by Black students. University president Jones allowed students to go on spring break two weeks early, fearful for student safety. [14] In response to these protests, a fraternity held a party celebrating Martin Luther King Jr.'s death with no repercussions.

After these events, African American students and other activists organized events and protests to bring awareness to white supremacist activities and ideologies on campus. Student led group AWARE, which primarily focused on issues of free speech, held "white awareness week," a week dedicated to educating primarily white students about Black Power.[15]

ORANGEBURG MASSACRE AS A HAUNTING

After the denial of permission to burn the Confederate Flag on campus, as well as Brett Bursey's public burning of it despite the legality, tensions grew on campus. In a February 1969 Gamecock article "Tension Sparks Dixie Incidents" by Carl Stepp, he reported that the "flag burning Friday by black students led to a confrontation with racial overtones."[16] The university president responded with a request to "cool things off," ignoring the threats of violence faced by Black students. Though no arrests were made at the time of the burning, both State Law Enforcement officers as well as Highway Patrolmen responded to the burning. The article then reports that: "The controversy began with a requisition by the Association of Afro-American Students for an end to the playing of "Dixie" and waving of the Confederate Flag at University functions. A confederate flag was burned Wednesday night in front of Jones's home. Thursday night a debate scheduled on the Horseshoe officially broke up after 20 minutes when speakers were unable to talk over the shouts and chants of the crowd. Confederate flag-wavers stayed around for a rally, however, then marched to the Confederate monument at the State House where they sang dixie, the national anthem, and the alma mater."[17]

This reaction on the part of White students shows how both "Dixie" and the Alma Mater were wrapped up in ideologies of both the Confederate flag and what it meant to be a student at the University of South Carolina. That Friday, after two more flags were burned on the Russell House (student union) patio, "At one point several costumed white females paraded a cart carrying a black-faced corpse draped with a confederate flag. The group was ushered into Russell House by administrators."[18] The quick ushering of white students into Russell House shows the ways campus administrators sought to avoid controversy and media attention, rather than confront the continued white supremacy and racial violence present on campus. Though Carolina was known for a relatively peaceful desegregation process, the threat of violence was never eradicated for Black students during the 1960s and '70s. South Carolina State law enforcement was present through the entire incident, though there were no arrests.

Though there were multiple flag burnings on campus, only Brett Bursey faced formal legal consequences.[19] Because burning the flag was not simple vandalism but breaking a state statute banning the mutilation of the flag, the case was not clear cut. Regardless, Physical Education major Steve Wilson testified that he witnessed Bursey burning the flag, without identifying any other participants.[20]

Following the flag burnings, upset students and alumni wrote about their love of the flag and "Dixie" in the Daily Gamecock. One student said, "it should be obvious from the response at the USC basketball games that [']Dixie['] is loved and cherished by the majority of the student body. In our present-day society, the majority should respect the minority, but the majority should not be ruled by the selfish whims of the minority. What will it be next, Southern fried chicken."[21] Other students attempted to understand both sides as reasonable.

As the discussion intensified, there were two more flag burnings on campus, this time by African American students (Brett Bursey was a white ally). In retaliation, white students broke into the AAAS office and destroyed their belongings. Even the spaces claimed as "safe," created in the "hold," were threatened by the violence of white students. Other white students threw bricks at the windows of African American students and marched to the state house in protest. Though USC avoided state sanctioned violence during integration, unlike other southern institutions, the narrative of peaceful integration is a myth that denies the reality for Black students attending USC in the years after desegregation. After these events, AAAS called for Black students to avoid confrontation, stating "the lives of black folk are too precious to lose in another massacre," referencing the Orangeburg Massacre.[22]

In a February 18, 1969, edition of the Gamecock, Robert Pratt wrote a letter to the editor claiming that "Dixie" is beloved by the entire nation. Pratt wrote "when laws are broken because of a misconception by a radical minority group whose presence thus far has only been to stir up racial dissension, then the basis for a democratic society has been destroyed."[23] John Lottich, a USC graduate from the class of 1966, threatened to "withhold my personal financial support from the University" if "Dixie" and the Confederate flag were banned. Lottich goes on to refer to African American protesters as a "miserable handful of assorted un-washed, functionally illiterate and thoroughly mixed-up individuals, who would attempt to have the majority of students and faculty live by the desires of the minority."[24] Relying on racial stereotypes and the refusal of South Carolina to educate its African American residents, Lottich portrays Black students as unwanted and lacking knowledge.

In response to these actions, the university set up a committee to study "race relations" on campus and though many students still supported both "Dixie" and the Confederate flag, the song was no longer played after the semester. This show of support was modest in comparison to the violence, destruction, and threats faced by Black students at the University.

In a September 1970 issue of the Gamecock, a staff writer reported the appointment of Charles McMillian as the head of the new Office of Minority Student Affairs. At the time of his appointment, McMillian said that the committee "should have come with the first 25 black students. A person with this capacity should have come earlier." The vice president of Student Affairs, Charles Witten said that the job was created "to fill the needs of students and to improve campus relations.[25] "For Witten and other administrators, these resources were designed to quell resistance on campus rather than to aid Black students.

The committee was created by university president Jones to "keep under review the needs and problems of minority group students, particularly, but not limited to black students and make recommendations to the President, the Provost and the Vice President of the University."[26] The committee was designed to focus on incidents of discrimination, curriculum of interest to minority students, the recruiting of African America students and faculty to the university, and attempts "to incorporate" African American students into the study body. The Office of Minority Student Affairs was created after a directive from the US Department of Education and Welfare.[27]

Though many thought the debates over "Dixie" were over, the Office of Minority Student Affairs was called in to help after the marching band played "Dixie" twice during a basketball game in which Casey Manning, an African American student, was playing. Without formally banning the song, OMSA got the band director to agree to stop playing it to avoid controversy.

In 1970, the year of the committee's founding, fewer than 100 "minority students" were enrolled at the University of South Carolina. Even by 1979, after the committee had been in place for almost a decade, it was relatively unknown to most African American students. McMillian reported that the Office of Minority Student Affairs was understaffed and could only help about 40 percent of eligible students. Nathaniel Smith, then president of The Association of Afro American Students, said, "a lot of people are hurting unnecessarily because they aren't aware there is a place for them to come with their problems, personal or otherwise."[28]

In the meeting minutes from October 18, 1972, it was reported that "Discussion revolved around a decision by the Student Union Lecture Committee to withdraw its support of Don L. Lee, a black poet, who was supposed to be invited to give a lecture during the annual ‹Black Week› at USC."[29] White students claimed they felt threatened by large numbers of African American students meeting in the Student Union, when only six students were present. The committee reported that "White students suggested that the Russel House is their Union, and that black students should be content with what they allow them to do."[30] Ownership of space was still essential to the experiences of Black students.

In 1973, the Office of Minority Student Affairs became involved in cheerleading tryouts after African American student Cynthia Mcleod was rejected from the senior cheerleading team because of her "style." The Afro-American Association presented this incident of discrimination to the administration as well as the Office of Minority Student Affairs. A new tryout judging system was developed and was required to include a representative from the Office of Minority Student Affairs.[31] There were no reports on the effects of this judging system, however.

In a 1979 report, The Office of Minority Student Affairs reported that minority students were faced with grade discrimination on campus. Director Charles McMillian said that "the most common problem is teachers discriminating with their grades."[32] McMillian also noted that there were very few faculty of color on campus. Again, there were few notes on attempts to correct these issues beyond frustrations with survey use.

The office of Minority Student Affairs was also involved in the creation of a Council on Legal Educational Opportunities (CLEO), which allowed for economically disadvantaged students to gain entrance to the law school. While this program was eventually discontinued, citing a lack of academic preparation rather than the institutional barriers to success faced by Black students, the advent of this program makes evident the recognition of institutional and socioeconomic barriers to success for minority students by the committee. The desegregation of the University of South Carolina allowed Black students to enroll at the University of South Carolina but did not directly address barriers to entrance from outside the doors of the University. According to the Committee, African American students were often from poor neighborhoods with subpar public schools, and while many of these students would be admitted to the university, they faced challenges unknown to many other students. The institution of the CLEO makes clear that the Committee on Minority Student Affairs, and the university more broadly, was both cognizant of these barriers and made small attempts to rectify the situation. The Committee on Minority Student Affairs concluded that secondary education in South Carolina was at fault for the failure of CLEO.

As the perceived failure of the CLEO program shows, attempts to address broader issues for African American students did not always succeed. These institutional barriers to success lasted long after the formal desegregation of the university and colored the experience of the African American students at the University of South Carolina.

Throughout the 1970s, the Committee for Minority Student Affairs was also concerned with the hiring of African American professors and the attendance and support at university events and speaker series with African American speakers. Many of these events were poorly attended, especially by White students and faculty. The Commission on minority affairs and the university president made a concerted effort to get students and faculty to show support for African American students and faculty, making clear the importance of not just integrating the university but fully engaging African American students and faculty within the university community.

The interest in recruiting and giving extra attention to African American faculty became more pronounced throughout the 1970s. The Committee on Minority Student Affairs had an interest in both attracting more African American faculty and giving more resources to African American professors. They realized that solely integrating the student body would not effectively change the racial dynamics of the university, and that African American members of the faculty were facing issues as well.

In 2017, the University of South Carolina officially recognized the only remaining slave residences on campus with a historical marker. A second marker, installed at the same time, acknowledges openly that much of the horseshoe was built by enslaved people. Fifty-four years after the University of South Carolina officially desegregated, the university first tacitly acknowledged the place enslaved

African Americans had in the creation and functioning of the university. Even as this happened, buildings across campus are still named after slave owners (The Thomas Cooper Library, for one) and portraits still dot the campus. The campus gymnasium is named after famed segregationist Strom Thurmond. The struggles for inclusion that students faced directly post desegregation are still relevant today as Black Gamecocks fight to remove the iconography and names of slave owners from campus.

Chapter Ten

"THE RIGHT TIME"

Performing Public History at the
University of South Carolina, 2010–2020

Katharine Thompson Allen & Lydia Mattice Brandt

T wo brick walkways line the "historic Horseshoe," the antebellum core of the University of South Carolina (USC) campus. Frustrated with the state's unwillingness to fund paths on the quadrangle during the Great Depression, students from two fraternities raised $500, secured a donation of seven thousand red bricks, and decided to do the work themselves.[1] Under the supervision of Professor Havilah Babcock, they enlisted the school's civil engineering program for survey and excavation work and hired professional brick masons to supervise the project. On November 23, 1931, acting president Leonard T. Baker laid the first ceremonial brick adjacent to Lieber College, marking the beginning of a performative exercise of blue-collar manual labor enacted by hundreds of students. Sensing an opportunity to raise additional funds, the project announced plans to place "bronze or iron tablets" in the walkways acknowledging the more than $1,500 raised by fraternities and other organizations for the effort. The "memorial sidewalks" that ran from Sumter to Bull Street ultimately included the initials of ten student groups and two faculty members, including Babcock. Contrasting bricks, rather than memorial tablets, ultimately spelled out these initials.[2]

Just feet from the white initials of Havilah Babcock (HB) are red-brick letters almost indistinguishable from the pavers around them: they spell "MEE," the initials of Black brick mason Marion Edgar Evans. The thirty-nine-year-old Evans lived with his family at 1106 Pine Street in Waverly, an upper-middle-class Black neighborhood. By all contemporary accounts, Evans and his wife, Irene, had a stable life and raised two entrepreneurial children, barber Marion Jr., and dressmaker Angeline. Their life together ended tragically on December 21,

1933—just a little over a year after Evans's initials appeared in the sidewalk of the all-white university—when he died from injuries sustained during a car accident.[3]

In the decades after Evans's death, articles in the *Gamecock* student newspaper embellished Babcock's recollections of the sidewalk project, specifically "how Marion Evans, an old Negro man, helped to lay the brick walks and put his own initials in the walk" and then "cancelled the debt of nearly $100 owed him for bricklaying to have them remain there."[4] In each retelling, Evans was simultaneously remembered as supremely competent and "clever," yet somehow foolish enough to vandalize a white-owned space—an act that would have been cause for lynching in his lifetime. This narrative allowed Babcock to explain how the initials of a Black man ended up alongside his own while characterizing himself as tolerant of and benevolent to USC's Black workforce.

As a *Gamecock* staff writer noted in 1959, "MEE" allowed the university to show "what it is today—a reflection of humanity."[5] These words rang false as the university remained segregated and continued to in the decades to come. More than sixty years after Evans's death, another version of this story ensured that white students—rather than Babcock and the administration—would take credit for memorializing him. In a letter to the Carolina Alumni Association in 1999, a civil engineering alumnus from the class of 1935 recalled that "one day our hired helper was not there and we decided to put his initials in the brick because of his fine help and being such a nice person. Thus our black helper had his initials put in the walk."[6] The guidebook *On the Horseshoe* (2015) and present-day university tours still share this story.[7]

Reframing the installation of MEE and the interpretation that accompanies it as acts of memorialization that benefited USC's white community offers a critical lens for examining the university's recent efforts to recognize Black individuals and achievements. Between 2013 and 2020, USC dedicated a garden and plaque to commemorate the fiftieth anniversary of the university's second desegregation (2013); a statue of the university's only Heisman Trophy winner, George Rogers (2015); two markers acknowledging the contributions of enslaved laborers on the Horseshoe (2017); a statue of Reconstruction-era faculty member, Richard T. Greener (2018); and a statue of basketball champion, A'ja Wilson (2021). While remarkable in both their range and number, these projects were often the result of ad hoc initiatives that were at turns reactive or opportunistic, and therefore have often failed to disrupt, much less transform, USC's identity as a campus controlled by and for white people.

While the university's top officials ensured that the garden and athlete statues —all noncontroversial in substance and form—were quickly funded and built, they did not provide the same support to the grassroots efforts to publicly acknowledge USC's history of slavery or to celebrate Richard T. Greener, the school's first Black faculty member. The administration moved forward with markers recognizing slavery and a statue honoring Greener only after student-led pressure. It relied solely upon unsponsored research, suggesting that concerns over public perception rather than a desire to comprehensively reevaluate the university's historical narrative drove how and when it decided to react.

THE STANDING HISTORICAL NARRATIVES OF THE UNIVERSITY OF SOUTH CAROLINA

Students and faculty who led efforts to research slavery and build the Greener monument sought to revise and confront existing institutional histories. Until this recent scholarship, only three histories shaped who and what was remembered at the University of South Carolina: those by Maximillian LaBorde (1859, expanded in 1874), Edwin L. Green (1916), and Daniel W. Hollis (1951, 1956).[8] While ostensibly published as institutional histories, these texts perform as chronicles of the university's perceived heroes, villains, tragedies, and triumphs. Each aligned with similar narratives emerging out of colleges and universities across the nation, in large part because they were all written by white men connected to these institutions (either as faculty or administrators). Although USC's story grew more sophisticated and reliant on primary sources over time, each author unsurprisingly narrated the events of the university from the perspective of the most powerful.

In alignment with national trends, these histories take for granted, willfully ignore, or blatantly misconstrue the role of Africans and African Americans on campus, and particularly the university's histories of slavery and the Reconstruction era. They are largely silent on the enslaved Black men, women, and children who made their heroes' lives possible and the institution itself economically feasible. Their telling of the university's remarkable post–Civil War history, meanwhile, follows the Dunning School's politicization of Reconstruction as a failure of "radical" proponents of racial equity.[9] From LaBorde's narrative to Hollis's nearly one century later, the antebellum period—before the indignities of the Confederacy's loss, integration, and the long period of stagnation and rebuilding that followed—consistently remained the institution's "golden age."[10]

"INVISIBLE NO MORE"?

On December 5, 2017, USC unveiled two historical markers on its antebellum campus that acknowledged slavery: one sits at the head of the Horseshoe, the other in front of the university president's residence and its slave dwelling/kitchen. In his dedication speech, "Invisible No More," President Harris Pastides noted, "From 1801 through February of 1865, enslaved people were absolutely an integral part of the daily operations at South Carolina College . . . visible yet invisible . . . from masonry to meal preparation, to setting up student chemistry labs." These individuals were now honored with "two beautiful and strong markers."[11] What was not readily apparent or acknowledged were the origins of the markers' language and content, which derived almost entirely from a one-semester graduate student project completed more than six years earlier. This scholarship, which debuted as the website "Slavery at South Carolina College, 1801–1865: The Foundations of the University of South Carolina," uncovered the names featured on the plaque in front of the president's house. This list, although incomplete, is not problematic in and of itself; as Pastides noted, "we may not [ever] know" the names of many of the enslaved individuals who lived and worked on campus. However, no attempt to document additional names was made prior to the marker's installation, and several scholars noted omissions on the very day of the markers' dedication. This outcome was inevitable given the reactionary administrative process, disconnected from new scholarship, which informed both markers' creation.[12]

"Slavery at South Carolina College" was the brainchild of Professor Robert Weyeneth, a tenured faculty member in USC's Department of History and director of the award-winning Public History program. Although admittedly not an expert of the antebellum period, he was aware of similar research taking place at other universities and recognized a gap in scholarship at USC. Weyeneth led a senior seminar in the fall of 2010 that aimed to document the enslaved people owned or whose labor was rented by the antebellum university and its faculty. The students' research was limited by time constraints and the fact that university archivist Elizabeth West hand-selected the antebellum records they could consult.

The three main historiographies of the antebellum institution also hamstrung the students' work because the texts obscured the centrality of the "peculiar institution" to the college's very identity. Written while he served as chairman of the faculty, Maximilian LaBorde's *History of the South Carolina College* (1859) enshrined the college as a prestigious institution populated with academic leaders who educated the state's elite.[13] The enslaving LaBorde regarded slavery as an unremarkable fact.[14] He described the construction of the college's physical plant, much of which survives today, in passive voice, a method that denied recognition of the enslaved laborers who performed the work. Mentions of "servants" appeared only in anecdotes about misbehaving students and hagiographic faculty biographies.[15]

More than fifty years later, Edwin Luther Green declared his *A History of the University of South Carolina* (1916) a successor to LaBorde's work.[16] Although

Green devoted half of his book to detailed descriptions of the antebellum campus, he still confined the institution of slavery to a series of line-item expenditures and avoided depictions that portrayed enslaved people as individuals with humanity. Furthermore, his book enshrined the myth that the college's administrators were kind and responsible masters and referred to the enslaved as "servants." His sole attempt at documenting the enslaved appeared in a chapter on university expenses. It included the names of several men bought and sold by the college— Henry, Jim Ruffin, Jim Blue, and Jack, its "first slave."[17]

If Green provided a glimpse of humans in bondage on campus, USC's next institutional historian succeeded in reframing the college's role in the institution of slavery as intellectual rather than physical. Daniel W. Hollis arrived at USC in 1947 and published *South Carolina College*, volume one of his two-volume university history, four years later. He interpreted the administration's (and faculty's) attitude toward slavery by acknowledging that it was "slavery and cotton" which united South Carolina, and that the college merely promoted that unity.[18]

Hollis also documented how the college's most prominent academics, including presidents Thomas Cooper and James Henley Thornwell, influenced attitudes toward slavery and states' rights in South Carolina, particularly as their former students began assuming roles in government.[19] Although the college's participation in and advocacy for slavery was not a central thesis of Hollis's work, he nonetheless documented how the institution served as a kind of antebellum, proslavery "think-tank" that played a role in South Carolina's eventual secession.[20]

Despite having access to just these three secondary narratives and a small set of university records, Weyeneth's undergraduate students realized they had an opportunity to create something new and meaningful. Most took a top-down approach by examining the "big names" on the antebellum campus, such as past presidents Cooper and Thornwell, and interrogating their roles in promoting and practicing slavery. Others researched the lives of enslaved people on campus, including where they might have lived as well as the purpose and consequences of the "Proviso of 1807," which barred students from bringing enslaved people to campus. The course culminated in a symposium at McKissick Museum. Attendees included local public history practitioners and some university administrators, faculty, and graduate students who planned to continue the work the following spring.[21]

Weyeneth's spring 2011 graduate course, "Historic Site Interpretation," built upon the undergraduates' scholarship. Enrollees included a mixture of graduate students pursuing an emphasis in public history. Most did not have any experience in identifying which extant records might discuss enslavement and thus relied primarily on the expertise of archivist Elizabeth West, and to a lesser extent,

Graham Duncan, South Caroliniana Library's manuscript specialist and arguably USC's only scholar on slavery and the institution.[22] After weighing time constraints and reviewing other universities' efforts, which ranged from comprehensive histories (e.g. Brown University), websites (University of North Carolina), markers (University of Alabama), and public statements of regret (University of Virginia), the students decided to build a website. They believed this platform "could potentially reach the most people and did not require significant material support from the university, beyond the encouragement and support of the instructor and university librarians."[23] The website's content challenged the university's primary historiographies by foregrounding the stories of the enslaved and the motivations of their enslavers while arguing for the preservation of structures on campus *because* of their connections to slavery.[24]

"Slavery at South Carolina College" was revelatory for its comprehensiveness and accessibility. It explored the "hiring-out" system utilized by the university, explicitly connected the college's construction and maintenance to slavery, named enslaved people when possible, and documented all of the "slave quarters" that once stood on campus, only one of which remained. The website also included selected digitized archival documents, at Weyeneth's insistence, that could silence any denials about the institution's active role in slavery.[25]

In the summer of 2011, Weyeneth worked with West, graduate student Katharine Thompson [Allen], and Kate Boyd, the director of the library's digital collections, to migrate the project to the latter's ContentDM system.[26] Although the university's administration had been aware of the project since its inception, their response to the final product was seen as "minimal" by the website's authors.[27] Over the next two years, the project's participants, both students and faculty, promoted the project on the National Council on Public History's website and in presentations at conferences, in undergraduate courses, and to USC's University 101 faculty; this outreach did not result in sustained or widespread support.[28] "Slavery at South Carolina College" did serve as the impetus for the approval of a $1.5 million restoration of the campus's historic wall. However, this effort did not foreground slavery in a meaningful way or actively build upon the website's scholarship.[29] Weyeneth felt that "it was up to the community to figure out what they wanted to do" with this research, but knowledge of the project quickly dwindled as students and faculty moved on to careers elsewhere. Years passed with no official acknowledgment or effort from the administration to promote the research or underwrite additional inquiry.

Four years later, students once again brought the university's complicity in slavery to the forefront. On November 16, 2015, approximately 150 students and faculty marched from Longstreet Theatre to the Osborne Administration

Building on the Horseshoe to present a list of twelve demands to USC's leadership.[30] Although President Harris Pastides was out of town, both Provost Joan Gabel and John Dozier, chief diversity officer and chair of the Diversity and Inclusion Advisory Committee (DIAC), met the group outside. Their demands, as well as an open letter to Pastides, appeared simultaneously on the petition platform Change.org. Listed first was a "demand that our university acknowledge that this institution was built on the backs of enslaved Africans. Further, we expect that this acknowledgment is included in tours, especially areas like the garden directly behind the president's house where slaves were once housed. This acknowledgement should be reflected in markers on historic buildings."[31]

Local observers perceived this student-led coalition, USC 2020 Vision, as building on protests at the University of Missouri that had led to the resignations of that system's president and chancellor. While Karli Wells and Clarie Randall, two USC 2020 Vision organizers, acknowledged that they had pushed the date of the protest forward because of the events at Missouri, they did so only as a means of "capitalizing on [USC administration's] fear." As Wells later recalled, "when people react and they're afraid of something, it's already on the forefront of their mind. The impression that I got from the administrators was their belief was that USC was better than all these other places [having protests]: [the idea that] USC doesn't have those problems. Which I think signifies how out of touch they were with the student population, or at least part of it."[32]

In response to the protestors' demands, DIAC formed a subcommittee on engagement, which relied on the "Slavery at South Carolina College" website as the definitive history of slavery at the university. At Weyeneth's suggestion, Jennifer Gunter and Alyssa Constad, history graduate students who participated in USC 2020 Vision, attended the subcommittee's meeting in March 2016.[33] According to Constad, the group debated where markers interpreting slavery could be placed but had not prepared language. In the following days and at the behest of committee member David J. Snyder, Gunter and Constad drafted language for two markers based on content from the website, one of which included the names of twenty-one enslaved people, their labor, and the dates they may have worked or lived on campus. The markers also called the antebellum campus by Weyeneth's favored phrase: a "landscape of slavery."[34]

Rather than introducing Gunter and Constad's text to the subcommittee, Snyder asked Weyeneth for another interpretation. Although Weyeneth considered his role in documenting slavery on campus as largely complete, he was nevertheless thrilled that something was happening and glad to contribute. That same day, he repurposed language from the "Slavery at South Carolina College" website almost verbatim as text for two markers:

A Landscape of Slavery

The modern Horseshoe is the campus of South Carolina College, as the University of South Carolina was called before the Civil War. Its buildings and historic wall were constructed by slave labor and built of slave-made brick. Slaves were also essential to the daily operations of the college. Whether they were owned outright by the faculty or the college itself, or hired from private parties, slaves maintained campus buildings, cleaned student tenements and faculty duplexes, and prepared meals at the student dining commons, faculty residences, and the president's house. Slaves lived and worked in now-forgotten outbuildings located behind the primary buildings; remarkably, one kitchen-house/slave-quarters survives. The Horseshoe is a surprisingly intact and well-preserved "landscape of slavery."

The Slave Quarters

This kitchen-house/slave-quarters stands as a tangible link to the enslaved people who lived and worked in this outbuilding. South Carolina College owned a number of slaves and hired countless others between 1801 and 1865. It is difficult to locate information about the enslaved, as college records rarely listed names or identifying information about individual slaves. Although slaves made significant contributions to the construction and maintenance of college buildings and to daily life on campus, in most cases we do not know who these slaves were, what labor they performed, or where they lived. Slaves who did appear by name in college records included Abraham, Amanda, Anna, Anthony, Charles, Henry, Jack, Jim, Joe, Lucy, Mal., Peter, Sancho and his wife, Simon, Toby, and Tom. Naming these individuals represents an effort to remember all of the enslaved who built South Carolina College.[35]

Snyder added a single sentence to the first marker that stated, "Many students and faculty in those years would become outspoken advocates for the slave system that led to the Civil War" and presented this language to the subcommittee. On June 7, 2016, the subcommittee approved a final version, which included only minor word substitutions as well as a less forceful statement on the college's advocacy for slavery.[36]

Over the next several months, Dozier worked with William Hubbard and Leah Moody, both members of USC's board of trustees, to ensure that the markers would be approved. By the time university architect Derek Gruner presented the project in April 2017 to the board's Building and Grounds Committee, DIAC's approved text had been substantially simplified. References to the college's "landscape of slavery," the role of the college's faculty and students in advocating for slavery, and even the duties performed by enslaved people on campus had been removed.[37]

Furthermore, Gruner noted that "the markers will be bronze plaques mounted on posts identical to those which already exist on the Horseshoe to commemorate the original nineteenth-century university buildings."[38] While ostensibly designed to keep the "sacred" Horseshoe landscape as unaltered as possible, their design symbolically positioned them as equal in importance to markers honoring the namesakes of buildings, including enslavers Edward Rutledge, Henry William DeSaussure, Charles C. Pinckney, Hugh S. Legare, and Francis Lieber.[39] The complete board approved the two edited markers "without discussion."[40]

According to Pastides upon their approval, the markers took a "long time because it's not only a sensitive matter, but the research that was done to support the wording took a lot of time."[41] This phrasing purposefully severed the creation of the markers from the protests eighteen months prior, with Pastides explicitly stating that, "The effort started through the material culture or public history department with grad students who came to see me . . . again well before the Vision 2020 group."[42] They also did not acknowledge that a much more organized effort to confront institutional history was underway at rival Clemson University. Following protests to rename Tillman Hall (dedicated to white supremacist politician Benjamin Ryan Tillman) in 2015, Clemson's board of trustees had denounced Tillman, formed the Task Force of the History of Clemson, and announced a new interpretive plan—including markers—in February 2016, just a month before the first drafts of USC's markers emerged from DIAC.[43]

Associate Professor Bobby Donaldson gave the keynote speech at the December 2017 unveiling. He spoke movingly of Sancho and Lucy Cooper, a husband and wife enslaved by Thomas Cooper, the college's second president. He called the markers "important corrections to the institution's history," even as he offered up a correction of his own—that "Sancho and his wife" were actually "Sancho and Lucy Cooper."[44] How then did "the culmination of years of research," as reported by local news outlets, lead to such an omission?[45] The obvious answer is there had not been "years of research," and so the original list of names was immediately outdated. As Dozier more accurately stated in a piece published by the university, "Bob Weyeneth's students conducted research several years ago that has given us the information we have today about the university's use of enslaved people." To Dozier's credit, he acknowledged that the markers were only a "step toward complete ownership of who we are as a university" that was "inspired by our students."[46]

Put simply, repurposing (and shortening) the list of twenty-one names discovered in 2011, including "Sancho and his wife," allowed DIAC to interpret slavery without further research and the complications inherent within. As even amateur genealogists know, the search for Sancho's wife would unearth far more than the name "Lucy." Probate records preserved by the South Carolina Department of Archives and History and digitized in 2015 for Ancestry.com include those of Professor Thomas Cooper. In his will, Cooper bequeathed to his wife not only Sancho, but also "Lucy, Sancho Jun[ior], Rachel, and any other that I may possess at my deceased." In sales papers dated thirty-two days later, Dr. Cooper's executor ordered the sale of all four people to offset his outstanding debts. Although both Sancho and "Lucy his wife" remained with Cooper's widow, both "negro boy" Sancho Junior and "negro girl" Rachel were sold separately.[47] Census records prompt darker questions. As late as 1830, while still president of the college, Dr. Cooper enslaved eight people, not four, including two girls under the age of ten.[48] Who were they? What became of them? Merely opening the door to these questions, even if their answers could not fit on a marker, might have forced the institution to reconcile, or at least acknowledge, its role in housing enslaved babies and young children, in revering the men who enslaved them, and in teaching the next generation of enslavers to do the same.[49]

This example does not discredit Weyeneth's students' work, but rather highlights that their "Slavery at South Carolina College" class project continued to carry the sole burden of documenting and interpreting the institution's role in slavery. DIAC's subcommittee on engagement decided against further inquiry in the name of speed and cost-effectiveness. In other words, markers that *seemed* right would work for the time being. After all, according to Snyder, DIAC only reconvened after the USC 2020 Vision protests, and "none of this happen[ed]" without their list of demands.[50] The narrative that emerges around this memorial, then, is a reactionary one that resulted in performatory reconciliation by an administration that saw the markers as an effective and inexpensive way to promote diversity and inclusion.

The markers now blend in among those that describe the origins of building names, and promises of additional university-supported scholarship remain unrealized. University ambassadors—students tasked with sharing the history of USC with prospective students and parents—are prepared to answer questions about slavery but do not actively discuss it on their tours. According to one ambassador this is because, "We don't want to make certain people feel uncomfortable, and we don't necessarily think that it contributes to the overall message that we are trying to bring."[51] The University of South Carolina seems to agree. As

Marker recognizing slavery on USC's Horseshoe, installed
December 2017. Photograph by Chandler Yonkers, 2021.

late as July 2020, its "Our History" page omitted the existence of enslaved people
on campus while touting the service of "noted European scholars Francis Lieber
and Thomas Cooper."[52]

RECONSTRUCTION AND THE STATUE OF RICHARD T. GREENER

Preliminary student and faculty research on slavery coincided with an effort to
celebrate pioneering Black Professor Richard T. Greener. While "Slavery at South
Carolina College" illuminated the university as enslaver, the Greener Memorial
Committee pushed back against the dominant institutional history of USC's
Reconstruction period as a stain on its record during which its biracial faculty,
student body, and board of trustees fell "into alien hands and sunk beneath
contempt."[53] Reconstruction featured prominently in the introduction to the
second edition of LaBorde's history, in which faculty member John L. Reynolds
bitterly chronicled the fight to "save the University for the white sons of the
State" and claimed that "a mixed school was impracticable. The colored people
neither needed nor desired it."[54] Edwin L. Green offered a similar perspective in
his 1916 university history, when he characterized the period as a "defilement" and
a "fraud upon the taxpayers . . . deliberately perpetrated in the name of progress

and enlightenment!"[55] Although tempered and well cited, Daniel Walker Hollis's mid-twentieth-century history held tight to the Dunning School's standard line on Reconstruction. He recognized that "the history of the University of South Carolina during the years of Congressional Reconstruction is unique among Southern Institutions," but observed that the University of Virginia and other schools were "fortunate enough to escape Radical rule."[56] Published a decade after the first serious challenge to end segregation at USC, his conclusion offered a warning for those looking to integrate the university once again: "A public institution can be destroyed in more ways than one, however; and one of the most effective ways is so to alter it that it no longer receives the approval of the people whose support it must have."[57]

The campus's only material recognition of Reconstruction erected prior to the Greener memorial confirmed and legitimized this narrative. In 1938, the Columbia Sesquicentennial Commission installed three identical highway markers explaining the history of the university, the most prominent of which still sits on Sumter Street in front of the Horseshoe.[58] Erected as part of a campaign of fifty plaques installed across the city and Richland County, the markers' text briefly summarized the milestones common to these institutional histories.[59] They note the founding of the college, that the "entire student body volunteered for Confederate service," and, most pointedly, "Radical control" from 1873 to 1877, followed by "Closed 1877–80."[60] While the integrated institution (as well as the politicians who supported it) were summarized as "radical," the post-Reconstruction legislature's decision to close the university rather than allow it to continue is left without comment.[61]

The university did not supplement or contradict these virulent written and public histories for decades. But in the fall of 2010, students in College of Education Professor Katherine Chaddock's "Evolution of Higher Education" class pondered why USC's remarkable Reconstruction period remained unrecognized. Her students questioned why there was a plaque in Cambridge, Massachusetts, to recognize Greener as the first Black graduate of Harvard University but that there was not one at USC, where he worked as the first professor of color from 1873 to 1877.[62] A year later, Chaddock organized an ad hoc, racially diverse group of faculty, students, alumni, and staff to discuss the possibility of publicly recognizing Greener.[63] The group's mission was "to establish a lasting public memorial to Richard T. Greener in honor of his service (librarianship and teaching) to the University of South Carolina; his influence on the positive achievements of the Reconstruction years in education; and his pioneering status as the first African American faculty member at the University (1873–77)." The Greener Memorial Committee hoped that "[s]uch a memorial [would] draw appropriate public attention not only to an important individual, but also to an era in the history of the institution, city and state that contributed to the beginnings of social justice across the races."[64]

The committee campaigned for six years before President Harris Pastides chose to finance a "lasting memorial" with unrestricted university funds in the fall of 2017. Throughout this period, the committee had to push back against widespread misunderstanding of the Reconstruction period, Greener's relative obscurity, and build support for the project—all while navigating the university's bureaucracy. What would the memorial look like? Where would it be located? Who should pay for it? This process prompted the committee to question if recognizing Greener could ever reconcile such a complicated and contested period in USC's history.

The Greener committee spent its first four years determining the monument's form and location. It was initially cautious about committing to a plan for a monument without garnering wider support from potential stakeholders. To build buy-in and gather ideas, it implemented a public competition to "guide the proposed design of a lasting memorial" with a "concept."[65] Open to all USC students, faculty, staff, and alumni, the Richard T. Greener Memorial Competition launched in February 2012 (coordinated with the university's calendar of events for Black History Month).[66] A jury representing students, the local preservation community, the Black Alumni Council, and faculty ultimately recognized three proposals.[67]

While the proposals represented a range of ideas, two of the three winners provided special "inspiration" for the committee as they "conceptualize[d] a way to permanently honor Richard Greener."[68] Undergraduate art student Shawn Glover proposed a representational sculpture of Greener sitting on a bench on the Horseshoe, arguing convincingly for the clarity of a figurative memorial and the impact of the historic quadrangle as its site.[69] Professor Robert Weyeneth's proposal celebrated Greener's role in rebuilding the university's library collection after the Civil War by renaming Thomas Cooper Library after him. Weyeneth found justice in replacing an enslaver's name with Greener's and suggested that a renaming debate "could become a catalyst for a productive discussion of modern race relations."[70]

Regardless of whatever form the memorial would take, its location was a persistent question in the early years of the project. The committee initially agreed with Glover's proposal that the Horseshoe was the most impactful site for any kind of memorial: it was the center of the historic campus and the space in which Greener lived and worked during the 1870s. But conversations with university landscape architect Ben Coonrod, university architect Derek Gruner, and university archivist Elizabeth West convinced the group that any insistence on the Horseshoe as the site for the memorial could doom the project.[71] Denise Wellman, director of the university's visitor's center (housed in McKissick Museum at the space's eastern end), had also recently faced considerable opposition for her idea to build a statue of the university's mascot, Cocky, on the Horseshoe.[72] The Horseshoe was widely viewed as a "sacred" place that should be frozen in the antebellum period glorified by the university's institutional histories.[73]

The committee quickly pivoted to Thomas Cooper Library as a memorial site that was both conceptually appropriate and more politically viable.[74] Noted in Weyeneth's competition entry as the "heart of the modern campus" and "the most important academic building on campus today," the library could also honor Greener's work as a librarian.[75] The committee initially proposed redesigning the reflecting pool plaza in front of Thomas Cooper Library, but dean of libraries Thomas McNally warned the group against introducing anything that would visually interrupt the iconic view from Greene Street (especially important on ESPN's College Gameday broadcasts) and cited cost as a potential roadblock.[76] Gruner was the first to see the potential in the monument's ultimate location: a grassy space that connected the library, a new student health center, and the Russell House student union.[77]

With a general consensus that the memorial should be located adjacent to Thomas Cooper Library, the committee refocused on determining its future form. It publicly solicited proposals for the memorial with a $200,000 budget in the fall of 2013.[78] The open request for proposals specified that the work must be "three-dimensional and constructed of materials suitable for long-term outdoor installation and easy maintenance" but did not dictate that it had to be a statue.[79] Nine artists submitted proposals, seven of which were figurative statues representing Greener. A jury similar in composition to that of the ideas competition chose a sculpture by artist John Hair in December 2013.[80] Hair described his proposed standing figure: "the visionary Greener gazes into the future, contemplating what grand things it might hold. He cradles a large book in his hands, safeguarding it, as he did the library collection."[81] USC's Design Review Committee—the first gatekeeper in the process of acquiring final authorization from the university's board of trustees—approved Hair's design and the site just east of the library in April 2014.[82]

Following the design's approval, funding became a challenging next step.[83] Without any promises of financial assistance from the administration, all assumed that the committee must raise funds privately. This was already the case for the Cocky statue. But in contrast to the Greener committee's members' lack of experience raising money, the fundraising effort for Cocky was backed by Wellman and others' extensive development experience and administrative clout, such as that of Vice President for Student Affairs Dennis Pruitt.[84] Similarly, the effort for a memorial garden and programming commemorating the fiftieth anniversary of the 1963 desegregation enjoyed the support of the administration with a fundraising campaign—"Embracing Change, Fulfilling the Dream"—led by the Educational Foundation, an independent development and investing group that supports the university.[85] While the Greener committee's ad hoc nature ensured representation of diverse perspectives, it was not an ideal organization to raise the hundreds of thousands of dollars necessary; even determining where to bank the funds was unclear.[86]

Fundraising also faced a catch-22: securing money for something that might not be built was not a strong position as the project sought approval from the board of trustees, but neither was proposing an unfunded project.[87] The Greener committee first approached the organizing committee for the desegregation commemoration, but that group was not interested in expanding its scope.[88] It then made unsuccessful entreaties to the development teams responsible for raising money for the law school (speaking to Greener's status as one of the school's first Black graduates), the libraries (because of the proposed location next to Thomas Cooper and its recent investment in purchasing Greener's USC law diploma), and the colleges of education and arts and sciences (the home colleges of the committee's co-chairs).[89]

In the fall of 2015, more than a year after the jury selected Hair's sculpture, the board of trustees gave approval for the committee to begin its own fundraising, and the group established a relationship with the university's development staff.[90] But meeting the sculpture's $200,000 cost seemed impossible. Despite promising names of potential donors, solicitation materials, and a featured spot on the university's new crowdsourcing fundraising platform, development never identified any donor candidates.[91] Although Pastides had always endorsed the committee, he did not offer university funds or direct staff to raise funds for the project as for other commemorations.

One year later, Pastides suddenly propelled the project forward by guaranteeing unrestricted funds from the Educational Foundation.[92] The board of trustees approved Hair's sculpture and its $225,000 price tag ("funded with gifts"); Pastides said it was "the first project to be authorized by the board of trustees without already being funded."[93] The finished statue was unveiled in February 2018 along with a short program planned by the committee. Three of Chaddock's students who had initially suggested a permanent memorial to Greener—Danny Bounds, Michael Jones, and Samantha White—were among those who unveiled the nine-foot-tall figure.[94] White told the local news, "at a time, where there was just a few

Richard T. Greener, Jon Hair (sculptor), unveiled February 2018. Photograph by Christian Anderson, 2021.

years ago there was a Confederate flag hanging over this state to now the state flagship having a monument for a brown person, an African American person, that's what growth does and what it means to be dedicated."[95] Evelyn Bausman, Greener's granddaughter, was also present at the event and presented family correspondence to the South Caroliniana Library.[96]

Pastides's decision to fund the statue and present it to the board came amidst discussions over the slavery markers and the USC 2020 Vision protests, as well as Clemson University's significant efforts to recognize African Americans and recontextualize campus history. As stated in the title of the fundraising brochure produced by the university's development office for the sculpture—"A Place of Honor at the Right Time in History"—the administration had waited until the "right time" to admit that the Greener committee would never raise the funds without administrative support, and the prolonged lack of action might reflect poorly on the university.[97]

But as with the slavery markers, scholarship that reckoned with the standing narrative of the university's Reconstruction-era history was not part of the administration's implementation of the Greener statue. Neither the board of trustees nor Pastides included any funding or support for research that would encourage comprehensive revision of the institution's narrative as part of the statue's construction. And yet dialogue and new research had always been a priority for the faculty-led Greener committee. After learning more about Greener in the process of advocating for the memorial, committee co-chair Katherine Chaddock wrote a biography, *Uncompromising Activist: Richard Greener, First Black Graduate of Harvard College*, published by Johns Hopkins University Press ahead of the monument unveiling.[98] The committee had also long imagined an annual public event to be an essential part of the memorial. Its members saw a series of speakers, symposiums, or roundtables to deepen the meaning of the sculpture and facilitate ongoing discussions of Greener's legacy, Reconstruction history, reconciliation, and racial justice. They had long insisted on an endowment for such programs as part of the fundraising plan.[99] Pastides did not advocate for scholarship on Greener or Reconstruction when he directed unrestricted funds for the statue. Faculty co-chairs Lydia Mattice Brandt and Christian Anderson applied to the provost's Excellence Initiative just weeks before the statue's unveiling, proposing a one-time $100,000 grant to endow an annual symposium. They spoke to how such an annual event could "provide a dialogical space to discuss and debate the values of racial equality and civic service embodied by the recently erected sculpture."[100] The initiative's $11 million fund, collected from all university departments' budgets for "transformative teaching, research, creative activity, and community engagement," instead went to just eight projects across the university.[101] Even though the statue's unveiling ceremony in February 2018 was called the "Inaugural Richard T. Greener Symposium," efforts to stimulate dialogue around the monument remain unrealized.

CODA

Less than a month after the statue's unveiling in March 2018, President Pastides drew a "stark contrast" between USC's recent "spirit to build" and other institutions' removal of monuments to Confederates and white supremacists. In an opinion piece in the *Charlotte Observer*, he claimed that USC's slavery markers and Greener statue would "build a pathway where our racial history casts no shadow" and boasted that "while the larger debate has resulted in statues coming down, there is ample opportunity to shift the narrative by erecting symbols celebrating America's greatest strength, our values of diversity and inclusion."[102] But *were* the markers and Greener statue "shifting the narrative"? Did they reckon with history, or was this "spirit to build" merely symbolic? Did they honor African Americans or serve—like the stories explaining "MEE"—to applaud the supposed progressiveness of a predominantly white institution?

The administration's reluctant attitude and hasty implementation of the slavery markers and Greener statue do stand in sharp contrast to three other permanent monuments to African Americans on the campus executed in the same period: statues of football player George Rogers and basketball player A'ja Wilson and the Desegregation Commemorative Garden. The administration and board of trustees championed and fast-tracked each of these projects, which benefited from substantial private donations. Although not publicly debated by the board, their respective locations likely played a role; adjacent to USC's sports complexes or tucked away behind the Osborne Administration Building, none threatened the Horseshoe's picturesque antebellum setting. Each also commemorated contemporary people (including the first Black students since Reconstruction, Robert G. Anderson, Henrie D. Monteith Treadwell, and James L. Solomon), and thus a lack of substantial historical scholarship did not preclude honoring them. The hard-earned successes of these individuals became entwined with USC, elevating the institution. Dialogue acknowledging USC's long-standing resistance to desegregation and its outsized impact on generations of Black students went unsaid; the university instead chose to cast 1963 as the moment when it became the progressive institution it sees itself as today.[103]

As the efforts for the Greener statue and slavery markers demonstrate, acknowledgement of the institution's history of slavery and Reconstruction was clearly a much more difficult "pathway" for the administration. Any overhaul of USC's hagiographic antebellum narrative would take significant additional research and reckoning with standing assumptions and sources. Discussions of slavery inevitably acknowledge that racial oppression lives on in systems and institutions like USC. Even explicitly identifying enslaved people can be confrontational: one can't name Sancho *Cooper* without recognizing that he was owned by the namesake of USC's library. The unique nature of the institution's Reconstruction story—the fact that it was the only public college in the former Confederacy to fully integrate—presents more subtle roadblocks. Unlike the relative finality offered by emancipation or even the desegregation of 1963, Reconstruction was a short-lived attempt at racial equity that historians like Green and Reynolds remembered as a failure and that USC's white leaders immediately countered with the systemic racism of Jim Crow.

In October 2019, new university president Robert Caslen appointed a Presidential Commission on University History, co-chaired by former president Pastides. Its establishment, years after USC 2020 Vision called attention to the administration's failing, exemplifies one way in which the administration continues to grapple with its history. Although its mission includes a "comprehensive and constructive review of our campus history," the details of who will conduct this research, how or if it will be funded, and how the findings will translate to racial justice for today's USC community remain unclear.

Instead, Caslen primarily charged the commission with investigating building namesakes and identifying "prominent African-American South Carolinians who could be considered for honorific naming of university buildings in the near future." Yet as historian Hilary Green has noted, renaming campus buildings—as well as "self-congratulatory narratives" like the installation of the markers or the Greener statue—could give the false sense of "solv[ing] racism" without addressing systemic inequality.[104] Renaming buildings, especially, focuses attention on historical white individuals' responsibility without fully addressing the complicity of the institution throughout time. This "highlight[s] the history of white individuals and white people" while "oftentimes [we do] not know much about the African American history that makes the university what it is today," according to Hannah White, student body vice president and a member of the commission. She calls this focus on white men a "crutch" that allows the university to continue to look away from its past misdeeds.[105]

After the murder of George Floyd in May 2020, the board of trustees promptly confirmed the commission's recommendation to remove the name of J. Marion Sims, a nineteenth-century gynecologist who practiced on enslaved women, from a residence hall. But the act was merely symbolic: renaming the building will require special dispensation from the legislature, and as Caslen noted in his first State of the University address, all renaming recommendations would be considered "in accordance with our state's Heritage Act."[106] Yet soon after the decree, Sims's name was replaced with an acronym on the university's website without comment.[107]

Even as the names of white supremacists are scrubbed from USC's website, the narratives that legitimized them endure in the histories by Laborde, Green, and Hollis; in tours and on the university's website; and on public markers like the one on Sumter Street. By nominally identifying and presumably obscuring the university's most obvious ties to white supremacy, the commission will ostensibly enact Pastides's vision of a university "where our racial history casts no shadow." But if the university is truly interested in a process of reconciliation, then it is imperative that the renaming process follow a different pattern than the one exemplified by the Greener statue and the slavery markers on the Horseshoe. Renaming cannot simply be an act of public relations and superficial celebration. There must instead be meaningful opportunities for community self-reflection and deep historical research that explore the totality of the university's complex past. This volume, which chooses to fully examine the history of racism at the university and to celebrate Black accomplishments, may help USC's community understand its responsibilities to the Africans and African Americans who have lived, worked, studied, and been exploited on its campus. The translation of these new narratives into public history will require the courage to admit that racial reconciliation should be the goal, but that history will always cast a shadow.

CONCLUSION

On January 18, 2020, A'ja Wilson, a former women's basketball star and arguably the University of South Carolina's most decorated athlete in its history, was honored with an unveiling of an eleven-foot bronze statue constructed in the WNBA standout's image and placed outside the Colonial Life Arena on the USC campus. As a Black woman born in Hopkins, South Carolina, Wilson holds deep roots in the state and a multigenerational legacy of oppression and triumph that mirrors the narratives of many African Americans rooted in the South. In her speech, Wilson made it clear that her statue's location on the University's ground was deeply personal, and though it was a triumphant moment for her, it also brought memories surrounding the horrors of Jim Crow racism that was all too familiar in her family history. Through tears and emotional pauses, she relayed a powerful, and personal, narrative that mirrors and encapsulates the historical investigations within this volume: "My grandmother, Hattie Rakes, grew up in this area, actually four blocks from the governor's mansion, to be exact. When she was a child, she couldn't even walk on the grounds of the University of South Carolina. She would have to walk around the campus just to get where she needed to go. If only she was here today to see that the same grounds she had to walk around now are the same grounds that house a statue of her granddaughter."[1]

In this moving tribute, Wilson shows how the violence of racism and segregation were never detached from the university, as her grandmother faced devastating consequences for even entertaining the idea that she could touch foot on the campus grounds. However, she simultaneously shares the possibilities of triumph through the efforts of activists and community members who dared to dream of a different, more equitable, future. Only through these efforts could a single family see such a significant change within two generations.

In many respects, Wilson's recollection resembles the words spoken by Simon P. Smith in 1873, who, as Evan Kutzler notes in his chapter, expressed significant elation at the thought that an institution that less than one decade before had enslaved him and many others, now invited the formerly enslaved and other marginalized people to join in the Reconstruction project. Such historical connections across time make the University of South Carolina a unique case study. Whether one was held in bondage on the campus grounds or barred from stepping foot on its grounds, the efforts of Black activists and progressive, multiracial legislatures in the state have ensured that all people, regardless of race, class, or gender, could obtain an education at the university and use their acquired skills to make a difference locally, nationally, and internationally.

Wilson's commemoration represents one of the many steps the University has recently taken in recognizing the significant contributions of Black Americans on campus. In 2021, a report was issued by the University of South Carolina's Presidential Commission on University History. It began with the words, "The University of South Carolina was founded in 1801 as South Carolina College. Located in Columbia, a block from the state's capitol, it was an institution of higher learning primarily for the Palmetto State's sons of the aristocracy." It continued, "From its inception, the university was the province of white men from wealthy families." This was the strongest, and clearest, statement ever released by a University of South Carolina task force looking back at the school's long and often racist past.[2]

The report and the existence of the Presidential Commission on University History was the culmination of years of protests, at USC and elsewhere, against the continued erasure of African American history on university and college campuses—and the privileging of white supremacists, slave holders, and segregationists by keeping the names of buildings and other facilities honoring them. As mentioned in previous chapters, however, this was not the first time the University of South Carolina was touched by the flame of protest that galvanized an entire nation. As has been the case with movements for social change in American society, the current Black Lives Matter movement has sought to not only change American law, but also how Americans perceive and remember their past. As the Presidential Commission on University History noted, "The documented history of this university is not perfect; the Horseshoe, for instance, was built by slave labor. Many periodicals do not reflect this." The commission acknowledged the barring of women and African Americans from enrolling at the university for many years—and noted that the tremendous growth of the university "negatively impacted historic, black neighborhoods adjacent to the campus."[3]

The central theme of *Invisible No More* is the centrality of African Americans to the history of the University of South Carolina. This story changed dramatically during the school's history, from including the enslaved in a broader narrative of the university than most people are familiar with, to locating within the poorly remembered—yet exciting and invigorating—history of the Reconstruction era the seeds for a different state of South Carolina. In the long run, those seeds gave birth to the drama of the civil rights movement in South Carolina, which included failed attempts to desegregate the school followed by the eventual victory of September 1963. That this victory was fueled by the creation of a law school at South Carolina State—which itself existed to avoid those earlier desegregation fights—was an additional reason for every person at USC to understand their unique, troubled, and fascinating history.

There continues to be need for additional scholarship on the history of the University of South Carolina. What about the Black men and women who have labored at the University? What do we know about the Black neighborhoods adjacent to the campus that were "negatively impacted" by its expansion? Let us also consider the plight of other racial and ethnic groups at the university, just to take one broad example. The struggle for women at the university is another such story—one that is glimpsed in consideration of the stories of African American women such as Henrie Monteith, or the women who followed after her as trailblazers for breaking both racial and gender barriers on campus. The battle for acceptance by LGBTQ community members at the University of South Carolina—not to mention other campuses across the so-called Bible Belt region of the nation—is another potential story to be followed up on in years to come.[4]

The University of South Carolina is by no means done with the continuing excavation of the story of African Americans on its campus. The Presidential Commission recommended that numerous building names be changed across the campus. It remains to be seen what the new names will be, but it has already been suggested by Dr. C. Dorn Smith, Chairman of the University of South Carolina Board of Trustees, that the names of several prominent African Americans be used to replace those of segregationists and slave owners. In his statement, Dr. Smith mentioned individuals such as "Richard Greener, Judge Ernest Finney, Robert Anderson, James Solomon, and Dr. Henrie Monteith Treadwell, among others." He called it "an issue that is past due."[5]

It is unclear how far the movement to change building names on campus will go. What is clear, however, is that the university will also have to confront a long-standing issue: low numbers of African American students and faculty alike. Black students were only 9.5 percent of the student body in 2020, in comparison to being 27 percent of the population of the state of South Carolina. Former university president Robert L. Caslen, who served from July 2019 until May 2021, acknowledged that African American students were "hugely underrepresented" on campus. As the University of South Carolina finally—and it appears, forcefully—looks to its Black past, it will be the future of Black students, faculty, and staff on campus that will define the ultimate legacy of the university when it comes to race.[6]

The university's ambitious goal of 15 percent African American students by 2022 is but another landmark in the history of African Americans at the Palmetto State's flagship institution of higher learning. The attempts to bring in new African American students, however, do stand in sharp contrast to the fate of African American students at the end of Reconstruction, driven away from the university by a Redemptionist government. For that matter, they clash significantly with the university's goal during the defense of Jim Crow segregation in the South during the 1930s, '40s, and '50s to find any legal way possible to dissuade African Americans from trying to desegregate the institution. Such tasks may appear daunting, but the historical context provided throughout this volume can help propel these goals forward.

We expect this volume's chapters to collectively provide a framework for future scholarship and unveil many possibilities for those hoping to continue researching African American history at the University of South Carolina. Graham Duncan, Robert Greene, II, and Brian Robinson discussed the structural roadblocks Black South Carolinians faced when trying to access the university and the benefits of education. Tyler D. Parry, Marcia Synnott, Christian Anderson, Jason Darby, and Evan Kutzler provide important biographical information on Black people tied to the University and their significant societal contributions both within and outside its walls. Lydia Brandt, Ramon Jackson, Katharine Allen, and Holly Genovese provide further context to the continued project of desegregation, examining the rather fraught relationships between student activists and institutional bureaucracies. And though this volume is the most detailed examination of Black people connected to the University of South Carolina, these chapters are not the last word on any of these topics. On the contrary, we hope they bolster increased interest in these largely understudied histories, inspire new questions, and lead toward a more concerted effort to excavate the past. We must continuously work to position African American history as a central component of the university's history, not a secondary one.

The intersections of race and representation at the University of South Carolina are both similar and unique when compared to broader national narratives. We offer this volume as an addition to the excellent research now being conducted across North America's university campuses in uncovering the histories of slavery and segregation that were so common throughout the United States, and we hope to see many more unique stories emerge in the near future. Memory of the past cannot, by itself, be a substitute for genuine change in the present. However, it is a critical supplement, a balm that helps everyone understand why such change needs to take place. African Americans will always remain visible at the University of South Carolina. To do that, those who came before must never be forgotten.

Afterword

Entrance into the University of South Carolina in 1963 gave me the honor of being witness to, and participant in, the dismantling of post–Reconstruction-era segregation in South Carolina's premier public educational institution. Throughout the Jim Crow period, the University of South Carolina adhered to a racist history of excluding African Americans, even after other leading public institutions in the southern United States had removed racial barriers to the entry of people of color. But the pathway was indelibly imprinted on the soil by my ancestors, brave African Americans who attended the university in a long-ago era. Their sacrifices and achievements were not lost on me, though I recall that the media reported nothing substantial about their heroic educational aspirations as a precursor to my enrollment.

My own journey began with a conversation one beautiful Sunday afternoon with my mother, Rachel Rebecca Monteith, and my aunt, Modjeska Monteith Simkins, both of whom were civil rights leaders and pioneers, in the family homestead living room. They requested that I apply to the University of South Carolina just to 'see what they do'. I agreed with them, but never honestly imagined that I would enroll in the university. My doubt was not based on any fear of the enrollment process. I was frankly very happy at the College of Notre Dame in Baltimore. I was excelling academically and had wonderful friends who all happened to be white. There were no other African Americans in my class or enrolled in the College of Notre Dame. Nevertheless, after a series of events I ultimately agreed to seek admission.

While I was studying in Baltimore, my family sent word that Attorney Matthew Perry, who was assisted by Attorneys Lincoln Jenkins and Ernest Finney, had discovered the South Carolina Supreme Court determined that I could not be denied admission based on race. My dilemma began at that point, and it took some time for me to decide to enroll. That decision came one evening when I attended a civil rights meeting at an area church and a senior citizen, a woman, asked plaintively, "Miss Monteith, are you going to enroll in the University?" My short answer was *yes,* as I have never known how to deny requests from my elders who had endured many years of marginalization. I have told many in later years this truth: If the university had admitted me, indicating that the reign of segregation was over, they would never have seen me. Monteith's did not, and still do not, take the word *no* easily, particularly if it is exclusionary in intent, based on race, gender, or class. And, there evidently was no one throughout the hierarchy of South Carolina's leadership with the authority or the gumption to declare an end to segregation. It was evident in South Carolina that true leadership, in which one leads without fear of recrimination, was not present.

Significantly for me, an important insight occurred when, at the court hearing prior to entry, I was asked as a final question by the State Attorney General, in which he asked if I thought I "would like it at the University of South Carolina?" My response was: "I don't know; I guess I will just have to wait and see." At that moment I fully understood that "they," the white community, did not understand my mission. I was not attending the University to be "liked," or even seeking to "like" it there. I had no intention of entering the university so that I could simply mix and mingle with white people, though I was glad to become friends with all who so desired. My mission was to break the bonds of tyranny and marginalization. That question, however, fully confirmed that my preparation had to involve self-reliance so that no one could disappoint me. I also recall each pivotal step collectively, beginning with my resolution to attend and eventually to graduate. My own internal peace was firmly rooted in, and guided by, my own actions and reactions to different circumstances. I dwell on these steps as I continue to be committed to thinking through issues, strategies, and tactics to ensure success of any endeavor. Failure was not an option as it would have unearthed other stereotypes, such as the common assumption by so many white Americans, "they just cannot compete."

The entry on September 11, 1963, was quiet. The January 11, 1963, issue of the *Gamecock* reported in an interview words and statements that reflected a comparison to other states in the Deep South. Beliefs like the following statement were commonplace: "I really did not expect violence; I would expect some difficulty but nothing like Mississippi." Prior to the official enrollment, my entire immediate and extended family were inundated with threatening and harassing phone calls, along with one incident of dynamite being thrown into my uncle's (Dr. Henry D. Monteith) yard. As a family we were taught to never let any threats or aggressions divert us from our mission for civil and social justice. I have even been told that the national press was kept away from the actual registration "ceremony." I only remember scenes but not sounds. Bystanders have told me that my eyes were everywhere, constantly scanning the scene, the environment. Scanning, using perception, to gain and maintain perspective was then, and now, a survival tactic. Overall, the crowd was subdued. I pondered why so many individuals felt so threatened by an African American woman, a mere teenager, seeking an education in her state's flagship institution.

I entered the university that day with two other African American students, Robert G. Anderson and James L. Solomon Jr., and we registered for classes without event. We were met by stone-faced individuals who offered neither solace, comfort, nor welcome, except for one professor, Dr. Willard Davis. I admit to being nonplussed by seeing one friendly face. He and I had a wonderful reunion many years later. His warmth was genuine. I am not aware of any leadership actions that might have created an authentic aura of welcome. The sense of alienation may still linger, and my subsequent visits cause me to reflect on the leaderful actions still needed.

After completing registration, I gave remarks to those gathered to witness the formal admissions process on behalf of Bob, Jim, and myself, at their request. I moved into Sims Dormitory. The insult, though perhaps unintended, was not lost on me that I lived in a dormitory named for an individual, Dr. J. Marion Sims, who had performed experimental surgery on African American women without the benefit of anesthesia.[1] I often reference this lack of knowledge and concern for the impact of this history on me, African American women, and the Black community at large, in speeches to community groups. I had hoped that someone would speak up on the Sims name and the implications for Black women. But no one said a mumblin' word. The inaction and insensitivity affirmed to me that the impact of racist historical events pain the psyche and have the potential to injure the spirit of those that must endure these mini and macro slights. I reflect on how that angst continues to reverberate for students of color today, who must soldier on amidst the "honorary" monuments that commemorate those that enslaved or otherwise dishonored their ancestors. The reality is that little has changed regarding reverence for the icons of segregation and the dark history of terrorism and exclusion that they evoke in the ensuing 58 years since I graduated.

Dormitory life was dull and drab, but I was fine with that. Having grown up on the outskirts of Columbia I was accustomed to not having people around, next door, and I had learned to read, listen to music, and entertain myself. The Sims housemother never smiled at me. She did not assume the "mother" role. Perhaps she did not like my being there on the campus, or even more poignantly, in the Sims Dormitory. Perhaps she had no orientation by her supervisor on how to act or react. It seemed to me that the men and women working in houses and fields throughout the university smiled because it was what they were supposed to do if they wanted to keep employment. Why was it different for me and for many who came behind me?

I did have a problem with some of the white women who lived across the hall from me, as they would leave food on the floor outside my door. They would place the food, knock on my door, and then run laughing back to their room. I at first kicked the food down the hall, but when the insult continued for weeks, I walked across the hall, knocked loudly on their door, and told them to cease and desist forever. The women did not open the door, but I had no more food placed outside my door after that interaction. I faced them; they hid from me. They stereotyped me as something less than. I wonder if this stereotype is acted on today.

Undeterred by any passive aggression, I began classes. Security was unobtrusively present. On my first day a young white woman recognized me and spoke to me. We walked to class together. In the class a male student tapped the young woman (who I will not name) on the shoulder and said that he had "heard" that there was a Negro in the class. She introduced me to him. I did encounter her on another walk to class and discerned that she did not want to be seen with me on a regular basis. Peer pressure existed then, and it continues unabated to this day, as I have observed and been told by many white students in recent years. It occurred to me then and now that it is white people who live in fear, and due to this fear, it is they who are not free! They were then, and perhaps now, bound by historical racist tradition, by fear of retribution among their social group. They do not seem to understand that if they free themselves then everyone will be free to live and everyone can thrive. I make this reflection because almost every year I still receive one or two emails, and even phone calls, from white women who entered Carolina when I did, or were students in other classes. These women now apologize that they did not step forward and befriend and assist me. I was even asked to write remarks for a Carolinian who had died, hoping my words could be read at the funeral. The remarks that I wrote were read at the service. How nice it would have been if we had known each other in life.

I should also recount my experience with some of the white men. I had a phone in my room, but a white man kept calling me on the dormitory public phone. I had asked not to be alerted to those calls. Naturally, the Sims housekeeper ignored my request, and it made me wonder why. The calls persisted, and I had to continually go to the public phone. They claimed I was "invited" to a party. I declined, but the calls continued, and I decided that I needed to end that intrusion. I agreed to go to the party. After I arrived, they invited me to "have a drink" and sit me at the bar by myself. No one came forward to meet and greet except one white male student. I saw the men gather in deep conversation, as they were surreptitiously sneaking peeks at me. I used my time to look around and see who was there and could probably generate an exact replica of some faces today.

Both white men and women were present. I had one drink, and despite their protests, I thanked them and left. I was in and out of there within 30 minutes. The phone calls stopped. But it was clear to me that their goal was to make me inebriated, as they constantly suggested I have another drink. These "gentlemen" affirmed to me that they objectified me and thought little of Black womanhood. They were prepared to foster actions that would confirm their perceptions of how Black women act, including assumptions of low morals or a lack of character. I did not reveal this incident to my family, as they would have taken me to the woodshed for even going to this party. But I learned from that same family that one does not run away from a challenge. And I knew that Aunt Modjeska, a role model, attended Ku Klux Klan rallies to see what they were saying and planning. And for me, the price of peace is almost always worth the encounter. Out of adversity comes strength. Perhaps things have now changed to a degree, so that African American womanhood is viewed in its holistic dimensions.

My general activities on campus were not limited, though I was not allowed to attend sports events, particularly football games. I was told that the crowds were not manageable and that the playing of the song "Dixie," a favorite ballad by those who long for the Confederacy's return, might be incendiary if I was present. Not attending a game was not an issue for me, as I understood USC's teams were not outstanding. Outstanding team sports came much later with the enrollment of large numbers of young African American men and women whose competence on the fields greatly benefit institutions of higher education in so many ways. The added value of Black athletes is often unstated, and in consequence, never sufficiently recognized.

Many times, in class and elsewhere, I had to hear and not hear, see and not see any slights against me, as any response I emitted might give pleasure to those who detected that I was pained by their comment or action. The professors were generally gracious, except for one woman professor in biology. This professor specifically drove home the point that some of the land that the university had purchased sat on a former public housing complex occupied by Black people, and she insisted that there remained many germs and parasites in the soil, as a consequence. She "may" have felt that she was doing no harm, but she was enforcing and reinforcing a stereotype. She looked at me when she made her remark. I did not speak (or "hear") or react, and neither did any of my classmates, unfortunately. Stereotypes have their own lifetime and ripple impact. I decided to just move along, as my goal was to graduate and respond later through my work and writing.

My major was biology, which meant that I was supposed to complete much of my laboratory work with a partner. But I rarely had a partner, and even when

I did, it was clear that they did not want to work with me. I expected this marginalization, so I simply continued to complete my work without them and pursued my ultimate goal: to disappoint my detractors by graduating. The isolation was not at all intimidating; it was just the way things were. I firmly believe that self-direction was further built as a part of my character that has served me well throughout life.

I never had a professor of color, Black or Brown. The only African Americans I encountered were either working in the cafeteria or were on the janitorial staff. The absence of people of color throughout the institution was a stark reminder that while I had made a first step, many more feet would have to cross the threshold to move the needle in the direction of equity and social justice. My subsequent visits to the campus in the ensuing years confirm that we have only just begun, though it is worth noting the wonderful programs that are being built with an outstanding faculty. So, I am grateful to know someone's leaderful hands are moving things along a positive trajectory.

I rarely saw Bob Anderson or Jim Solomon on campus. Bob endured significant harassment as white male students bounced basketballs outside of his window at night and made other noises so that he could not study or sleep. Unfortunately, such juvenile behavior, forms of which were surely taught to them by their ancestors, ultimately took its toll on Bob, and he withdrew from the university. My Aunt Modjeska had offered him rooms, which he used, at the Simbeth Hotel, of Green Book fame, so that he could relax on weekends. This was just temporary, and Simbeth was isolated from other amenities that might have been healing to his soul and spirit. Bob, a sensitive and kind human being, though he has transitioned, is still owed an apology. It pains me even today that no one came to his aid. I know others certainly heard the balls bouncing outside Bob's room, or the other forms of noisy harassment he endured. In this way it seems our society has not progressed nearly enough, and I wonder whether these students recognized their role in this persistent diminution of the human spirit in others. Bob's treatment mirrors the treatment that African American men still disproportionately bear simply because of the color of their skin and their manhood. Why do white men fear African American men? I wonder who will come for the persecutors when and/if they encounter difficulties, or if they attempt to cross into unchartered territory? I was then, and am now, a firm believer in what goes around comes around.

I would be remiss if I did not include my friends and supporters in this reflection. Important work was done by the South Carolina Council on Human Relations to bring together students from the university with me so that I would have a few friendly faces and associates when I enrolled. I recall being very pleased that efforts were made to smooth the pathway and reduce isolation. I made some friends from that group. And I made a particularly good friend with a student, who happened to be white, Isabelle Secrest Mims, who continues to be my fast-and-close friend even today. Isabelle was in my wedding as a maid of honor. She and I went shopping together, had lunch off- and on-campus together, and were just comfortable in our friendship. We truly did not see race as barrier. We never thought about it or spoke about race.

The many friendships I gained at this time were a direct result of enrolling at USC, and many of these friendships were made with other individuals of color, most of whom have transitioned. It has been a while. I specifically enjoyed working with students in the newly implemented Upward Bound program. Through the state's civil rights networks, I was also fortunate to engage with other students from South Carolina who had similarly stepped into the gauntlet. I reference particularly Harvey Gantt and Lucinda Brawley-Gantt who desegregated Clemson University, and Millicent Brown who broke segregationist policies in Charleston. Millicent and I speak regularly. We are "sisters" and continue to encourage each other to stay on the road to freedom. We have both committed ourselves to reflecting on the past and assisting those who will lead into the next frontier. There is much yet to be done. In sum, despite not having a broad social network at USC, I benefitted greatly through these relationships, a tactic that I have similarly used in the ensuing years.

My college studies ended after one year at the College of Notre Dame, Baltimore, and two years and one summer at USC. My graduation from the university fulfilled two historic changes, as I was the first African American since the Reconstruction era, and the first African American woman to graduate from the institution. However, it was a quiet event with no media or other fanfare. Perhaps this was a good thing, if it meant that the graduations of people of color were to become commonplace at the university. I have no concern for my own profile in the media. But I do have a concern that some in South Carolina media do not spread the good news about the victories that indicate the civil rights of Black people are being gradually achieved, or even a knowledge surrounding the road yet to be travelled. Perhaps key leaders suppose that "if we don't tell them they won't come," but I also think that media can foster proactive discussions around race, racism, the path forward, and the added value of equal treatment. Their participation in this process is crucial.

My journey as a student at USC may be at an end today. But it was there that I learned much about thriving when you are your own best friend, when others would marginalize you, and when the way forward is not defined as there was no direct role model. There is almost always a light, faint though it might be at the time, at the end of the tunnel. I thrived, I learned, I received many blessings in the form of lifelong friendships, and in knowing that there are times when you must go it alone. I am blessed to have had the honor of walking a pathway toward justice. I am overjoyed that so many other students of color have enrolled in THEIR state-sponsored educational institution. I am on a mission. And here I stand! As my mantra I use a quote stated regularly by Russ Mawby, former CEO, W.K. Kellogg Foundation, in closing his speeches:

I AM ONLY ONE
BUT I AM ONE
I CANNOT DO ALL THINGS
BUT I CAN DO SOME THINGS
OF THE THINGS THAT I CAN DO
SOME OF THEM I SHOULD DO
AND FOR THE THINGS THAT I SHOULD DO
BY THE GRACE OF God
I WILL DO!

And the walls came tumbling down. Amen! Hallelujah!!!
Dr. Henrie Monteith Treadwell
University of South Carolina
Class of 1965

Notes

FOREWORD

1. Isidora Stankovic, "Spaces of Memory—'The Presence of Absence,' Cultural Memory, and Oblivion Mechanisms," *Culture*, no. 8 (2014): 87.

INTRODUCTION

1. Bristow Merchant, "The Slaves Who Built USC Are Virtually Unknown. How the College is Trying to Fix That," *The State*, https://www.thestate.com/news/local/education/article188153414.html, December 5, 2017, accessed on February 23, 2021. More is said about this statement and the ceremony in the final chapter of this book.

2. "Protestor Drowned Out by USC Students," *Cola Daily*, August 22, 2020, https://www.coladaily.com/communities/columbia/protester-drowned-out-by-USC-students/article_e3a30414-e430-11ea-9cfb-3fe9d1fa3560.html, accessed February 23, 2020.

3. "Students Jeer Klan in South Carolina," *New York Times*, February 24, 1949, 15.

4. Lucas Daprile, "USC Students Reboot NAACP Chapter as Energy Increases Around Building Controversy," *The State*, February 20, 2021, https://www.thestate.com/news/local/civil-rights/article249337670.html, accessed February 23, 2021.

5. Craig Steven Wilder, *Ebony and Ivy: Race, Slavery, and the Troubled History of America's Universities* (New York: Bloomsbury, 2013); *Slavery and the University: Histories and Legacies*. Edited by Leslie M. Harris, James T. Campbell, and Alfred L. Brophy (Athens: University of Georgia Press, 2015).

6. Rhondda Robinson Thomas, *Call My Name, Clemson* (Iowa City: University of Iowa Press, 2020); Maurice C. Daniels, *Ground Crew: The Fight to End Segregation at Georgia State* (Athens: University of Georgia Press, 2019); B. J. Hollars, *Opening the Doors: The Desegregation of the University of Alabama and the Fight for Civil Rights in Tuscaloosa* (Tuscaloosa: University of Alabama Press, 2013); Robert A. Pratt, *We Shall Not Be Moved: The Desegregation of the University of Georgia* (Athens: University of Georgia Press, 2002); Melissa Kean, *Desegregating Private Higher Education in the South: Duke, Emory, Rice, Tulane, and Vanderbilt* (Baton Rouge: Louisiana State University Press, 2008); F. Erik Brooks, *Pursuing a Promise: A History of African Americans at Georgia Southern University* (Macon: Mercer University Press, 2006).

7. Stefan Bradley, *Harlem Vs. Columbia: Black Student Power in the Late 1960s* (Urbana: University of Illinois Press, 2009); Stefan Bradley, *Upending the Ivory Tower: Civil Rights, Black Power, and the Ivy League* (New York: New York University Press, 2019).

8. Graham Duncan, "Peculiarly Suited for the Services of the Institution"; 2006; [typescript], South Caroliniana Library, Columbia, South Carolina.

Chapter One: SLAVERY ON CAMPUS

1. Minutes of the Board of Trustees of the South Carolina College, 6 December 1804, Volume 1, p. 42 (hereinafter cited as Trustees' minutes).

2. United States Census, 1800 and 1820.

3. Thomas Cooper, *Statutes at Large of South Carolina*, Volume 5 (Columbia, SC: A.S. Johnston), 403–5.

4. United States Census, 1800 and 1810. Theodore Gaillard and William Johnson had no enslaved persons listed in their households in 1800 or 1810. William Dobein James cannot be identified in the census of either year but left nine enslaved men and women to his children in his 1827 will. Lewis Trezevant cannot be identified in the census in either year.

5. Trustees' minutes, 6 December 1804, Volume 1, p. 42, and printed as *By-Laws of the South Carolina College: Enacted by the Trustees at Their Annual Meeting in Dec., 1804* (Columbia, SC: D. and J. J. Faust, 1805).

6. Daniel Walker Hollis, *University of South Carolina: Volume 1, South Carolina College* (Columbia: University of South Carolina Press, 1951), 26–27.

7. *Laws of the South Carolina College: Provisionally Adopted by the Trustees at their Annual Meeting in Dec., 1806* (Columbia, SC: D. and J. J. Faust, 1807).

8. Trustees' minutes, November 28, 1807, Volume 1, p. 128.

9. Trustees' minutes, June 27, 1808, Volume 1, p. 147.

10. Minutes of the Faculty of the South Carolina College, February 25, 1808 (hereinafter cited as Faculty minutes).

11. Faculty minutes, February 25, 1808, Volume 1, p. 30.

12. For an overview of the practice of hiring out see Jonathan D. Martin, *Divided Mastery: Slave Hiring in the American South* (Harvard University Press, 2004), 1–16.

13. Hollis, 49, 151, 153.

14. West, Elizabeth Cassidy and Katharine Thompson Allen, *On the Horseshoe: A Guide to the Historic Campus of the University of South Carolina* (Columbia: University of South Carolina Press), 54.

15. Records of the Vice President of Finance and Office of the Treasurer (hereinafter Treasurer's records), Box 1.

16. "Report of the Professors of the South Carolina College Respecting the Commons," Steward's Hall Box 1, Commons Folder.

17. Letter, June 12, 1841, Camden, [South Carolina], William Carlisle to William Martin, Columbia, South Carolina, Steward's Hall Box 1, Commons Folder.

18. In 1842, the position of steward was renamed "bursar," and paid an annual salary rather than a per student fee. Hollis, 145.

19. Trustees' minutes, May 9, 1849.

20. John Hammond Moore, *Columbia & Richland County: A South Carolina Community, 1740–1990* (Columbia: University of South Carolina Press, 1993), 128–30.

21. Faculty minutes, October 16, 1845.

22. See letter, March 16, 1850, Committee of Students to William Campbell Preston that declared that the "Coffee, Tea, and Chocolate . . . are so inferior as to be unfit to be drunk;" meat "cut into huge slices, covered with grease rather than gravy so that even were they good in themselves which (is often otherwise)—the appearance of the dish is forbidding;" and "Chickens and Turkeys (when furnished) are cooked or made to undergo some process, so that their peculiar taste and flavor is lost and they become a red and tasteless aggregation of muscular fiber."

23. Faculty minutes, April 10, 1820.

24. Letter, May 4, 1850, Thornwell to Preston.

25. Faculty minutes, January 17, 1810.

26. Faculty minutes, January 27 and May 10, 1817; January 21, 1822; June 2, 1823; February 9, 1825; October 27 and November 20, 1828; May 9, 1836; February 6 and 13, 1837; April 4, 1838; and March 25, 1849.

27. Faculty minutes, February 25, 1808.

28. Faculty minutes, April 30, 1813; May 11, 1818; October 7, 1822, and January 6, 1823; and Trustees' minutes, April 26, 1815, November 30, 1821, and December 3, 1823.

29. Trustees' minutes, April 26, 1815, and November 30, 1821.

30. Trustees' minutes, April 26, 1815.

31. Trustees' minutes, November 28, 1815.

32. Report of Committee on Schools On Certain, Representations Made by the Trustees and Faculty of the South Carolina College Asking that Jack, a Slave, may be Purchased for the Institution's Use. Series S165005, Year 1816, Item Number 0004, South Carolina Department of Archives and History.

33. Reports of Professor Richard T. Brumby, Trustees' minutes, May 3, 1854, and November 28, 1855.

34. Trustees' minutes, December 31, 1816.

35. Faculty minutes, January 5, 1818.

36. Faculty minutes, June 29, 1819.

37. Faculty minutes, February 14, 1820.

38. Hollis, 72–75, 104.

39. Faculty minutes, April 23, 1821. Letter, April 22, 1821, S[outh] Carolina College, Thomas Cooper to the Board of Trustees of the South Carolina College, Thomas Cooper Papers.

40. Trustees' minutes, May 3, 1821.

41. Faculty minutes, April 10, 1820.

42. First Presbyterian Church of Columbia, Session Book, April 7 and July 8, 1820, and April 6, July 7, and October 13, 1821.

43. First Presbyterian Church of Columbia, Session Book, October 13, 1821.

44. Faculty minutes, March 4, 1822.

45. Trustees' minutes, April 28, 1823.

46. Trustees' minutes, November 26, 1828, and November 24, 1829. Examples of receipts for clothing, April 7, July–October, and December 24, 1847, Treasurer's records, Box 1.

47. Trustees' minutes, November 29, 1833. *Savannah Daily Republican*, October 1, 1833.

48. Faculty minutes, December 4, 1824.

49. Trustees' minutes, November 29, 1833.

50. *Laws of the South Carolina College: Adopted by the Board of Trustees at their Annual Meeting in Dec. 1835.* Chapter XV: Of the Marshall, and the College Buildings (Columbia, SC).

51. Accounts and receipts, April 10, 1837; October 25, October, November, and December 28, 1843; 5 and February 24, March 4 and 25, April 2, and October 6 and 28, 1844; and undated, Treasurer's records, Box 1.

52. Faculty minutes, May 23, 1836.

53. Faculty minutes, March 3, 1845.

54. Trustees' minutes, May 7, 1851.

55. Trustees' minutes, May 9, 1849.

56. Accounts, June 1849 and October 30, 1850, Treasurer's records, Box 1.

57. Trustees' minutes, November 30 and December 3, 1853, May 3 and 8, 1854, November 28 and December 5, 1855, and November 26, 1856.

58. Faculty minutes, April 20, 1814.

59. Faculty minutes, January 14, 1850.

60. Faculty minutes, February 25, 1850.

61. Faculty minutes, March 21, 1851 and Trustees' minutes, May 7, 1851.

62. Faculty minutes, January 28, 1852.

63. Faculty minutes, February 16, 1852.

64. Faculty minutes, October 30, 1825.

65. Faculty minutes, April 15, 1833.

66. Trustees' minutes, May 3, 1848.

67. Faculty minutes, October 30, 1825.

68. Report of Committee on Schools On Certain, Representations Made by the Trustees and Faculty of the South Carolina College Asking that Jack, a Slave, may be Purchased for the Institution's Use. Series S165005, Year 1816, Item Number 0004, South Carolina Department of Archives and History.

69. Trustees' minutes November 26, 1828.

70. Trustees' minutes, November 26, 1845.

71. Trustees' minutes, November 30, 1853.

72. *By-Laws of the South Carolina College: Revised and Adopted by the Board of Trustees at the Regular Meeting in May, 1853."*

73. Faculty minutes, February 25, 1808.

74. David S. Shields (ed.), *Pioneering American Wine: Writings of Nicholas Herbemont, Master Viticulturist* (Athens: University of Georgia Press, 2009), 9.

75. For a discussion of Herbemont's views on the institution of slavery see Shields, 15–23.

76. Trustees minutes, May 3, 1854.

77. Account, December 1838, Treasurer's records, Box 1.

78. Account book, 1846–1847 and 1880–1882, James Carroll LaBorde papers.

79. Hollis, 142–144.

80. Maximilian LaBorde, *History of the South Carolina College with an Appendix Prefaced by a Life of the Author by J.L. Reynolds, D.D.* (Charleston, SC: Walter, Evans, and Cogswell, 1874), xi–xvi.

81. Hollis, 262 and 268.

82. LaBorde account book.

83. Trustees' minutes, December 7, 1833.

Chapter Two: "IRRESPECTIVE OF RACE OR COLOR"

1. "A Famous Class Reunion," *New York Age*, December 21, 1911.

2. Edwin Luther Green, *A History of the University of South Carolina* (Columbia, SC: The State Company, 1916), 411.

3. "A Famous Class Reunion," *New York Age*, December 21, 1911.

4. "A Famous Class Reunion," *New York Age*, December 21, 1911.

5. "A Famous Class Reunion," *New York Age*, December 21, 1911.

6. James Lowell Underwood, "African American Founding Fathers: The Making of the South Carolina Constitution of 1868," in *At Freedom's Door: African American Founding Fathers and Lawyers in Reconstruction South Carolina*, ed. James Lowell Underwood and W. Lewis Burke (Columbia, SC, 2000), 2; Joel Williamson, *After Slavery: The Negro in South Carolina During Reconstruction, 1861–1877* (New York: W. W. Norton, 1975); Thomas Holt, *Black Over White: Negro Political Leadership in South Carolina During Reconstruction* (Urbana: University of Illinois Press, 1977).

7. White, "Free and Open."

8. John H. Roper, "The Radical Mission: The University of South Carolina in Reconstruction," (MA Thesis, University of North Carolina-Chapel Hill, 1973); Pamela Mercedes White, "'Free and Open': The Radical University of South Carolina, 1873–1877" (MA Thesis: University of South Carolina, 1975); John Herbert Roper, "A Reconsideration: The University of South Carolina During

Reconstruction (1974)," in *South Carolina in the Civil War and Reconstruction Eras: Essays from the Proceedings of the South Carolina Historical Society*, ed. Michael Brem Bonner and Fritz Hamer (Columbia, SC, 2016), 184–194; Michael David Cohen, *Reconstructing the Campus: Higher Education and the American Civil War* (Charlottesville, VA, 2012); Eric Foner, *Reconstruction: America's Unfinished Revolution, 1863–1877* (New York, 1988), 368; Thomas Holt, *Black Over White: Negro Political Leadership in South Carolina during Reconstruction* (Urbana: The University of Illinois Press, 1977), 180–182; Walter Edgar, *South Carolina: A History* (Columbia, SC, 1998), 391–393, 407–408; Jacob L. McCormick, "The Extracurriculum of the University of South Carolina: The First Century, 1805–1906" (PhD diss., University of South Carolina, 2005), 145–146, 154, 161–164, 172.

9. "Jan. 14, 1868: South Carolina Constitutional Convention," *Zinn Education Project* (Jan. 14, 2019), https://www.zinnedproject.org/news/tdih/South-Carolina-Constitutional-Convention; J. Woodruff, *Proceedings of the Constitutional Convention of South Carolina; Including the Debates and Proceedings* (Charleston, SC: Denny and Perry, 1868).

10. Woodruff, *Proceedings*, 891.

11. Woodruff, *Proceedings*, 890.

12. Woodruff, *Proceedings*, 892.

13. Woodruff, *Proceedings*, 892.

14. Woodruff, *Proceedings*, 894.

15. Woodruff, *Proceedings*, 900.

16. Woodruff, *Proceedings*, 902.

17. "Sad End of the University," *Daily Columbus Enquirer*, March 31, 1869.

18. "The University of South Carolina has just opened its fall term under rather peculiar circumstances," *Lowell Daily Citizen*, October 22, 1869, p. 1.

19. "Editorial Notes," *The Independent . . . Devoted to the Consideration of Politics, Social, and Economic Tendencies*, April 30, 1868.

20. Benjamin Ginsberg, *Moses of South Carolina: A Jewish Scalawag During Radical Reconstruction* (Baltimore, MD: Johns Hopkins University Press, 2010).

21. "The South Carolina University," *New York Times* (July 4, 1869), 3.

22. "General Notes," *The Congregationalist*, November 6, 1873.

23. Bernard E. Powers Jr., *Black Charlestonians: A Social History, 1822–1885* (Fayetteville: The University of Arkansas Press, 1994), 6. Also see William C. Hine, "Black Politicians in Reconstruction Charleston, South Carolina: A Collective Study," *The Journal of Southern History* 49(4) (1983): 555–584.

24. Cornelius Chapman Scott, "When Negroes Attended the State University," *The State*, May 8, 1911.

25. "Negro Rule vs. the Arts and Sciences—South Carolina College," *The Georgia Weekly Telegraph and Journal and Messenger*, January 9, 1877

26. John Herbert Roper, "A Reconsideration: The University of South Carolina During Reconstruction," in *The Proceedings of the South Carolina Historical Association, 1974*, ed. Hewitt D. Adams (Columbia: The South Carolina Historical Association, 1975), 47; White, "Free and Open," 30–32; Parry, "The Radical Experiment of South Carolina," 565.

27. William Henry Heard, *From Slavery to the Bishopric in the A.M.E. Church, An Autobiography* (Philadelphia: A.M.E. Book Concern, 1928), 28.

28. Heard, *From Slavery to the Bishopric*, 28.

29. Heard, *From Slavery to the Bishopric*, 32.

30. Heard, *From Slavery to the Bishopric*, 32.

31. Heard, *From Slavery to the Bishopric*, 32.

32. Heard, *From Slavery to the Bishopric*, 36.

33. Heard, *From Slavery to the Bishopric*, 37.

34. Alfred Sidney Johnson, ed., *The Cyclopedic Review of Current History*, volume 8 (Boston, MA: Current History Company, 1898), 151.

35. "Rev. O.L.W. Smith," *The Star of Zion*, January 21, 1897.

36. White, "Free and Open," 2.

37. "Notes and Opinions," *Chicago Daily Tribune*, February 25, 1873.

38. Monroe, Alphus Majors, *Noted Negro Women: Their Triumphs and Activities* (Chicago: Donohue and Henneberry, 1893), 67.

39. James T. Haley, "Clarissa M. Thompson," *Afro-American Encyclopedia; or, the Thoughts, Doings, and Sayings of the Race* (Nashville, TN: Haley and Florida, 1895), 569.

40. Ronald E. Butchart and Amy F. Rolleri, "Secondary Education and Emancipation: Secondary Schools for Freed Slaves in the American South, 1862–1875," *Paedagogica Historica* 40, no. 1–2 (2004): 169.

41. Majors, *Noted Negro Women*, 67.

42. Michael David Cohen, *Reconstructing the Campus: Higher Education and the American Civil War* (Charlottesville: University of Virginia Press, 2012), 121.

43. Haley, "Clarissa M. Thompson," 568; Majors, *Noted Negro Women*, 66.

44. Haley, "Clarissa M. Thompson," 567–568. Also see Elizabeth Marsden, "Clarissa Minnie Thompson Allen (?-?)," in *Encyclopedia of African American Women Writers*, Volume 1, ed. Yolanda Williams Page (Westport, Conn.: Greenwood Press, 2007), 9.

45. Thompson Allen, Clarissa Minnie; Brown, Gabrielle; Willey, Eric; and MacDonald, Jean, "Treading the Winepress; or, A Mountain of Misfortune" (2019). Undiscovered Americas. 2. https://ir.library.illinoisstate.edu/ua/2.

46. Debbie Clare Olson, "Allen, Clarissa Minnie Thompson (?-?)," in *Writing African American Women: An Encyclopedia of Literature by and about Women of Color, Volume 1: A-J*, ed. Elizabeth Ann Beaulieu (Westport, Conn.: Greenwood Press, 2006), 6; "HBW History," http://www2.ku.edu/~phbw/about_us_history.html, accessed 3 Feb. 2021; Gabrielle Brown, "Editor's Introduction," in *Treading the Winepress*, vii–x.

47. Haley, "Clarissa M. Thompson," 570.

48. Haley, "Clarissa M. Thompson," 569–570.

49. Joseph D. McGee, "Thousands at Last Rites for Celia Saxon," *The Chicago Defender*, February 16, 1935.

50. Majors, *Noted Negro Women*, 111–112.

51. McGee, "Thousands at Last Rites for Celia Saxon."

52. "Condition of Negroes as Reported to Fosdick," *The State*, March 3, 1918.

53. Joseph D. McGee, "Thousands at Rites of Mrs. Celia Saxon," *The Chicago Defender*, February 16, 1935. For information on Josiah Morse see Amy Scully, "Josiah Morse, The First Jewish Professor at the University of South Carolina: The Role of Mixed Bias in the American University System," (MA Thesis, The University of South Carolina, 2011).

54. Katherine Mellen Charron, *Freedom's Teacher: The Life of Septima Clark* (Chapel Hill: University of North Carolina Press, 2009), 123.

55. "To the Editor of the *Daily Union-Herald*," Students, 1875, Fisk P. Brewer Papers, South Caroliniana Library, Columbia, SC.

56. "Sad End of the University," *Columbus Daily Enquirer*, March 31, 1869.

57. "Educational Meeting, Friday, December 12, 1873," Fisk P. Brewer Papers, South Caroliniana Library, University of South Carolina.

58. Jesse Kess, "Blind Man with Math Degree," https://blindmanwithmathdegree.blogspot.com/.

59. "Personal Gossip," *The Daily News (Denver)*, August 20, 1886, 4.

60. "Southern Testimony," *Whig and Courier*, November 7, 1876.

61. Fisk Parsons Brewer and William P. Vaughn, "South Carolina University—1876 of Fisk Parsons Brewer," *The South Carolina Historical Magazine* 76 (4) (1975): 231

62. "To the Editor of the *Daily Union-Herald*," Students, 1875, Fisk P. Brewer Papers, South Caroliniana Library, Columbia, SC.

63. Henry J. Fox, "The Negro," *The Methodist Quarterly Review* (January 1875), 27.

64. Fox, "The Negro," 27.

65. "Nubs of News," *Rocky Mountain News*, May 5, 1877. Also see "Washington—Current Notes of the Capital," *The Galveston Daily News*, May 25, 1877.

66. "Sectionalism in Education," *The Milwaukee Sentinel*, August 22, 1877, 4.

67. "The University of South Carolina," *The Georgia Weekly Telegraph and Journal and Messenger*, May 15, 1877.

68. William C. Hine, *South Carolina State University: A Black Land-Grant College in Jim Crow America* (Columbia: University of South Carolina Press, 2018), 1–6.

69. Hine, *South Carolina State University*, 4

70. Majors, *Noted Negro Women*, 67.

71. E. Horace Fitchett, "The Influence of Claflin College on Negro Family Life," *The Journal of Negro History* 29, no. 4 (1944): 431.

72. T. McCants Stewart, "Prof. William M. Dart Dead," *The New York Freeman* Nov. 7, 1885; Majors, *Noted Negro Women*, 67.

73. Katherine Reynolds Chaddock, *Uncompromising Activist: Richard Greener, First Black Graduate pf Harvard College* (Baltimore: Johns Hopkins University Press, 2017), 78–79.

74. Tyler D. Parry, "The Radical Experiment of South Carolina: The History and Legacy of a Reconstructed University," *The Journal of African American History* 105, no. 4 (2020): 560–561.

75. James A. Padgett, "Ministers to Liberia and their Diplomacy," *The Journal of Negro History* 22, no. 1 (1937): 78–79, 83.

76. Chaddock, *Uncompromising Activist*, 128.

77. Kess, "The Law Students of the Radical University: Edgar Caypless," *Blind Man with Math Degree*, https://blindmanwithmathdegree.blogspot.com/2021/.

78. For an examination of this erasure see Parry, "The Radical Experiment of South Carolina," 561–562. For an example see William Gilmore Simms, *The History of South Carolina* (Columbia, SC: The State Company, 1918), Chapter 33.

Chapter Three: RICHARD T. GREENER AT THE
RECONSTRUCTION-ERA UNIVERSITY

1. The first and only Black graduate of a state university prior to the end of the Civil War was abolitionist Isaiah G. DeGrasse, an 1836 graduate of Newark College (now the University of Delaware) according to Robert Bruce Slater, "The First Black Graduates of the Nation's 50 Flagship State Universities," *The Journal of Blacks in Higher Education* 13 (Autumn, 1996), 74. Slater documents the first Black graduates in private institutions, noting that a very few Blacks earned degrees before the Civil War—the first were at Amherst and Bowdoin in 1826, Middlebury in 1823, and Dartmouth in 1828—in his article "The Blacks who First Entered the World of White Higher Education," *The Journal of Blacks in Higher Education*, No. 4 (Summer, 1994), 47–56. Also, Oberlin College admitted Blacks in 1835 and women in 1837. Slater's articles demonstrate how extraordinarily rare these cases were. Even by 1870, Greener's graduation was an exceptionally unusual case.

2. The deal between political parties surrounding the 1876 Presidential election led to the removal of federal peacekeeping forces from the former Confederate states. Eric Foner, *Reconstruction: America's Unfinished Revolution, 1863–1877* (New York: Harper Perennial, 1988/2014), 575–587. Regarding the repeal of Scholarship Act see Bernard F. Powers, *Black Charlestonians: A Social History, 1822–1885* (Fayetteville: University of Arkansas Press, 1994), 157.

3. George Brown Tindall. *South Carolina Negroes, 1877–1900* (Columbia: University of South Carolina Press, 1952), 227.

4. Edwin L. Green, *A History of the University of South Carolina* (Columbia, SC: The State Company, 1916), 94.

5. W. E. B. Du Bois, *Black Reconstruction in America* (New York: The Free Press, 1935/1998), 381.

6. Edgar Wallace Knight, "The Schools in South Carolina from 1870 to 1876," in *The Influence of Reconstruction on Education in the South* (New York: Teachers College, Columbia University, 1913), 83. The Trinity College/Columbia University professor decried the lack of opportunity for "native white leadership" to determine the fortunes of postwar South Carolina.

7. Bernard A. Weisberger, "The Dark and Bloody Ground of Reconstruction Historiography," *The Journal of Southern History* 25, no. 4 (November 1959): 427–447.

8. See Chapter IV, "The Radical University, 1873–77" (pp. 61–79) in Daniel Walker Hollis, *University of South Carolina: College to University (Vol. II)* (Columbia: University of South Carolina Press, 1956).

9. Pamela M. White, "'Free and Open': The Radical University of South Carolina, 1873–1877" (Master's thesis, University of South Carolina, 1975).

10. Samuel Eliot Morison makes no mention of Greener (or of W. E. B. Du Bois for that matter) in *Three Centuries of Harvard* (Cambridge, MA: The Belknap Press of Harvard University Press, 1936). Andrew Schlesinger mentions him in passing (pp. 121 and 136) in *Veritas: Harvard College and the American Experience* (Chicago: Ivan R. Dee, 2005). *Harvard: A to Z* by John T. Bethell, Richard M. Hunt, and Robert Shenton (Cambridge, MA: Harvard University Press, 2004) omits him from the index but nonetheless has a paragraph about him in its entry on "Firsts (Men)" (p. 143). The one history that deals with his time at Harvard in detail is "Richard T. Greener: The First Black Harvard College Graduate" (pp. 37–58), in Werner Sollors, Caldwell Titcomb, Thomas A. Underwood, and Randall Kennedy (eds.). *Blacks at Harvard: A Documentary History of African-American Experience at Harvard and Radcliffe.* New York University Press, 1993.

11. John Hope Franklin, *From Slavery to Freedom: A History of American Negroes* [Second Edition]. (New York: Alfred A. Knopf, 1965), 392–393. He also wrote extensively about the history of the era in *Reconstruction After the Civil War* (University of Chicago Press, 1961/2012).

12. In 1994 a made-for-cable movie, "Assault at West Point: The Court-Martial of Johnson Whittaker" (Harry Moses, dir.), Samuel L. Jackson appeared as Greener (co-starring with Sam Waterston as former South Carolina governor Daniel Chamberlain), dramatizing the trial of Greener's former University of South Carolina student, whom he had recommended for an appointment at the US Military Academy. However, the movie seems to have had a limited audience on premium cable and is still only available on VHS tape (and is available on YouTube at https://youtu.be/oZmuaP_TX7w).

13. Carolyn B. Matalene and Katherine Chaddock Reynolds, *Carolina Voices: Two Hundred Years of Student Experiences* (Columbia: University of South Carolina Press, 2001).

14. The play was performed on campus and throughout the state in 2001 as part of the University's bicentennial and later published in Jon Tuttle, *Two South Carolina Plays* (Spartanburg, SC: Hub City Writers Project, 2009), 23–57. Tuttle relied on Mounter's research as he was working on the play, which he discusses in the introduction. Mounter also gives his perspective in a chapter, "Rebuilding Richard Greener" (pp. 59–67).

15. One such example is the story broadcast on "All Things Considered" on National Public Radio on April 23, 2012: "Discovery Sparks Interest In Forgotten Black Scholar," available at https://www.npr.org/2012/04/23/151227283/discovery-sparks-interest-in-forgotten-black-scholar.

16. This is detailed in Chapter 10.

17. There is also a portrait of Greener (commissioned of Larry Lebby in 1984) that is part of the McKissick Museum's collection and has hung in the President's Office since 2008, at President

Harris Pastides's request. (See Figure 1.) The Black Alumni Council sponsors the Richard T. Greener Scholarship.

18. We also briefly refer to other aspects of Greener's life—his time at Harvard and elsewhere before coming to the University of South Carolina and his career afterward as dean of the Howard University School of Law, as the administrator of the Grant Memorial, as a diplomat for the United States in Vladivostok, Russia, and his activism and work as a lawyer—but refer readers to Mounter's and Chaddock's volumes for deeper understanding of these aspects of Greener's life. See Michael Robert Mounter, "Richard Theodore Greener: The Idealist, Statesman, Scholar and South Carolinian" (PhD diss., University of South Carolina, 2002) and Katherine Reynolds Chaddock, *Uncompromising Activist: Richard Greener, First Black Graduate of Harvard College* (Baltimore, Johns Hopkins University Press, 2017).

19. Michael David Cohen, *Reconstructing the Campus: Higher Education and the American Civil War* (Charlottesville: University of Virginia Press, 2012), 101.

20. James D. Anderson, *The Education of Blacks in the South, 1860–1935.* (Chapel Hill: The University of North Carolina Press, 1988).

21. William P. Vaughn, "Integration in Public Higher Education." In *Schools for All: The Blacks and Public Education in the South, 1865–1877* (Lexington: University of Kentucky Press, 1974); Hollis, *University of South Carolina*, 61–63.

22. Hollis, *University of South Carolina*, 22–23.

23. Hayne was also the biracial nephew of a former US Senator and SC Governor Robert Y. Young.

24. See chapter IV, "The Radical University, 1873–77" (pp. 61–79) in Hollis, *University of South Carolina*.

25. John Herbert Roper, "A Reconsideration: The University of South Carolina During Reconstruction (1974)," in *South Carolina in the Civil War and Reconstruction Eras: Essay from the Proceedings of the South Carolina Historical Association* (Columbia: University of South Carolina Press, 2016), 192.

26. W. Lewis Burke Jr., "The Radical Law School: The University of South Carolina School of Law and its African American Graduates," in *At Freedom's Door: African American Founding Fathers and Lawyers in Reconstruction South Carolina* (Columbia: University of South Carolina Press, 2000), 91.

27. Roper, "A Reconsideration," 189.

28. Collectively known as the Reconstruction Amendments, the Thirteenth, Fourteenth, and Fifteenth Amendments of the US Constitution abolished the practice of slavery (outside of incarceration), provided for equal protections of all citizens under the law, and extended universal male suffrage.

29. The irony of the proposed bill is that the roots of the military college lie in Charleston being able to easily martial a standing militia to suppress slave revolts like the 1739 Stono Rebellion and the failed 1822 Vesey Rebellion and it played an important role in the Civil War. See Christian K. Anderson, "The South Carolina Military Academy During the Civil War: Training Ground for the Confederacy," in R. Eric Platt and Holly Foster (Eds.), *Persistence Through Peril: Episodes of College Life and Academic Endurance in the Civil War South* (Jackson: University Press of Mississippi, 2021).

30. Blinzy L. Gore. *On a Hilltop High: The Origin and History of Claflin College to 1984.* (Spartanburg: The Reprint Company Publishers, 1993), 57–59.

31. Lee also served as board chairman. Browley was abolitionist Harriet Tubman's nephew.

32. John S. Reynolds. *Reconstruction in South Carolina, 1865–1877* (Columbia: The State Company, 1905), 229.

33. Vaughn, *Schools for All*, 111.

34. Colyar Meriwether, "Collegiate Education," in *History of Higher Education in South Carolina, With a Sketch of the Free School System* (Washington; Bureau of Education, 1889), 55.

35. Cohen, *Reconstructing the Campus*, 81–85; 114–17.

36. Cohen, *Reconstructing the Campus*, 117.

37. Cohen, *Reconstructing the Campus*, 121–22.

38. Chaddock, *Uncompromising Activist*, 47.

39. "Memoir of Richard Theodore Greener," Harvard Class of 1870 Class Book (pp. 329–332). Harvard University Archives, Call #HUD 270.714.

40. Chaddock, *Uncompromising Activist*, 30. The ICY later became Cheyney University of Pennsylvania, the nation's first Historically Black College or University.

41. Arthur Clifton Willis. *Cheyney: Mother of Higher Education of African-Americans, 1837–1981*. (Philadelphia: Arthur C. Willis, 1994), 43.

42. Chaddock, *Uncompromising Activist*, 38–40. Catto was born in Charleston, SC, and moved as a boy to Philadelphia.

43. Quoted in Chaddock, *Uncompromising Activist*, 40.

44. Chaddock, *Uncompromising Activist*, 41.

45. Willis, *Cheyney*, 44.

46. Chaddock, *Uncompromising Activist*, 44, 47. The Preparatory School later became known as the M Street High School and then Paul Laurence Dunbar High School, its current name. Dunbar was one of the first public high schools in the nation to serve Black students.

47. Chaddock, *Uncompromising Activist*, 49.

48. *Anderson Intelligencer* (Anderson, SC), Nov. 20, 1872, 1. The section of the newspaper with this quote has a column called, "All Sorts of Paragraphs," collected from other newspapers. This one came from *The Georgetown Times*. Anderson is located in the Upstate section of the state while Georgetown is in the Lowcountry, both areas where Greener would later encounter hostility while he was doing his speaking tours.

49. The College Library where Greener served as librarian now serves as an archival and special collections library and was renamed the South Caroliniana Library in 1940, one hundred years after its opening. The Thomas Cooper Library, beside which stands a statue of Greener, is currently the University's primary library.

50. Chaddock, *Uncompromising Activist*, 49–50.

51. Gerhard Weiss, "The Americanization of Franz Lieber and the Encyclopedia Americana," in Lynne Tatlock and Matt Erlin (Eds.), *German Culture in Nineteenth-Century America Book Subtitle: Reception, Adaptation, Transformation* (Rochester, NY: Camden House, 2005), 283.

52. Keil, Hartmut. "Francis Lieber's Attitudes on Race, Slavery, and Abolition." *Journal of American Ethnic History* 28, no. 1 (2008): 13–33.

53. Matthew J. Mancini, "Francis Lieber, Slavery, and the 'Genesis' of the Laws of War," *The Journal of Southern History* 77, No. 2 (MAY 2011): 325–348.

54. Hollis, *University of South Carolina*, 66.

55. Maximilian LaBorde, *History of the South Carolina College from its Incorporation December 19, 1801, to Nov. 25, 1857, Including Sketches of its Presidents and Professors with an Appendix* (Columbia, SC: Peter B. Glass, 1859). The 463-page volume contains a wealth of detail about the antebellum South Carolina College, but not surprisingly contains no information or even mention of the College's use of enslaved laborers except one passing reference to a professor's "servant" on page 62.

56. Hollis, *University of South Carolina*, 66.

57. Trustees' minutes, October 10, 1873, quoted in Hollis, *University of South Carolina*, 67. Green quotes a portion of this resolution in his history, adding only briefly to it in his description of the 1873 integration, and directs the reader to the appendix of his book.

58. Hollis, *University of South Carolina*, 68.

59. Brewer, Fisk Parsons, and William P. Vaughn. "'South Carolina University: 1876' of Fisk Parsons Brewer." *The South Carolina Historical Magazine* 76, no. 4 (1975): 230.

60. Chaddock, *Uncompromising Activist*, 55.

61. Annual examination on the Latin Reader by Allen and Greenough, June 1875, Miscellaneous 19th and 20th Century materials, Box 10, Folder: Richard Greener, University of South Carolina Archives, Columbia, South Carolina.

62. White, "Free and Open."

63. Chaddock, *Uncompromising Activist*, 56.

64. Annual examination on the Latin "Odes of Horace," June 1875, Miscellaneous 19th and 20th Century materials, Box 10, Folder: Richard Greener, University of South Carolina Archives, Columbia, South Carolina.

65. Annual examination on the Logic of Jevons, given by Richard Greener to junior class students, June 1875, Miscellaneous 19th and 20th Century materials, Box 10, Folder: Richard Greener, University of South Carolina Archives, Columbia, South Carolina.

66. Annual examination on the metaphysics of Hamilton to junior class students, June 1875, Miscellaneous 19th and 20th Century materials, Box 10, Folder: Richard Greener, University of South Carolina Archives, Columbia, South Carolina.

67. Annual examination on history given by Richard T. Greener to senior class students, June 1875, Miscellaneous 19th and 20th Century materials, Box 10, Folder: Richard Greener, University of South Carolina Archives, Columbia, South Carolina.

68. Correspondence from J. K. Jillson to Richard T. Greener, 17 June 1875, Miscellaneous 19th and 20th Century materials, Box 10, Folder: Richard Greener, University of South Carolina Archives, Columbia, South Carolina.

69. Correspondence from Richard T. Greener to Chairman and Faculty of the University of South Carolina, February 12, 1874, Miscellaneous 19th and 20th Century materials, Box 10, Folder: Richard Greener, University of South Carolina Archives, Columbia, South Carolina.

70. Correspondence from Richard T. Greener to T. McCants Stewart and C. J. Babbitt, November 6, 1875, Miscellaneous 19th and 20th Century materials, Box 10, Folder: Richard Greener, University of South Carolina Archives, Columbia, South Carolina.

71. Bernard F. Powers. *Black Charlestonians: A Social History, 1822–1885.* (Fayetteville: University of Arkansas Press, 1994). Prior to his political career, Francis L. Cardozo served as the second principal of the Avery Normal Institute in Charleston; the school was formally established in 1865 by the American Missionary Association to educate the children of the city's Black elite. Twenty-nine students born or raised in Charleston attended the University during this era.

72. Chaddock, *Uncompromising Activist*, 57.

73. Asa H. Gordon. *Sketches of Negro Life and History in South Carolina* [Second Edition]. (Columbia: University of South Carolina Press, 1929/1971), 93. Both Howard University in Washington, DC, and Howard Academy in Columbia, SC, were both named in honor of Union General Oliver Otis Howard, director of the Freedman's Bureau Department of Refugees, Freedom, and Abandoned Lands.

74. Carolyn B. Matalene and Katherine Chaddock Reynolds, *Carolina Voices: Two Hundred Years of Student Experiences* (Columbia: University of South Carolina Press, 2001), 58.

75. Powers, *Black Charlestonians*, 156.

76. Correspondence from H. R. Pinckney to Richard T. Greener, 31 January 1875, Miscellaneous 19th and 20th Century materials, Box 10, Folder: Richard Greener, University of South Carolina Archives, Columbia, South Carolina.

77. *The Christian Recorder*, July 9, 1874, 1 quoted in Chaddock, 54.

78. Matalene and Reynolds, *Carolina Voices*, 59.

79. Richard Theodore Greener, *Charles Sumner: The Idealist, Statesman and Scholar, An Address Delivered on Public Day, June 29, 1874 at the Request of the Faculty of the University of South Carolina* (Columbia, SC: Republican Printing Company, 1874).

80. Greener, *Charles Sumner*, 7.

81. Greener, *Charles Sumner*, 38–39.

82. Greener, *Charles Sumner*, 39.

83. Rutledge College was the first building erected at South Carolina College and in 1848 was renamed for brothers John and Edward Rutledge. John represented South Carolina in the Constitutional Convention of 1787 and also served as governor and Supreme Court justice. Edward was the youngest signer of the Declaration of Independence and also served as governor. See Elizabeth Cassidy West and Katharine Thompson Allen, *On the Horseshoe: A Guide to the Historic Campus of the University of South Carolina* (Columbia: The University of South Carolina Press, 2015), 8.

84. Richard T. Greener, "Civil Rights Again," *Columbia Union Herald*, Jan. 12, 1875, quoted in Chaddock. *Uncompromising Activist*, 60.

85. Greener would years later serve as the administrative head of the Ulysses S. Grant Monument Association.

86. See Foner, *Reconstruction*; Douglas R. Egerton, *The Wars of Reconstruction: The Brief, Violent History of America's Most Progressive Era* (New York: Bloomsbury Press, 2014); and Henry Louis Gates Jr. *Stony the Road: Reconstruction, White Supremacy, and the Rise of Jim Crow* (New York: Penguin Press, 2019).

87. Mounter, "Richard Theodore Greener," 167. This quote is the title of Chapter 8 of Mounter's dissertation, which details his campaigning on behalf of Republican candidates and the danger he faced.

88. Mounter, "Richard Theodore Greener," 169.

89. Mounter, "Richard Theodore Greener," 172–173.

90. US House of Representatives, *Testimony Taken by the Select Committee on the Recent Election in South Carolina*, 44th Congress, 2nd Session, 231–232.

91. Richard T. Greener, "The White Problem" *Lend a Hand: A Record of Progress* 12 (May 1894): 366.

92. Chaddock. *Uncompromising Activist*," 59.

93. Chaddock. *Uncompromising Activist*, 59.

94. Chaddock. *Uncompromising Activist*, 60.

95. Chaddock. *Uncompromising Activist*, 53.

96. "Report of the Sub-Committee of the Board of Trustees of the University of South Carolina Relative to the Library of the University," Oct. 31, 1874, quoted in Chaddock, *Uncompromising Activist*, 61.

97. Quoted in Mounter, "Richard Theodore Greener," 144.

98. Chaddock. *Uncompromising Activist*, 61.

99. Dale F. Harter, "For the Love of Books: Richard T. Greener's Brief Career as the University of South Carolina's First African-American University Librarian," *Proceedings of the South Carolina Historical Association* (1997): 56.

100. Correspondence from Justin Winsor to Richard T. Greener, 21 October 1875, Miscellaneous 19th and 20th Century materials, Box 10, Folder: Richard Greener, University of South Carolina Archives, Columbia, South Carolina.

101. *Charleston News and Courier*, Nov. 1, 1875.

102. Harter, "For the Love of Books," 56.

103. *Charleston News and Courier*, Nov. 1, 1875

104. Correspondence from Richard T. Greener to Nathaniel Barnwell, 30 August 1877,

Miscellaneous 19th and 20th Century materials, Box 10, Folder: Richard Greener, University of South Carolina Archives, Columbia, South Carolina.

105. Chaddock. *Uncompromising Activist*, 62

106. Mounter, "Richard Theodore Greener," 149.

107. Chaddock, *Uncompromising Activist*, 60, 67, 159. Belle's story is recounted by Heidi Ardizzone in *An Illuminated Life: Belle da Costa Greene's Journey from Prejudice to Privilege* (New York: W.W. Norton, 2007).

108. Mounter, "Richard Theodore Greener," 150–51.

109. Correspondence from D. H. Chamberlain to Richard T. Greener, 12 November 1875, Miscellaneous 19th and 20th Century materials, Box 10, Folder: Richard Greener, University of South Carolina Archives, Columbia, South Carolina.

110. Henry G. Fulmer, "Richard T. Greener and the Radical University Library," *Ex-Libris* (University of South Carolina Libraries, 1995): 37.

111. Matalene and Reynolds, *Carolina Voices*, 59.

112. Letter from Richard T. Greener to Francis Grimké, November 18, 1907, 4–5. Francis James Grimké Papers, Moorland-Spingarn Research Center, Howard University. Greener wrote this letter from Orangeburg while visiting there to give talks at South Carolina State and Claflin universities.

113. Harvard had a law department dating to 1817 but its law school was organized by the newly appointed President Charles Eliot (1869) who hired Christopher Columbus Langdell as the school's first dean. Langdell instituted a host of reforms to legal education, some of which appear to have made their way to the young law school in South Carolina.

114. Chaddock, *Uncompromising Activist*, 41–41, 46.

115. Burke, *At Freedom's Door*, 90.

116. Bruce A. Kimball, "The Langdell Problem: Historicizing the Century of Historiography, 1906–2000s." *Law and History Review* 22, no. 2 (2004): 277.

117. W. Lewis Burke Jr., "The Radical Law School: The University of South Carolina School of Law and Its African American Graduates, 1873–1877," in James Lowell Underwood and W. Lewis Burke Jr. (eds.) *At Freedom's Door: African American Founding Fathers and Lawyers in Reconstruction South Carolina* (Columbia: University of South Carolina Press, 2000): 92–93.

118. Ibid., 93.

119. Burke, *At Freedom's Door*, 93–110

120. Ibid., 93–94.

121. W. Lewis Burke Jr., *All for Civil Rights: African American Lawyers in South Carolina 1868–1968* (Athens: The University of Georgia Press, 2017).

122. Burke, Jr., "The Radical Law School," 90–114.

123. Burke, *At Freedom's Door*, 108–109.

124. Gordon, *Sketches of Negro Life and History in South Carolina*, 95; Benjamin W. Arnett. *The Budget: Containing the Annual Reports of the General Officers of the African M. E. Church of the United States of America*. Xenia: Torchlight Printing Company, 1881.

125. The original name was the Colored Normal, Industrial, Agricultural and Mechanical College of South Carolina. As part of the 1896 state constitution, the SC Agricultural College & Mechanics' Institute was separated from Claflin University to create the state's new agricultural and mechanical college for Black students. The institution is today known as South Carolina State University.

126. John F. Potts, Sr., *A History of the Palmetto Education Association*. Washington: National Education Association, 1978, 37.

127. Charles E. Wynes, "T. McCants Stewart: Peripatetic Black South Carolinian," *The South Carolina Historical Magazine* 80, no. 4 (October 1979): 315.

128. Powers, *Black Charlestonians*. 157. Stewart was the first Black attorney licensed to practice in both Hawai'i and the US Virgin Islands.

129. Burke, *At Freedom's Door*, 115; Ronald E. Butchart, *Schooling the Freed People: Teaching, Learning, and the Struggle for Black Freedom, 1861–1876* (Chapel Hill: University of North Carolina Press, 2010), 136, 236.

130. Powers, *Black Charlestonians*, 148. Butchart, *Schooling the Freed People*. Before coming to the University, Mortimer A. Warren was one of Francis L. Cardozo's successors as principal of Avery Normal Institute in Charleston, SC.

131. Chaddock, *Uncompromising Activist*, 57.

132. Burke, "The Radical Law School," 115.

133. USC Law degree awarded to Richard T. Greener, 12 December 1876, Richard Theodore Greener Papers, 1876, University of South Carolina Archives, Columbia, South Carolina. Also see: https://youtu.be/Y-LH4yocqGw.

134. SC Law license bestowed upon Richard T. Greener, December 20, 1876, Richard Theodore Greener Papers, 1876, University of South Carolina Archives, Columbia, South Carolina. His undergraduate diploma was eventually purchased by Harvard.

135. Chaddock, *Uncompromising Activist*, 89–105.

136. Burke, "The Radical Law School," 115.

137. Henry H. Lesesne, *A History of the University of South Carolina, 1940–2000*. (Columbia: University of South Carolina Press, 2001), 143; Baker, *Paradoxes of Desegregation*, 149.

138. Account page signed by Richard T. Greener, 1 November 1875, Miscellaneous 19th and 20th Century materials, Box 10, Folder: Richard Greener, University of South Carolina Archives, Columbia, South Carolina.

139. Correspondence from Richard T. Greener to the University of South Carolina Board of Trustees, 29 June 1877, Miscellaneous 19th and 20th Century materials, Box 10, Folder: Richard Greener, University of South Carolina Archives, Columbia, South Carolina.

140. George Brown Tindall, "Negroes in Politics," in *South Carolina Negroes, 1877–1900*, (Columbia: University of South Carolina Press, 1952).

141. Scott, 1911. Republican Robert Lloyd Smith served two terms in the Texas state legislature.

142. William Sinclair is the author of *The Aftermath of Slavery: A Study of the Condition and Environment of the American Negro*, a seminal work about slavery, Reconstruction and early Jim Crow America first published in 1905.

143. Roper, "A Reconsideration," 191.

144. Ibid., 191–192.

145. Monroe Alphus Majors, *Noted Negro Women, Their Triumphs and Activities* (Chicago: Donohue & Henneberry, 1893).

146. Clarissa Minnie Thompson Allen (Brown, Wiley, MacDonald, eds.), *Treading the Winepress or, A Mountain of Misfortune*, (Normal, Ill: Downstate Legacies/Illinois State University, 2019).

147. Cohen, *Reconstructing the Campus*, 126–127.

148. Hollis, *University of South Carolina*, 71

149. Cohen, *Reconstructing the Campus*, 114.

150. Brewer, "South Carolina University: 1876": 231.

151. Tyler D. Parry, "The Radical Experiment of South Carolina: The History and Legacy of a Reconstructed University," *The Journal of African American History* 105, no. 4 (Fall 2020): 565.

152. Michael Sugrue, "'We Desired Our Future Rulers to Be Educated Men': South Carolina College, the Defense of Slavery, and the Development of Secessionist Politics," in Roger Geiger (ed.), *The American College in the Nineteenth Century* (Nashville: Vanderbilt University Press, 2000): 91–114.

153. Frances Marchant, "Richard Theodore Greener: A Story of a Busy Man," *Gloucester Bulletin*, 1882.

Chapter Four: LAYING THE MOUNTAINS LOW

1. Simon Peter Smith to Edward Franklin Williams, July 7, 186[7], Edward Franklin Williams Papers [hereafter WP], Box 13, Folder 12, Amistad Research Center [hereafter ARC], Tulane University, New Orleans [hereafter TU]. All original spellings are kept. Occasionally punctuation has been added in brackets. On slavery and the university, see Maurie D. McInnis and Lois P. Nelson, eds., *Educated in Tyranny: Slavery at Thomas Jefferson's Virginia* (Charlottesville: University of Virginia Press, 2019); Leslie M. Harris, James T. Campbell and Alfred L. Brophy, *Slavery and the University: Histories and Legacies* (Chapel Hill: University of North Carolina Press, 2019); Craig Steven Wilder, *Ebony and Ivory: Race, Slavery, and the Troubled History of America's Universities* (New York: Bloomsbury Press, 2013).

2. Dorothy Sterling, ed., *The Trouble They Seen: Black People Tell the Story of Reconstruction* (Garden City, NY: Doubleday, 1976), 344–345; 318–319, 478–479. Smith to Williams, December 26, 1873, WP, Box 13, Folder 13, ARC, TU; James M. McPherson, *The Abolitionist Legacy: From Reconstruction to the NAACP* (Princeton, NJ: Princeton University Press, 1975), 16. Other mentions, in passing, include Damon L. Fordman, *Voices of Black South Carolina: Legend and Legacy* (Charleston, SC: The History Press, 2009), 70; Leon F. Litwack, *Trouble in Mind: Black Southerners in the Age of Jim Crow* (New York: Vintage, 1999), 560n14.

3. Allison Baker, Jennifer Betsworth, Rebecca Bush, Sarah Conlon, Evan A. Kutzler, Justin McIntyre, Elizabeth Oswald, Jamie Wilson, and JoAnn Zeise, *Slavery at South Carolina College, 1801–1865: The Foundations of the University of South Carolina*, https://delphi.tcl.sc.edu/library/digital/slaveryscc/index.html; Evan A. Kutzler, Sarah Conlon, Jamie Diane Wilson, and JoAnne Zeise, "Revealing Slavery's Legacy at a Public University in the South," 3 parts, October 22, 2014, October 22, 2014, and October 27, 2014, https://ncph.org/history-at-work/revealing-slaverys-legacy-part-1/l; Duncan A Buell and Heidi Rae Cooley, "Critical Interactives: Improving Public Understanding of Institutional Policy," *Bulletin of Science, Technology & Society* 20, no. 10 (Spring 2012): 1–8; Richard Lee Walker, "Ghosts of the Horseshoe: A Mobilization of a Critical Interactive," (PhD diss., University of South Carolina, 2014). In this early stage, I became indebted to Andrew Salinas, an archivist at the time who went out of his way to confirm the richness of Smith's letters and photocopy part of the collection.

4. Jamie Lovegrove, "University of South Carolina unveils plaques recognizing slave contributions to campus," *The Post and Courier* (Charleston, SC), December 5, 2017; Bristow Marchant, "The slaves who built USC are virtually unknown. How the college is trying to fix that," *The State* (Columbia, SC), December 5, 2017; Bristow Marchant, Instagram post, December 5, 2017.

5. On the language of writing and speaking about slavery, see P. Gabrielle Foreman, et al., "Writing about Slavery? Teaching about Slavery," a community-sourced document, April 2, 2020, https://docs.google.com/document/d/1A4TEdDgYslX-hlKezLodMIM71My3KTNozxRvoIQTOQs/mobilebasic.

6. Smith to Williams, September 24, 1870, WP, Box 13, Folder 13, ARC, TU; 1880 US Census, District of Columbia, population schedule, Enumeration District 20, pg. 187A (stamped), dwelling 216, family 264, Simon P. Smith, digital image, Ancestry.com (http://ancestry.com: accessed 30 April 2020); citing NARA microfilm publication T523, roll 121.

7. George Smith Will, January 17, 1855 (executed on July 24, 1858), Richland County, South Carolina, Wills Record, No. L, 1840–64, 453–556; 1860 US Census, Richland County, South Carolina, population schedule 2, pg. 116 (stamped), John A. Smith; Smith to Williams, July 4, 1870 [incomplete, unsigned], WP, Box 13, Folder 13, ARC, TU; 1900 US Census, District of Columbia, population, pg. 13B (stamped), dwelling 157, family 174, 318 A Street SE, Harrison Smith et al.; digital image, Ancestry.com (http://ancestry.com : accessed 31 December 2019); citing NARA microfilm publication T523, roll not listed;

8. Kevin M. Levin, *Searching for Black Confederates: The Civil War's Most Persistent Myth* (Chapel Hill: University of North Carolina Press, 2019), 16, chs. 2–3. On mobility in the Civil War era, see Yael A. Sternhell, *Routes of War: The World of Movement in the Confederate South* (Cambridge, Mass.: Harvard University Press, 2012). On refugee camps, see Amy Murrell Taylor, *Embattled Freedom: Journeys through the Civil War's Slave Refugee Camps* (Chapel Hill: University of North Carolina Press, 2018). Thanks to Christopher Barr, former park ranger at Chickamauga-Chattanooga National Military Park and now park ranger at Reconstruction Era National Historic Park, for suggesting Smith might have been enslaved alongside the Confederate army.

9. Ronald E. Butchart, *Schooling the Freed People: Teaching, Learning, and the Struggle for Black Freedom, 1861–1876* (Chapel Hill: University of North Carolina Press, 2010), xvii.

10. *Acts of the State of Tennessee, Passed at the Second Session of the Thirty-Fourth General Assembly, for the Years 1865–66* (Nashville, TN: S. C. Mercer, 1866), 372–373; "Historical Note," WP, ARC, TU.

11. Smith to Williams, September 7, 1886, WP, Box 13, Folder 16, ARC, TU.

12. Lewis F. Clark to Williams, July 16, 1867, WP, Box 13, Folder 12, ARC, TU.

13. Clark to Williams, December 1, 1869, WP, Box 13, Folder 12, ARC, TU. See also Smith to Williams, January 11, 1873, May 10, 1873, Box 13, Folder 13, WP, ARC, TU; Smith to Williams, February 14, 1874, March 20, 1874, June 22, 1874, March 9, 1874, WP Box 13, Folder 14, ARC, TU.

14. *Annual Catalogue of the Normal and Preparatory Department of Howard University, Washington, DC, 1867* (Washington, DC: Gibson Brothers, no date), no page numbers, image 9–10, https://dh.howard.edu/cgi/viewcontent.cgi?article=1000&context=hucatalogs.

15. In 1868–69, Smith lived in room 36 of "B.H." The next year, he lived in room 23 of Minor Hall. *Catalogue of the Officers and Students of Howard University, District of Columbia, 1868–69* (Washington, DC: Judd & Detweiler, 1869), 8; *Catalogue of the Officers and Students of Howard University, District of Columbia, 1869–70* (Washington, DC: Judd & Detweiler, 1870), 11; Rayford W. Logan, *Howard University: The First Hundred Years 1867–1967* (New York: New York University Press, 1969), 20–23, 37; *Catalogue of the Officers and Students of Howard University, District of Columbia, 1871–62* (Washington, DC: Reed & Woodward, Printers, 1872), 24; *Catalogue of the Officers and Students of Howard University, District of Columbia, 1874–76* (Washington, DC: O. H. Reed:, 1876), 13.

16. Smith to Williams, January 31, 1868, May 25, 1868, June 12, 1868, WP, Box 13, Folder 12, ARC, TU.

17. *Catalogue of the Officers and Students of Howard University, District of Columbia, 1869–70* (Washington, DC: Judd & Detweiler, 1870), 66; Logan, *Howard University*, 53–54; Smith to Williams, November 19, 1869, December 23, 1869, Box 13, Folder 12, WP, ARC, TU; Ledger of the Military Department, 101, 102, 106, 111, 117, Digital Howard, Howard University; Smith to Williams, April 14, 1871, WP, Box 13, Folder 13, ARC, TU.

18. Smith to Williams, March 20, 1869, Box 13, Folder 12, WP, ARC, TU; Smith to Williams, March 14, 1873, Box 13, Folder 13, WP, ARC, TU; Smith to Williams, January 5, 1875, Box 13, Folder 14, WP, ARC, TU.

19. Smith to Williams, September 24, 1870, April 14, 1871, WP, Box 13, Folder 13, ARC, TU; Smith to Williams, February 15, March 20, 1874, WP, Box 13, Folder 14, ARC, TU.

20. Smith to Williams, February 02, 1869, WP, Box 13, Folder 12, ARC, TU; Smith to Williams, February 15, 1871, December 16, 1871, April 22, 1872, August 15, 1872, October 10, 1873, WP, Box 13, Folder 13, ARC, TU.

21. John Herbert Roper, "A Reconsideration: The University of South Carolina during Reconstruction (1974)," in Michael Brem Bonner and Fritz Hamer, eds., *South Carolina in the Civil War and Reconstruction Eras: Essays from the Proceedings of the South Carolina Historical Association* (Columbia: University of South Carolina Press, 2016), 190; *Catalogue of the Officers and Students of Howard University for the Academic Year 1873–74* (Washington, DC: O. H. Reed, 1874), 12–15.

22. Smith to Williams, June 11, 1877, WP, Box 13, Folder 14, ARC, TU.

23. Smith to Williams, June 11, 1877, WP, Box 13, Folder 14, ARC, TU; Sanborn Fire Insurance Map Company, Columbia, South Carolina, March 1888, Sheet 3, University of South Carolina Digital Collections; Beasley & Emerson, *Columbia South Carolina City Directory, 1875–1876*, 75.

24. Smith to Williams, June 11, 1877, WP, Box 13, Folder 14, ARC, TU; Roper, "A Reconsideration," 188–189.

25. Smith to Williams, June 11, 1877, WP, Box 13, Folder 14, ARC, TU.

26. Smith to Williams, July 19, 1877, August 21, 1877, WP, Box 13, Folder 14, ARC, TU.

27. Smith to Williams, August 4, 1877, WP, Box 13, Folder 14, ARC, TU; Walter Edgar, *South Carolina, A History* (Columbia: University of South Carolina Press, 1998), 407–08.

28. Smith to Williams, August 21, 1877, WP, Box 13, Folder 14, ARC, TU.

29. *Catalogue of the Officers and Students of the Chicago Theological Seminary, Chicago, Illinois, 1877–78*, 7; *Catalogue of the Officers and Students of the Chicago Theological Seminary, Chicago, Illinois, 1878–79*, 6; "Personals. Notes Concerning Prominent People," *The Inter Ocean* (Chicago, Ill.), October 17, 1886; "Anniversary Exercises. The Seminary Commencement," *Inter Ocean*, April 24, 1879.

30. Edward Whitin to Williams, April 21, 1879, WP, Box 13, Folder 14, ARC, TU.

31. Smith to Williams, June 17, 1878, July 29, 1879, October 17, 1879, WP, Box 13, Folder 14, ARC, TU; [No Title], *The Field and Fireside* (Marietta, Ga.) July 31, 1879.

32. *The American Missionary* 34, no. 2 (February 1880), 37; Smith to Williams, December 8, 1879, WP, Box 13, Folder 14, ARC, TU; Rev. Simon P. Smith, "District of Columbia. Lincoln Mission," *The American Missionary* 34, no. 5 (May 1880), 141.

33. Smith to Williams, April 7, 1880, WP, Box 13, Folder 15, ARC, TU.

34. Smith to Williams, June 28, 1880, WP, Box 13, Folder 15, ARC, TU.

35. Smith to Williams, June 14, 1880, August 3, 1880, WP, Box 13, Folder 14, ARC, TU; "Gen. Garfield's Acceptance," *The People's Advocate* (Alexandria, VA), July 24, 1880; "Poor Wade," *People's Advocate*, August 28, 1880; "The Pulpit and Politics," *People's Advocate*, October 23, 1880; "God in Politics," *People's Advocate*, November 20, 1880; "Why Colored Men Should be Appointed to Office," *People's Advocate*, December 18, 1880; Adelaide M. Cromwell, *Unveiled Voices, Unvarnished Memories: The Cromwell Family in Slavery and Segregation, 1692–1972* (Columbia and London: University of Missouri Press, 83–84; "Personals," *Inter Ocean*, October 17, 1886; "A Colored Preacher's Suit," *Inter Ocean*, October 23, 1886; "Recovering Damages," *Inter Ocean*, June 8, 1889.

36. Smith to Williams, November 25, 1880, May 20, 1881, WP, Box 13, Folder 15, ARC, TU; Smith to Williams, June 10, 1887, August 3, 1887, August 8, 1887, December 10, 1887, December 29, 1887, WP, Box 13, Folder 16, ARC, TU; James Powell to Williams, July 12, 1887, December 21, 1887, WP, Box 13, Folder 16, ARC, TU. *The Sixty-Fourth Report of the American Home Missionary Society, Presented to the Executive Committee, at the Annual meeting, June 3, 1890* (New York: The American Home Missionary Society, 1890), 93, 95; *The Congregational Year-Book, 1893* . . . . (Boston: Congregational Sunday School and Publishing Society, 1893), 260; *The Congregational Year-Book, 1894* (Boston: Congregational Sunday School and Publishing Society, 1894), 256; *The Congregational Year-Book, 1895* (Boston: Congregational Sunday School and Publishing Society, 1895), 294.

37. Smith to Williams, December 8, 1879, WP, Box 13, Folder 14, ARC, TU; Smith to Williams, April 11, 1881, WP, Box 13, Folder 15, ARC, TU; 1880 US Census, District of Columbia, population schedule, Enumeration District 67, pg. 431 (stamped), dwelling 24, family 26, 704 East Capitol Street, Charles R., Angeline, Martha E., Carrie E. and Ellsworth W. Prior, digital image, Family search.org (http://familysearch.org : accessed April 8, 2010); citing NARA microfilm publication T9, roll 123; Smith to Williams, February 26, 1885, September 11, 1885, WP, Box 13, Folder 16, ARC, TU.

38. Smith to Williams, September 7, 1886, November 8, 1886, February 23, 1887, WP, Box 13, Folder 16, ARC, TU; "A Caterer," *The Crisis*, Vol. 13, no. 4 (February 1917), 186.

39. Smith to Williams, May 4, 1888, September 5, 1888, August 18, 1888, WP, Box 13, Folder 17, ARC, TU.

40. *The Congregational Year-Book, 1895,* 294; *Minutes of the General Assembly of the Presbyterian Church,* 378.

41. Smith to Williams, April 6, 1907, WP, Box 13, Folder 17, ARC, TU; *Charlottesville, Virginia, City Directory* (1906), 96–97; 1910 US Census, Charlottesville, Albemarle County, Virginia, population, pg. 7B (stamped), dwelling 156, family 203, 520 Pearl St., William E. Jackson et al.; digital image, Ancestry.com (http://ancestry.com: accessed 9 April 2020); citing NARA microfilm publication T624, roll 1625. Many thanks to Sam Towler, Edwina St. Rose, and Miranda Burnett for helping confirm that Katie Smith did not own the house at 520 Pearl St. but was related to the family who owned it. I regret not being able to uncover more on Katie Smith's life and experiences. Simon Smith never used Katie's full name in his correspondence with Williams. In fact, it was only through a lucky find—her death certificate—that I learned her name. Katie A. Smith, North Carolina Death Certificate, May 3, 1911, North Carolina State Archives, Raleigh.

42. Smith to Williams, May 20, 1908, May 15, 1911; May 25, 1911; August 1, 1911; January 29, 1914, WP, Box 13, Folder 17, ARC, TU; Rev. Simon Peter Smith, North Carolina Death Certificates, Cumberland County, April 28, 1914, North Carolina State Archives; S. P. Smith Will, March 12, 1913, Cumberland County, North Carolina. Smith is buried in Brookside Cemetery.

Chapter Five: STRUGGLE FOR EDUCATIONAL
ACCESS IN SOUTH CAROLINA

1. "The Suffrage Question" *New York Times,* February 13, 1866; Education and Its Influence on the Character of the State" *The Anderson Intelligencer,* September 21, 1865.

2. "The Suffrage Question" *New York Times,* February 13, 1866.

3. "Education as an Element of Reconstruction" *The American Journal of Education,* June 1866; "National Education" *American Educational Monthly,* August 1865, 235; "The Right to Educate" *The American Educational Monthly,* January 1870, 31.

4. "The Despotic Principle" *The American Monthly,* May 1865; "Who will be Harmed by Emancipation?" *The Universal Quarterly and General Review,* October 1862, 329.

5. "The Power Whites of South and the Freedom" *Journal of Freedom* Saturday, October 14, 1865.

6. Gustavus Frankenstein "The Great Southern Convention in Charleston" Debow's Review 16, no. 6 (June 1854): 632–41.

7. James D. Anderson, Education in the South, 6.

8. "Education in the South: There is some" *New York Times,* September 6, 1865.

9. Janet Duitsman Cornelius, When I Can Learn to Read My Title Clear, 10.

10. "Education and its influence on the character of the state," *The Anderson Intelligencer,* September 21, 1865.

11. Claude H. Nolen, *African American Southerners in Slavery, Civil War and Reconstruction* (McFarland, 2005), 169. Education's racialization did not start with reconstruction; one could return to the antebellum period or the Civil War. See Horace Mann Bond, *The Education of the Negro in the American Social Order* (Octagon Books, 1934). Ronald E. Butchart, *Schooling the Freed People: Teaching, Learning, and the Struggle for Black Freedom, 1861–1876* (University of North Carolina Press, 2010).

12. "Education in the South: There is some" *New York Times,* September 6, 1865.

13. "Education for poor whites in the South" *New York Times,* October 1865.

14. "Education for poor whites in the South" *New York Times,* October 1865.

15. "How the Freedmen's Schools are Supported" *The Daily Phoenix,* July 13, 1867; American Freedmen's Union Commission, The session in Baltimore-Public Meeting Address by Reverend Henry Ward Beecher, October 14, 1866; Bishop Elliot of Georgia "On the Education of the Freedmen" *Debow's review,* September 1866. White supremacy was used in this sense as an appeal to white solidarity and to flatten class tension.

16. Bond, Horace Mann Bond, *The Education of the Negro in the American Social* Order (New York: Octagon Books, 1970), 54–57; Joel Williamson, After Slavery: The Negro in South Carolina During Reconstruction, 1861–1877 (New York: W. W. Norton, 1975), 221.

17. Bond, Horace Mann Bond, *The Education of the Negro in the American Social* Order (New York: Octagon Books, 1970), 54–57.

18. Joel Williamson, *A Rage for Order: Black-White Relations in the American South Since Emancipation* (Oxford University Press, USA, 1986); Joel Williamson, *The Crucible of Race: Black-White Relations in the American South since Emancipation* (Oxford University Press, 1984), 82–83.

19. "They Don't Like Schools," *Charleston Daily,* May 29, 1868.

20. "Governor Scott," *Charleston Daily* July 10th, 1868; "Free Schools" *The Atlanta Constitution,* December 10th, 1869.

21. "Refuse To Take Their Own Pills," Edgefield, SC, October 23, 1873.

22. The News and Herald, April 21, 1877 South Carolina and South Carolina College; Joel Williamson, After Slavery: The Negro in South Carolina During Reconstruction, 1861–1877 (New York: Norton, 1975), 232. Williamson noted that 91 students obtained state aid to attend South Carolina college. Kershaw County Commissioner report 1873; The Orangeburg Times, March 6, 1872; "Educational Provisions of the Civil Rights Bill" *The American Educational Monthly,* November 1874; "Mixed Schools" *The American Educational Monthly,* January 1875, 28.

23. "Close the free schools," *The Charleston News,* Wednesday, May 22, 1872; "Popular Education" *The Charleston Daily News,* October 10, 1871; Annual Report of the Commissioners of Education for the year 1872 (Washington: Government printing office), 313.

24. "About the Taxes" *The Charleston Daily News,* April 26, 1872.

25. State Superintendent of Education of the State of South Carolina 1872 General Remarks. It is important to note that it was not just democratic leadership against public schools but also sectarian educational institutions. This is best illustrated when the state wanted to reopen South Carolina college after its closure in 1877. However, many religious colleges wanted it to remain closed. John Whitney Evans, "Catholics and the Blair Education Bill," *The Catholic Historical Review* 46, no. 3 (1960): 273–298.

26. State Superintendent of Education of the State of South Carolina 1872 General Remarks; Report of Commissioner of Education 1871–1872.

27. "Free education, *The Atlanta Constitution,* November 19, 1871; "The Free School Question" The Atlanta Constitution, December 30, 1871.

28. "Atlanta's Public Schools: The Second Annual Report of the Superintendent Mr. B. Mallon" *The Atlanta Constitution,* October 14, 1873.

29. Tindall, *South Carolina Negroes, 1877–1900,* 212.

30. Warren D. Wilkes "Commonest on Education" *The Anderson Intelligencer,* July 26, 1866; "Educational Needs of the South" *The Daily Phoenix,* June 22, 1867; South Carolina General Assembly, *Reports and Resolutions,* 1886. Tindall, *South Carolina Negroes, 1877–1900,* 211–212.

31. "Popular Education and the State Debt," *Anderson Intelligencer,* October 12, 1876; Joel Williamson, After Slavery: The Negro in South Carolina During Reconstruction, 1861–1877 (New York: Norton, 1975), 228. Williamson noted that the Democratic campaign of 1876 followed the education plan of reconstruction.

32. "The Democratic Platform," *The Fairfield News and Herald,* August 9, 1882.

33. "Interests in the Schools," *The News and Herald,* September 15, 1877; "The Court" *The Abbeville Press and Banner,* June 5, 1878.

34. "Education of the Masses" *Anderson Intelligencer,* January 30, 1873.

35. "Education in the South," *Debow's Review* May 1868; "Education of the People," *The Atlanta Constitution,* July 15, 1875.

36. "Education," *The Charleston Daily,* July 8, 1868.

37. William J. Cooper, *The Conservative Regime: South Carolina, 1877–1890* (Univ of South Carolina Press, 2005), 39.

38. "Democratic Enthusiasm," *The Anderson Intelligencer*, September 7, 1882.

39. "Our School System," *The Orangeburg Democrat*, October 17, 1879.

40. *The Newberry Herald*, August 24, 1882; *The Abbeville Press and Banner*, September 12, 1883.

41. "Dr. Mayo and Education," *The Fairfield News and Herald*, July 18, 1888.

42. "Our School System," *The Orangeburg Democrat*, October 17, 1879; "Our Free Education" *The Newberry Herald*, August 31, 1882; "The Democratic Platform" *The Fairfield News and Herald*, August 09, 1882, "the public schools" *The Abbeville Press and Banner*, September 12, 1883; *The Abbeville Press and Banner*, September 19, 1883.

43. "Common School Teachers," *The Abbeville Press and Banner,* April 09, 1884; *The Newberry Herald,* August 24, 1882.

44. Going, "The South and the Blair Education Bill," 271–272; National Aid in the Establishment and Temporary Support of Common Schools, Henry Blair, 1887; Timothy J. Conlan, *Intergovernmentalizing the Classroom: Federal Involvement in Elementary and Secondary Education* (Advisory Commission on Intergovernmental Relations, 1981), 13–14.

45. "The Blair Bill," *The Crisis Magazine,* 17; "The Educational bill" *The Herald Newberry SC,* April 24, 1884; Daniel W. Crofts, "The Black Response to the Blair Education Bill," *The Journal of Southern History* 37, no. 1 (1971): 47.

46. The Educational bill," *The Herald Newberry SC,* April 24, 1884.

47. "What is the Sentiment of the State?" *The Abbeville Press and Banner*, May 1884.

48. "Federal Education," *The Abbeville Press and Banner*, May 21, 1884.

49. "The Nation and The Schools," *The Yorkville Enquirer*, May 08, 1884.

50. Kantrowitz, *Ben Tillman and the Reconstruction of White Supremacy*, 222.

51. Eelman, *Entrepreneurs in the Southern Upcountry*, 207.

52. George Brown Tindall, *South Carolina Negroes, 1877–1900* (Columbia: University of South Carolina Press, 2003), 216.

53. "A word in reply to 'tax-payer,'" *The Abbeville Press and Banner*, August 09, 1882; "Popular Education," *The Abbeville Press and Banner*, January 17, 1883; "Knowledge is Power," *The Abbeville Press and Banner,* March 05, 1884; "Educational Relations of the Races," *The Atlanta Constitution*, January 9, 1884; "Education of Two Races In The South," The Independent, March 21, 1889; *The Newberry Herald and News October 11, 1893*, Newberry had more black in public schools than whites. "To the Friends of Education in Sumter County: The need of our public schools," *The Watchman and Southron*, July 31, 1889.

54. "Negro Education" *The Abbeville Press and Banner*, May 21, 1884.

55. "Does "Confiscation" confiscate?-The Negro Tax" *The Abbeville Press and Banner*, May 14, 1884; The *News and Courier* challenged the Press and Banner for using the word "confiscation," which they contended was done to stir up tension over the two-mill tax and education. However, no property was confiscated and/or sold for raising the school fund for that was not in possession of the state. The *Press and Banner* noted that it was true and that the word confiscation was not placed in the right context but argued that the state confiscated property and then sold property from whites that could not pay their taxes for "negro education." They noted, "while it is true that no land in this county has been 'forfeited to the state,' yet the state officials have exposed thousands of acres to sale, and a great number of parcels of land in this county are now held by titles received from the state because the proper owners were unable to pay this negro tax."

56. William Taylor, "Toward a Definition of Orthodoxy: The Patrician South and the Common Schools." *Harvard Educational Review* 36, no. 4: (420).

57. "The Unstable Foundation," *The Anderson Intelligencer*, July 17, 1890; "The Governor's Message," *Keowee Courier*, December 4, 1889.

58. "Democratic Platform," *Laurens Advertiser*, June 28, 1892.

59. "Governor Ellerbe," *Laurens Advertiser*, January 26, 1897.

Chapter Six: BEFORE 1963

1. Mark E. Lett. "Finney: 'The Law Works'—12 Lives/12 People Changing South Carolina," *The State*, June 5, 2011, pg. 1.

2. Jacquelyn Dowd Hall, "The Long Civil Rights Movement and the Political Uses of the Past," *Journal of American History* 91, no. 4 (March 2005): 1235.

3. Sundiata Cha-Jua and Clarence Lang, "The 'Long Movement' As Vampire: Temporal and Spatial Fallacies in Recent Black Freedom Studies," *The Journal of African American History* 92, no. 2 (Spring 2007): 265–288.

4. Patricia Sullivan, *Days of Hope: Race and Democracy in the New Deal Era* (Chapel Hill: University of North Carolina Press, 1996).

5. Henry Brown, "Plessy v. Ferguson," https://www.ourdocuments.gov/doc.php?flash=false&doc =52, accessed February 19, 2021.

6. Charles Thompson, "Harlan's Great Dissent," https://louisville.edu/law/library/special -collections/the-john-marshall-harlan-collection/harlans-great-dissent#:~:text=The%20one%20lonely %2C%20courageous%20dissenter,the%20races%20in%20rail%20coaches., accessed February 19, 2021.

7. Douglas O. Linder. "Before *Brown*: Charles H. Houston and the *Gaines* Case," https:// web.archive.org/web/20040615204134/http://www.law.umkc.edu/faculty/projects/ftrials/trialheroes /charleshoustonessayF.html, accessed January 1, 2021.

8. Interview with C. Bruce Bailey. "Quest for Civil Rights: C. Bruce Bailey," https://digital.tcl .sc.edu/digital/collection/p17173coll18/id/192/rec/1, accessed on February 19, 2021.

9. "South Carolina Historic Properties Record, Paris Simkins House," http://schpr.sc.gov/index .php/Detail/properties/12193, accessed February 19, 2021.

10. Interview with C. Bruce Bailey.

11. Patricia Sullivan. *Days of Hope: Race and Democracy in the New Deal Era*, p. 100.

12. Interview with C. Bruce Bailey.

13. Jason Morgan Ward, *Defending White Democracy: The Making of a Segregationist Movement and the Remaking of Racial Politics, 1936–1965* (Chapel Hill: University of North Carolina Press, 2011), pp. 38–66.

14. Peter F. Lau, *Democracy Rising: South Carolina and the Fight for Black Equality Since 1865* (Lexington: University Press of Kentucky, 2006), pp. 174–176.

15. Lau, p. 176.

16. Brian Hicks, *In Darkest South Carolina: J. Waties Waring and the Secret Plan That Sparked a Civil Rights Movement* (Charleston: Evening Books, 2018), p. 11.

17. Hicks, p. 160.

18. Henry H. Lesesne. *A History of the University of South Carolina, 1940–2000* (Columbia: University of South Carolina Press, 2001), p. 69.

19. Patricia Sullivan, *Lift Every Voice: The NAACP and the Making of the Civil Rights Movement* (New York: The New Press, 2010).

20. Sullivan, *Lift Every Voice*.

21. *Wrighten v. Board of Trustees*, https://casetext.com/case/wrighten-v-board-of-trustees, accessed February 20, 2021.

22. William C. Hine. *South Carolina State University: A Black Land-Grant College* (Columbia: University of South Carolina Press, 2018).

23. Hine, *South Carolina State University: A Black Land-Grant College*.

24. "John H. Wrighten, Civil Rights Lawyer and Legal Figure, Succumbs," *Jet*, October 28, 1996, p. 18.

25. Alfred D. Moore III, "Turning the Tide of Segregation: The Legacy of the Law School at South Carolina State College," https://www.jbhe.com/2017/09/turning-the-tide-of-segregation-the -legacy-of-the-law-school-at-south-Carolina-state-college/, accessed February 21, 2021.

26. Moore.

27. Jim Felder, "SC State is Owed Special Treatment," *The Times and Democrat,* January 11, 2015, https://thetandd.com/news/opinion/s-c-state-is-owed-special-treatment/article_1278dc90-995b-11e4 -ab51-7b9fdc970777.html, accessed on February 21, 2021.

28. Rebecca L. Miller, "Raised for Activism: Henrie Monteith and the Desegregation of the University of South Carolina," *The South Carolina Historical Magazine,* Vol. 109, No. 2, April 2008, p. 121.

29. Lesesne, pp. 129–131.

30. Doug Williams, "It Was a Long Road to Integration," *Gamecock,* December 6, 1973, p. 1.

31. Alexis Stratton, "Celebrating Black and White Progress," *Gamecock,* September 10, 2003, p. 7.

32. Amanda Coyne, "50 Years Later, September 11, 2013," *Gamecock,* September 11, 2013, p. 1–4.

Chapter Seven: THE LEGACY OF DESEGREGATION

1. Marcia G. Synnott, "Protesting the History of Slavery and Segregation on University Campuses," *The Proceedings of the South Carolina Historical Association, 2017,* pp. 79–91. Dylann Roof demonstrated racial hatred by shooting ten worshippers, nine of whom died, on June 17, 2015, at the Emanuel African Methodist Episcopal Church in Charleston. In response, the South Carolina legislature agreed to remove the nylon Confederate battle flag from the Statehouse grounds and send it, on July 10, to the Confederate Relic Room and Military Museum. A two-thirds vote of the General Assembly is required by the Heritage Act (2000) to remove this Confederate battle flag and any monuments or markers from the State House grounds. Alice Spearman Wright, Interview by Marcia G. Synnott, July 11, 1983, Linville Falls, NC, digitized version and transcript at the Oral History program (OHP), South Caroliniana Library (SCL); [Elizabeth C. Ledeen], The Purpose of the Student Program of the South Carolina Council on Human Relations [SCCHR, c. December 1960]; and Student Program of the SC Council on Human Relations, January 9, 1961, SCCHR, Box 10, file 1961 Student Council, 1960–1969 & n.d., SCL.

2. Howard H. Quint, *Profile in Black and White: A Frank Portrait of South Carolina* (Washington, DC: Public Affairs Press, 1958), pp. 93–94. Marcia G. Synnott, "Carolinians Will Discover the Way— Somewhere between 'Now' and 'Never'" (*Columbia Record,* April 16, 1964), Media & Civil Rights History Symposium, School of Journalism and Mass Communications, University of South Carolina at the Inn at USC, April 3, 2015. Marcia G. Synnott, "Desegregation in South Carolina, 1950–1963: Sometime 'Between "Now" and "Never,"'" in *Looking South: Chapters in the Story of An American Region,* ed. Winfred B. Moore Jr. and Joseph F. Tripp. Contributions in American History, No. 136. (New York; Westport, CT.; London: Greenwood Press, 1989), pp. 51–64.

3. George McMillan, "Integration with Dignity: The Inside Story of How South Carolina Kept the Peace," *Saturday Evening Post,* March 16, 1963, pp. 15–21. Orville Vernon Burton, "Dining with Harvey Gantt: Myths and Realities of 'Integration with Dignity,'" in *Matthew J. Perry: The Man, His Times, and His Legacy,* ed. W. Lewis Burke and Belinda F. Gergel; Introduction by Randall L. Kennedy (Columbia: University of South Carolina Press, 2004), pp. 183–220. Calvin Trillin, *An Education in Georgia: Charlayne Hunter, Hamilton Holmes, and the Integration of the University of Georgia* (Athens: University of Georgia Press: Brown Thrasher Book Series, 1992); Robert A. Pratt, *We Shall Not Be Moved: The Desegregation of the University of Georgia* (Athens: University of Georgia Press, 2010). Charlayne Hunter-Gault, *In My Place* (New York: Vintage Books, 1992); James Silver, *Mississippi: The Closed Society* (Oxford, 1964; University Press of Mississippi, Reprint Edition (May 25, 2012); E. Culpepper Clark, *The Schoolhouse Door: Segregation's Last Stand at the University of*

Alabama (New York: Oxford University Press, 1995). Marcia G. Synnott, "Federalism Vindicated: University Desegregation in South Carolina and Alabama, 1962–1963," *Journal of Policy History* I, no. 3 (July 1989): 298–302; 292–318. Rhoda E. Johnson, "Making A Stand for Change: A Strategy for Empowering Individuals," in *Opening Doors: Perspectives on Race Relations in Contemporary America,* ed. by Harry J. Knopke, Robert J. Norrell, Ronald W. Rogers (Tuscaloosa and London: University of Alabama Press, 1991), 153–164. See also: Craig Steven Wilder*, Ebony and Ivy: Race, Slavery, and the Troubled History of America's Universities* (New York: Bloomsbury Press, 2014); Melissa Kean, *Desegregating Private Higher Education in the South: Duke, Emory, Rice, Tulane, and Vanderbilt* (Baton Rouge: Louisiana State University Press, 2008); and Stefan M. Bradley, *Upending the Ivory Tower: Civil Rights, Black Power, and the Ivy League* (New York: NYU, 2018).

4. "'First in Secession-Last in Desegregation,'" *Record* (Columbia), January 26, 1963, p. 1 (John Hammond Moore, *Columbia and Richland County: A South Carolina Community, 1740–1990* (Columbia: University of South Carolina Press, 1993), p. 425). Henrie Monteith Turner Treadwell, Interview by Marcia G. Synnott, November 14, 1980, Atlanta, Digitized version and transcript, OHP, SCL. Her married name was Turner at the time of this interview. Mrs. R. Rebecca Monteith to Governor Ernest F. Hollings, February 5, 1962, Governor Ernest F. Hollings Papers, file Education, S. C. Department of Archives and History, Columbia. See Rebecca Miller Davis, "Raised for Activism: Henrie Monteith and the Desegregation of the University of South Carolina," *South Carolina Historical Magazine* 109:2 (April 2008): 121–47; and Marcia G. Synnott, "African American Women Pioneers in Desegregating Higher Education," Chapter 7, in Peter Wallenstein, ed., *Higher Education and the Civil Rights Movement, White Supremacy, Black Southerners, and College Campuses* (Gainesville: University Press of Florida, 2008), pp. 199–228. [*Henrie Dobbins] Monteith, a Minor, by her Mother and Next Friend, Mrs. R. Rebecca Monteith, Plaintiff v. The University of South Carolina et al.* (1963), Civil Action No. AC-1005, in the District Court of the United States for the Eastern District of South Carolina, Columbia Division, files of the Legal Defense Fund 1000–1495, New York City. Thomas F. Jones, Interview by Marcia G. Synnott, July 29, 1980, Massachusetts Institute for Technology, Cambridge, MA, digitized version and transcript at the Oral History program, OHP, SCL; and Daniel R. McLeod, Interview by Marcia G. Synnott, Office of the Attorney General, Columbia, SC, May 15, 1980, digitized version and transcript, OHP, SCL. Minutes of the Board of Trustees, January 1, 1961, to January 1, 1962, No. 11, USC; and President Thomas F. Jones Papers, 1963–1964, Box 5, Record Group 2 (President), file Integration, USC Archives and Special Collections, Columbia. WIS-TV News, July 11, 1963, 11:05 P.M.; WIS-TV News, July 20, 1963, 11:05 P.M., Charles Caton reporting, transcript, courtesy of Joe Wieder, Ways and Means Corporation, 1231 Lincoln Street, Columbia, SC. (WIS-TV film footage has been donated to USC.). During Reconstruction, Black women studied at the State Normal School, housed in Rutledge College on campus.

5. Harvey B. Gantt, Interview by Marcia G. Synnott, July 14, 1980, Charlotte, NC, digitized version and transcript, OHP, SCL.

6. Carolyn Click, "USC in '63: Black students step onto campus, into history," *State*, August 17, 2013.

7. James Lewis Solomon, Interview with Solomon and Howard R. Boozer by Marcia G. Synnott, May 13, 1981. South Carolina Commission on Higher Education, 1429 Senate Street, Columbia, SC, digitized version and transcript, OHP, SCL. Dennis Myers, "University Reportedly Has 13 More Negroes," *The State*, Sept. 5, 1964, clipping, SCCHR, Box 40, Colleges and Universities: University of South Carolina.

8. Henrie Monteith Turner Treadwell, Interview by Synnott, November 14, 1980, OHP, SCL.

9. Carolyn Click, "USC in '63: Black students step onto campus, into history," *State*, August 17, 2013. Henrie Monteith Turner Treadwell, Interview by Synnott, November 14, 1980, Atlanta, OHP. SCL. Monteith wrote a letter to the *Gamecock,* published May 10, 1963, thanking students for offers of "personal support" when she desegregated USC.

10. Carolyn Click, "USC in '63: Black students step onto campus, into history." Robert Anderson, as quoted by WIS-TV News, August 6, 1963, 11:05 P.M.; and WIS-TV News, September 11, 1963, 7:00 P.M. and 11:05 P.M., reports, by Charles Caton; WIS-TV News, September 12, 1963, 7:00 P.M. Report, Charles Caton, transcripts, courtesy of Joe Wieder, Ways and Means Corporation, 1231 Lincoln Street, Columbia, SC

11. Henrie Monteith Turner Treadwell, Interview by Synnott, November 14, 1980, Atlanta, OHP, SCL. At the May 1964 meeting of the Columbia Council on Human Relations, Matthew Perry analyzed *Brown v. Board of Education* in "The Desegregation Decision from Ten Years' Perspective," Reports of Program Director, June–August 1964 and September–November 1964, SCCHR Box 9, file Prog. Dir. Report 1964–1969, #289.

12. Spearman, quarterly report, Mar. 1964–May 1964, Box 9, no. 281; Ginnie Good, job report, Career and Service Office, Spring Quarter, 1964; "South Carolina-My Burden," July 33,1964, file "June-July 2, 1964," Box 3. Marcia G. Synnott: "Moderate White Activists and the Struggle for Racial Equality on South Carolina Campuses." In Robert Cohen and David Snyder, eds., *Rebellion in Black and White: Southern Student Activism in the 1960s* (Baltimore: Johns Hopkins University Press, 2013): pp. 114, 116; 106–125.

13. Henrie Monteith Turner Treadwell, Interview by Synnott, November 14, 1980, Atlanta, OHP, SCL. Henrie Monteith, form letter to Dear_____, Dec. 13, 1965, SCCHR, Box 10, file Student Council 1965, SCL. Her uncle, Dr. Henry D. Monteith, served on the South Carolina Council's board of directors, 1965–1968. The Operation Search committee hired a part-time black USC student as a "college counselor." Although he resigned at the end of the 1965 fall semester, he personally contacted the 119 Black South Carolina high school seniors identified by the National Scholarship Achievement program for Negro students (Elizabeth C. Ledeen, Reports of Program Director, March–May 1964, June–August 1964, September 1965–November 1965, and December 1965–February 1966, SCCHR Box 9, file Prog. Dir. Report 964–1969, #289. Minutes, executive committee of the SCCHR, Feb. 25, 1964, Box 8, no. 258.

14. Henrie Monteith Treadwell, Interview by Synnott, November 14, 1980, Atlanta, OHP, SCL. Davis, "Raised for Activism: Henrie Monteith and the Desegregation of the University of South Carolina," *SCHM*, pp. 121–47.

15. Henrie Monteith Turner Treadwell, Interview by Synnott, November 14, 1980, Atlanta, OHP, SCL. Synnott interviewed Dr. Turner on her return from Jackson, Mississippi, where she had interviewed James Meredith, November 8, 1980, and Chancellor John D. Williams at Ole Miss, October 28, 1980, OHP, SCL. Not one member of the University of Mississippi's board of trustees thought Meredith's admission "was a historical moment at all, that it was just another incident involving a black that was trying to crack the segregation barrier." Files on Integration, Papers of President Thomas F. Jones, USC Archives and Special Collections.

16. Henrie Monteith Turner Treadwell, Interview by Synnott, November 14, 1980, Atlanta, OHP, SCL.

17. Henrie Monteith Turner Treadwell, Interview by Synnott, November 14, 1980, Atlanta, OHP, SCL. Synnott interviewed Constance Baker Motley in New York City, September 16, 1980, OHP, SCL. Constance Baker Motley, *Equal Justice Under the Law: An Autobiography* (New York: Farrar, Straus and Giroux, 1998).

18. Henrie Monteith Turner Treadwell, Interview by Synnott, November 14, 1980, Atlanta, OHP, SCL.

19. Henrie Monteith Turner Treadwell, Interview by Synnott, November 14, 1980, Atlanta, OHP, SCL. "Edward W. Brooke III, 95, Senate Pioneer, Is Dead," *New York Times*, Jan 3, 2015.

20. Henrie Monteith Turner Treadwell, Interview by Synnott, November 14, 1980, Atlanta, OHP, SCL. Black students in Marcia G. Synnott's history classes said they still remembered the "difficult integration in their high school," but experienced at USC "an easy relationship, comfortable, between

whites and blacks. "Black First-Year Students at the Nation's Leading Research Universities," *JBHE* Weekly Bulletin, February 20, 2020.

21. James Lewis Solomon, Interview by Synnott, May 13, 1981, Columbia, OHP, SCL.

22. James Lewis Solomon, Interview by Synnott, May 13, 1981, Columbia, OHP, SCL.

23. James Lewis Solomon, Interview by Synnott, May 13, 1981, Columbia, OHP, SCL.

24. James Lewis Solomon, Interview by Synnott, May 13, 1981, Columbia, OHP, SCL.

25. James Lewis Solomon, Interview by Synnott, May 13, 1981, Columbia, OHP, SCL.

26. James Lewis Solomon, Interview by Synnott, May 13, 1981, Columbia, OHP, SCL.

27. James Lewis Solomon, Interview by Synnott, May 13, 1981, Columbia, OHP, SCL.

28. Henry H. Lesesne, *A History of the University of South Carolina, 1940–2000* (Columbia: University of South Carolina Press, 2002), pp. 146–150, 232, 257. Moore, *Columbia and Richland County*, p. 440. Allen Wallace, "Scholarship honors legacy of USC's first African American football coach," February 3, 2020: https://www.sc.edu/USC/posts/2020/02/coach_harold_white_scholarship.php?utm_source=%40USC+Today&utm_campaign=446ccab412-.

29. Lesesne, *A History of the University of South Carolina, 1940–2000*, p. 257.

30. "George Rogers Statue Unveiling and Dedication Saturday University" . . . *www.game cocksonline.com/sports/m-footbl/spec-rel/091115aaa.html* September 11, 2015-Columbia, SC Lesesne, *A History of the University of South Carolina, 1940–2000*, pp. 276, 294. *Marcia G. Synnott*, essay on *George Rogers* in David L. Porter, ed., *Biographical Dictionary of American Sports, Football* (New York; Westport, CT.; London: Greenwood Press, 1987), pp. 509–510.

31. Chloe Barlow, "Students who integrated USC experienced racism, isolation," Civil Rights Series, written February 2, published in the *Gamecock*, Monday, February 3, 2020, VOL. 114, NO. 4, pp. 1, 13; a longer version is available online. Treadwell, Interview by Synnott, November 14, 1980, Atlanta, OHP, SCL. Files on Integration, Papers of President Thomas F. Jones, USC Archives and Special Collections. Henrie Monteith Treadwell, keynote address at "The Origins of Contemporary Desegregation at the University of South Carolina, A Twenty-five Year Retrospective 1963–1988," November 18–19, 1988, videotaped by Dr. Grace Jordan McFadden, who videotaped her interview with Robert Anderson, November 18, 1988. See Dr. McFadden's oral history collection. Treadwell, quoted in the *State*, November 11, 1988, pp. 1D, 5D. In addition to interviewing Dr. Treadwell, in 1980, Synnott heard her presentations at USC in 1988, 2003 (40th anniversary of desegregation), 2010, and 2014 (50th anniversary of desegregation). Davis, "Raised for Activism: Henrie Monteith and the Desegregation of the University of South Carolina," *SCHM*, pp. 121–147. Anderson and Treadwell recalled their experiences at USC in the *Gamecock*, November 21, 1988, republished in *Carolina Voices: Two Hundred Years of Student Experiences*, ed. Carolyn B. Matalene and Katherine C. Reynolds (Columbia: University of South Carolina Press, 2001), pp. 179, 178–181.

32. "Black Enrollments Plummet at the University of South Carolina," *Journal of Blacks in Higher Education* (*JBHE*) Number 59 (Spring 2008): 28–29. Dave Ward, "Black admissions fall by 32 percent," *The Daily Gamecock*, March 19, 2008, 1–2. *The State* "Education Guide," October 15, 2010, p. 6.

33. Brad Muller, "On to Life" June 2012. In 2013, Dr. Henrie Monteith Treadwell published *Beyond Stereotypes in Black and White: How Everyday Leaders Can Build Healthier Opportunities for African American Boys and Men* (Santa Barbara, CA: Praeger, an Imprint of ABC-CLIO, LLC, 2013).

34. Chris Horn, "Alumni, friends mourn historic figure from desegregation era. Remembering Robert Anderson (1944–2009), "*USC Times*, 20, no. 7 (April 23, 2009): 1, 6.

35. Robert Anderson-USC: Museum of Education www.museumofeducation.info › 1963-anderson. Robert G. Anderson Jr. (1944–2009). Matalene and Reynolds, eds., Carolina Voices, p. 179. Robert Anderson, as quoted in the November 21, 1988, *Gamecock. A History of the University of South Carolina* by Henry H. Lesesne, p.148.

36. Eric Adelson, "Jadeveon Clowney walks in footsteps of Henrie Monteith," Yahoo! Sports http//sports.yahoo.com/, August 30, 2013. Treadwell's son Malcolm Turner was named Athletic Director at Vanderbilt in 2019.

37. Carolyn Click, "USC in '63: Black students step onto campus, into history," *The State*, August 17, 2013. List of Events-University of South Carolina, www.sc.edu/desegregation/events.htm. University of South Carolina 50th Anniversary of *Desegregation . . . Garden* Dedication.

38. Minutes-Board of Trustees | University of South Carolina *https://sc.edu/about/offices_and _divisions/*board . . . Plaque Unveiling Commemorates James L. Solomon Jr . . .www.sc.edu › study › mathematics › about › news › solomon_event. Honoring the First James L. Solomon Jr. was the University of . . .www.sc.edu › colleges_schools › artsandsciences › about › news › Apr 22, 2019—Lecture presented by Johnny Houston, co-founder of the National Association of Mathematicians. James L. Solomon and the End of Segregation at the . . . www.ams.org › journals › notices › rnoti-p192. Feb 2, 2020.

39. Chloe Barlow, "Students who integrated USC experienced racism, isolation," *Gamecock*, Monday, February 3, 2020.

40. Celebration of African-American Women's History presented . . . www.onecolumbiasc.com › event › celebration-of-african-american-w . . . Presented by *McKissick Museum*, Columbia SC. Feb 4, 2020. Celebration of *African-American* Women's *History* on USC's campus, featuring Nikky Finney and Dr. Henrie D. Monteith Treadwell. Columbia City of Women announces 2020 honorees . . . www.thecolumbiastar.com › articles › columbia-city-of-women-announces . . . Mar 12, 2020. Professor Finney is the daughter of Chief Justice Ernest A. Finney Jr. (1931–2017), the first African American appointed to the South Carolina Supreme Court since Reconstruction. She won the National Book Award for Poetry in 2011 and was elected in April 2020 to membership in the American Academy of Arts and Sciences. Dr. Treadwell is recognized for her leadership in public health and social justice.

Chapter Eight: PEACE, LOVE, EDUCATION, AND LIBERATION

1. "Orangeburg Violence, Tragedy Arouse Students Around State," *Gamecock*, February 16, 1968, 1; "Picketers Protest Death of Youths," *Gamecock*, February 16, 1968, 1.

2. "Students Flay Policy, Police," *Gamecock*, February 16, 1968, 1.

3. Ibram Rogers (Ibram X. Kendi), *The Black Campus Movement: Black Students and the Racial Reconstitution of Higher Education, 1965–1972* (New York: Palgrave Macmillan, 2012), 1–4.

4. Walter Edgar, *South Carolina: A History* (Columbia: University of South Carolina Press, 1998), 541. Edgar writes that Black South Carolinians were "less strident in their demands than activists elsewhere" because they "did not wish to destroy their towns over principle" due to their being part of their communities and not outsiders. He claims that the state's small size "allowed people to know one another across the racial divide and fostered a 'tradition of civility' that undid segregation—with dignity."; John G. Sproat, "Firm Flexibility: Perspectives on Desegregation in South Carolina" in Robert H. Abzug and Stephen Maizlish, eds., *New Perspectives on Race and Slavery in America: Essays in Honor of Kenneth M. Stampp* (Lexington: University Press of Kentucky, 1986), 180. Sproat describes the incident in Orangeburg as "a momentary, unexpected breakdown of 'control' rather than evidence of a larger pattern of racial animus or resistance to a vibrant movement for progressive change; Marcia Synott echoes this sentiment in her essay entitled "Desegregation in South Carolina: Sometime Between 'Now and Never,'" in Winfred Moore Jr. and Joseph Tripp, eds., *Looking South: Chapters in the Story of an American Region* (New York: Greenwood Press, 1989), 51–64; Jack Bass and Scott Poole, eds., *The Palmetto State: The Making of Modern South Carolina* (Columbia: University of South Carolina Press, 1999), 111–116, 196. Oddly, Jack Bass's documentation of the Orangeburg Massacre and its aftermath did not convince him that South Carolina transitioned into a multicultural society with anything but "relative ease." He credits "progressive governors" in the

1950s and '60s for affecting "profound change . . . with a minimum of turmoil."; Philip Grose, *South Carolina at the Brink: Robert McNair and the Politics of Civil Rights* (Columbia: University of South Carolina Press, 2006), 206. Grose acknowledges that civil rights protests occurred in South Carolina but claims that many of the most important moments, such as the desegregation of Clemson and the University of South Carolina, were highly organized affairs forged through communication between veteran activists, law enforcement officials, and white politicians. Orangeburg, in his view, was caused by the lack of communication between these parties and, most importantly, the interjection of Black youth and college students into ongoing political debates.

5. Rogers, *The Black Campus Movement.*

6. On Voorhees, see Grose, *South Carolina at the Brink*, pp. 263–264.

7. Ibram Rogers, "The Black Campus Movement and the Institutionalization of Black Studies, 1965–1970," *Journal of African American Studies* 16, no. 1 (2012): 36.

8. Eva Moore, "Learning Our Story," *The Post and Courier*, April 3, 2013; "Former City Councilman's Papers Tell Tale of Black Public Life," *Free Times*, February 25, 2015.

9. Luther Battiste III. Interview with the author. Digital recording. Columbia, SC, August 23, 2011.

10. Luther Battiste III. Interview with students from the African American Studies program. Digital recording. Columbia, SC, May 15, 2005.

11. Dr. Harry Wright. Interview with the author. Digital recording. Columbia, SC. August 30, 2011.

12. Interview with Dr. Harry Wright, August 30, 2011.

13. Interview with Dr. Harry Wright, August 30, 2011.

14. Interview with Dr. Harry Wright, August 30, 2011.

15. Luther Battiste III. Interview with the author. Digital recording. Columbia, SC, August 23, 2011; "Eye on the South: Civil Rights," *USC Times*, April 20, 2015, 12.

16. Memorandum from C.H. Witten to Harry Wright, et al., 21 December 1967, Records of the Office of the President, Thomas F. Jones, 1967–1968, Box 10, Folder: Student Affairs/Student Activities: Organizations-Association of Afro-American Students, South Caroliniana Library, University of South Carolina.

17. "Black Power Called 'Way of Modernity,'" *Gamecock*, November 1, 1968, 1. Interview with Harry and Ernestine Walker, October 26, 2012.

18. Interdepartmental Major Program in Afro-American Studies, April 1970, Records of the Office of the President, Thomas F. Jones, 1969–1970, 8.

19. Memorandum from Bruce Marshall to Robert Ochs, May 18, 1971, Records of the Office of the President, Thomas F. Jones, 1970–1971, Box 8, Folder: Faculty and Staff Committees-Afro-American Studies, South Caroliniana Library, University of South Carolina. Marshall explains that the recruitment of qualified Black faculty was the "central preoccupation" of the hiring committee. Only two of the thirty vitae submitted to the American Historical Society and American Political Science Association's placement offices were from qualified Black candidates. "Neither of them indicated an interest in pursuing the matter," Marshall lamented.

20. Interview with Willie Harriford, August 12, 2011.

21. "Education as a Reform Mechanism," *Journal of Correctional Education* 27:4 (1976), 2–4; "USC's first African American Full Professor Continues to Drive Change," *The Daily Gamecock*, April 5, 2020.

22. Interview with Dr. Harry Wright, August 30, 2011; "Big Man on Campus," *Jet*, August 1971, 107. During our interview, the Walkers shared an enlightening story that reveals the limits of racial tolerance at Carolina during this period. During the Homecoming court elections, Harry Walker was approached by another student, David Yarborough, who informed him that the Homecoming King asked who had won the competition. A sitting legislator sought the information because it

was tradition for an elected official to kiss the Queen during halftime of the Homecoming game. "He wanted to make sure that he was not going to have to kiss this girl in front of all these people," Walker explained. There was also an "underground buzz" over the possibility that the Student Body president, a white student, would also have to kiss the Black co-ed. "I just took great solace in understanding that my boyfriend would not do that," Ernestine laughed.

23. Interview with Harry and Ernestine Walker, October 26, 2012.

24. Ibid; Interview with Luther Battiste, August 23, 2011.

25. "Walker, Cannon, and Smith Announce for Student Offices," *Gamecock,* March 3, 1971, p. 5; John Gash, "Smith Campaign is 'Love,'" *Gamecock,* March 22, 1971, p. 5.

26. "Spears Expected to Announce Bid," *Gamecock,* May 19, 1971, 1; Interview with Luther Battiste, August 23, 2011.

27. Interview with Luther Battiste, August 23, 2011; Interview with Harry and Ernestine Walker, October 26, 2012; Campaign poster, "Let's Get Things Together," Luther Battiste Papers, South Carolina Political Collections, University of South Carolina; "Big Man on Campus," 106–7.

28. "Big Man on Campus," 107–108, 110; Interview with Harry and Ernestine Walker, October 26, 2011.

29. "2020 Vision at the University of South Carolina," https://www.change.org/p/university -of-south-Carolina-president-harris-pastides-2020-vision-at-the-university-of-south-Carolina-2, accessed March 15, 2021; Andrew Shain, "USC Students Call for Greater Campus Diversity," *The State,* https://www.thestate.com/news/local/article45053961.html, November 16, 2015, accessed on March 15, 2021.

30. "Group of USC Students Walks out of Class in Protest," https://www.wistv.com/story /30524972/group-of-usc-students-walks-out-of-class-in-protest/, posted November 16, 2015, accessed March 15, 2021.

Chapter Nine: "WHAT'S NEXT, SOUTHERN FRIED CHICKEN?"

1. For more on the Orangeburg Massacre, see Jack Bass and Jack Nelson, *The Orangeburg Massacre,* 2002.

2. "Desecration or Mutilation of United States, Confederate or State Flags," 16–17–220 SC § 16–17–220 (2012).

3. "Desecration or Mutilation of United States, Confederate or State Flags," 16–17–220 SC § 16–17–220 (2012).

4. Carl Stepp, "Dixie Questions Draws Reaction, Little Action" *Gamecock,* February 14, 1969.

5. "Dixie Land." *Gamecock,* February 14 1969.

6. Stefano Harney and Fred Moten, *The Undercommons: Fugitive Planning & Black Study* (Wivenhoe: Minor Compositions, 2013).

7. Stefano Harney and Fred Moten, *The Undercommons: Fugitive Planning & Black Study* (Wivenhoe: Minor Compositions, 2013), 26.

8. Harney and Moten, *The Undercommons,* 26.

9. *Gamecock,* September 11, 1967, p. 2.

10. Robert Cohen, ed., *Rebellion in Black and White: Southern Student Activism in the 1960s* (Baltimore: The Johns Hopkins University Press, 2013), 3.

11. Robert Cohen, ed., *Rebellion in Black and White: Southern Student Activism in the 1960s* (Baltimore: The Johns Hopkins University Press, 2013).

12. Christian McWhirter, "The Birth of Dixie," *New York Times,* March 31, 2012; Opinionator, https://opinionator.blogs.nytimes.com/2012/03/31/the-birth-of-dixie/.

13. Karen L Cox, *Dixie's Daughters: The United Daughters of the Confederacy and the Preservation of Confederate Culture,* 2004.

14. Erin Gregg, "The Silencing of Dixie," student paper for Dr. Valinda W. Littlefield, 2013.

15. Alyssa Constad, "Antagonistic Describes the Scene:" Local News Portrayals of the New Left and the Escalation of Protest at the University of South Carolina, 1970" (University of South Carolina, 2016), 28.

16. Carl Stepp, "Tension Sparks Dixie Incidents," *Gamecock*, February 18, 1969.

17. Stepp, "Tension Sparks Dixie Incidents."

18. Carl Stepp, "Tension Sparks Dixie Incidents," *Gamecock*, February 18, 1969.

19. "Legal Technicalities Confuse Flag Case," *Gamecock*, April 29, 1969.

20. "Legal Technicalities Confuse Flag Case," *Gamecock*, April 29, 1969.

21. Henry Kesane, *A History of the University of Carolina, 1940–2000*. Columbia SC: The University of South Carolina Press.

22. Jack Bass and Jack Nelson, *The Orangeburg Massacre*, 2002.

23. "Dixie Beloved by the Entire Nation," *Gamecock*, February 18, 1969.

24. John Lottich, *Gamecock*, February 18, 1969.

25. "Minority Affairs Post Filled," *Gamecock*, September 28, 1970.

26. "Minority Affairs Post Filled," *Gamecock*, September 28, 1970.

27. *Gamecock*, February 5, 1979.

28. *Gamecock*, February 5, 1979.

29. Thomas F. Jones Papers, Box 6, 1972–1973, Box 6, South Carolinian Library.

30. Thomas F. Jones Papers, Box 6, 1972–1973, Box 6, South Carolinian Library.

31. "Prince: Cheerleading Squad Discriminatory," *Gamecock*, March 1, 1973.

32. *Gamecock*, February 5, 1979, p. 5.

Chapter Ten: "THE RIGHT TIME"

1. "Students Begin Paving Walkways," *State* (Columbia), November 24, 1931. Kappa Sigma Kappa (KSK) and Omicron Delta Kappa (ODK) initiated the effort. Alumnus Deems Haltiwanger, the manager of Richland Shale Products Company, donated the bricks.

2. "Debt Definitely Lifted from Paving Project at University," *State* (Columbia), June 4, 1932. The *Gamecock* noted that students at the University of Southern California began laying brick sidewalks more than a year later. "Better Late," *Gamecock*, January 6, 1933. See also "Students Begin Paving Walkways," *State* (Columbia), November 24, 1931; "Boys Don Overalls, Co-Eds Cry Wares to Pave Walks," *Columbia Record*, November 20, 1931; "Work Begins on Sidewalks of Carolina," *Columbia Record*, November 24, 1931; "Campus Sidewalks Now Over Three Years Old," *Gamecock*, December 14, 1934.

3. 1930 US Federal Census, Columbia, Richland County, SC, District 00325, pg. 8A, Irene Evans, image 14; "City Directory of Columbia, SC" (Columbia: The State Company, 1928), 569; "Hill's Columbia City Directory" (Richmond: Hill Directory Company, 1930), 296. Beginning in 1930, city directories listed Marion Evans as a notary. Both of Evans's children sat for Columbia's premiere Black photographer, Richard Samuel Roberts. See Thomas L. Johnson and Phillip C. Dunn, *A True Likeness: The Black South of Richard Samuel Roberts, 1920–1936* (Columbia: University of South Carolina Press, 2019). Angeline Evans ran Angie Evans Dress Making and Art Shoppee out of the family's residence. See "Accident Fatal to Negro Man," *State* (Columbia), December 22, 1933; "Funeral Invitation," *State* (Columbia), December 23, 1933. His wife remained in their home and later operated the Irene B. Evans Tourist Home, which appeared in the Green Book in the 1940s and '50s.

4. "Babcock Speaks at Annual ODK Banquet May 25," *Gamecock*, June 8, 1945; "Enigmatical Initials 'MEE' on Well-Known Campus Brick Walks Add to Caroliniana," *Gamecock*, April 15, 1947; "Worst Faults Beneath Brick," *Gamecock*, February 27, 1959. By the 1959 retelling, Evans' labor was worth $125, or almost one-tenth of the project's total cost, and he exchanged it for "something my

grandchildren can come and see, and remember me by." At the time, the university remained closed to Black students; even in the 1950s, Evans' grandchildren would not have been welcome to visit the Horseshoe in any capacity other than as laborers.

5. "Enigmatical Initials 'MEE' on Well-Known Campus Brick Walks Add to Caroliniana," *Gamecock*, April 15, 1947.

6. Letter from vertical files, University Archives, South Caroliniana Library, USC.

7. Elizabeth West and Katharine Thompson Allen, *On the Horseshoe: A Guide to the University of South Carolina* (Columbia: University of South Carolina Press, 2001).

8. Henry Lesesne, *History of the University of South Carolina: 1940–2000* (Columbia: University of South Carolina Press, 2001), did not cover the antebellum or Reconstruction periods but does touch upon early attempts at integration beginning in the 1940s.

9. On the historical memory of Reconstruction, see Bruce E. Baker, *What Reconstruction Meant: Historical Memory in the American South* (Charlottesville, University of Virginia Press, 2007); David W. Blight, *Race and Reunion: The Civil War in American Memory* (Cambridge, Mass.: The Belknap Press of Harvard University Press, 2001).

10. Kim Campbell, "Monumental Memory: A Survey of the Markers and Memorials on the University of South Carolina Horseshoe" (report for the Horseshoe Committee, USC, June 4, 2013). Campbell wrote the report for a class taught by Robert Weyeneth and then passed the document to the committee at his suggestion.

11. Harris Pastides, "Invisible No More," speech delivered at the dedication of historical markers on the Horseshoe, December 5, 2017, https://sc.edu/about/our_leadership/president/speeches/2017 _12_speech_at_dedication_of_plaques_honoring_enslaved_workers.php.

12. Pastides, "Invisible No More." In his remarks, Bobby Donaldson acknowledged that "Sancho and his wife" were named Sancho and Lucy Cooper. "Slaves Who Built USC are Virtually Unknown–Now College is Trying to Fix That," *State* (Columbia), December 6, 2017. Historic Site Interpretation Class taught by Robert Weyeneth at USC, "Slavery at South Carolina College, 1801–1865," last updated May 2011, https://delphi.tcl.sc.edu/library/digital/slaveryscc/index.html. This website remains static and largely hidden at the time of this publication.

13. M. LaBorde, *History of the South Carolina College . . .* (Columbia: Peter B. Glass, 1859), v.

14. In 1850, LaBorde enslaved 29 people; by 1860, this number had grown to 36. 1850 US Federal Census-Slave Schedule, Richland County, SC, Maximillian LaBorde, image 1, image 32, Ancestry .com, accessed August 23, 2020. 1860 US Federal Census-Slave Schedule, Richland County, SC, Max[imillian] LaBorde, image 38, Ancestry.com, accessed August 23, 2020.

15. For examples, see LaBorde, *History of the South Carolina College*, 62, 89, 389, 277–79, 284.

16. Edwin L. Green, *A History of the University of South Carolina* (Columbia: The State Company, 1916), 5. Green was forced to omit biographical sketches due to the volume's length.

17. Green, *A History of the University of South Carolina*, 307–8. While descriptions of the antebellum steward's hall and library received entire chapters, the enslaved people who worked there received a brief or no mention.

18. Daniel Walker Hollis, *University of South Carolina: College to University* (Columbia: University of South Carolina Press), vol. 1, 23, 103, 238, 265.

19. For Cooper's influence, see Hollis, *University of South Carolina*, 102. For Thornwell's, see Hollis, *University of South Carolina*, 164–5.

20. This turn-of-phrase is credited to USC Professor Thomas Brown. Robert Weyeneth in email to the authors, October 25, 2020.

21. Robert Weyeneth in discussion with the authors, April 6, 2020.

22. Graham Duncan, "Peculiarly Suited for the Services of the Institution: Slavery at South Carolina College," (March 2006), https://delphi.tcl.sc.edu/library/digital/slaveryscc/papers/duncan

.pdf, accessed August 23, 2020. Duncan's research was the first—and remains the most thorough—attempt to interrogate the role slavery played in shaping the antebellum campus.

23. Evan A. Kutzler, Sara Conlon, Jamie Diane Wilson, and JoAnn Zeise, "Revealing Slavery's Legacy at a Public Institution in the South (Part 1)," *History @ Work* (blog), October 22, 2014, https://ncph.org/history-at-work/revealing-slaverys-legacy-part-1/.

24. Evan A. Kutzler et al., "Revealing Slavery's Legacy at a Public Institution in the South (Part 2)," *History @ Work* (blog), October 24, 2014, https://ncph.org/history-at-work/revealing-slaverys-legacy-part-2/.

25. Kutzler et al., "Revealing Slavery (Part 2)"; Weyeneth in discussion with authors.

26. Weyeneth in discussion with authors. The students used the free website hosting platform Weebly. Part of this migration entailed reworking the introductory page to reflect the project and its findings to new audiences.

27. Weyeneth wrote to both the president, Harris Pastides, and the dean of the college, Mary Anne Fitzpatrick, and spoke to the chair of the department of history, Lawrence Glickman, prior to the semester to ensure that they weren't "blindsided" by the work or any final products, and all expressed nominal support. Weyeneth in discussion with authors. The students also noted that there "could also be greater official acknowledgment of slavery from the university administration." See Evan A. Kutzler et al., "Revealing Slavery's Legacy at a Public Institution in the South (Part 3)," *History @ Work* (blog), October 27, 2014, https://ncph.org/history-at-work/revealing-slaverys-legacy-part-3/.

28. Kutzler et al., "Revealing Slavery"; "Documenting Slavery at South Carolina College: A Collaborative Effort," Tri-State Archivists Conference, Furman University, October 2013. Weyeneth in discussion with authors.

29. Weyeneth in discussion with authors; Kutzler et al., "Revealing Slavery (Part 3)." Two other faculty members, Duncan Buell and Heidi Rae Cooley, spent several semesters developing "Ghosts of the Horseshoe," a mobile interactive based upon the website's findings. See "Ghosts of the Horseshoe," accessed August 26, 2020, http://calliope.cse.sc.edu/ghosts/.

30. Claire Randall, "Rise Up: 2020 Vision and a New Era of Intersectional Grassroots Activism" (undergraduate thesis, USC, 2017), 3.

31. "2020 Vision at the University of South Carolina," accessed August 26, 2020, https://www.change.org/p/university-of-south-Carolina-president-harris-pastides-2020-vision-at-the-university-of-south-Carolina-2. The petition opened with a letter to president Pastides, stating: "The university has done a disservice in failing to address our history of racism that impacts our culture today; USC, like many universities, was built on the backs of enslaved people, and it is necessary for our university to formally recognize this. USC must acknowledge and take responsibility for its history of white supremacy that permeates campus even now."

32. Randall, "Rise Up," 29–30. Attempts to have productive conversations about racism on campus, including racist incidents, began after the murder of Michael Brown in 2014. See "Gamecock Snap sheds new light on 4/20," *Gamecock*, April 21, 2015; "In our opinion: Students must unite through action," *Gamecock*, April 9, 2015.

33. Although created by Chief Diversity Officer John Dozier as a means of providing his position with oversight and guidance and nominally chaired by professor David J. Snyder, DIAC had no clout with the administration without Dozier's endorsement. John Dozier, discussion with authors, May 29, 2020; David J. Snyder, discussion with authors, December 13, 2019.

34. Jennifer Gunter, email to Alyssa Constad, March 29, 2016; Jennifer Gunter, email to Alyssa Constad, April 9, 2016. Constad also drafted a proposal to repurpose the only extant slave quarter as a museum dedicated to the subject. This proposal was never acted upon.

35. Robert Weyeneth, email to David J. Snyder, April 20, 2016. Weyeneth's text included sixteen

names and the unnamed "wife" of Sancho. The additional four names included by Constad and Gunter relied on the determination made by previous graduate students that, for example, Jack, "the first college slave," was a different man than the Jack hired by Marshal Broom from 1858–1860. See "Remembering the Slaves," https://delphi.tcl.sc.edu/library/digital/slaveryscc/remembering-the -slaves.html.

36. Documents presented to authors from David J. Snyder. The draft approved by the subcommittee included the sentence, "Many students and faculty in those years fought to justify the slave system that led to the Civil War." Word substitutions included replacing "slaves" with "enslaved people" or "enslaved workers." Snyder, discussion with authors.

37. Buildings and Grounds Committee, Board of Trustees, USC, minutes, April 21, 2017, https:// sc.edu/about/offices_and_divisions/board_of_trustees/documents/minutes_archive/2017/b-g_042117 .pdf.

38. Buildings and Grounds Committee, minutes, April 21, 2017.

39. For a description of Rutledge and Pinckney's Richland County plantation, see Mark Kinzer, *Nature's Return: An Environmental History of Congaree National Park* (Columbia: University of South Carolina Press, 2017). "Francis Lieber," *South Carolina Encyclopedia,* https://www.scencyclopedia. org/sce/entries/lieber-francis/, accessed August 23, 2020. 1820 US Federal Census, Richland County, South Carolina, Henry W[illiam] DeSaussure, image 2, Ancestry.com, accessed August 23, 2020.

40. "Slaves Integral to USC's History to be Acknowledged," *State* (Columbia), April 22, 2017.

41. "Slaves Integral to USC's History to be Acknowledged." Pastides took credit for appointing the committee "to research the issue and draft language for the plaques." See Avery G. Wilks, "Slaves built USC's earliest buildings, new plaques will acknowledge," *Charlotte Observer,* April 21, 2017, https://www.charlotteobserver.com/news/local/article146113204.html; "USC unveils 2 plaques dedicated to contributions made by slaves to build campus," WIS News, December 5, 2017, https:// www.wistv.com/story/37001329/usc-unveils-2-plaques-dedicated-to-contributions-made-by-slaves-to -build-campus/. The *State* article also noted that the school was raising money for Greener and anticipated the statue's dedication in Fall 2017 (it was not dedicated until February 2018).

42. See interview with Harris Pastides, *State* (Columbia), April 21, 2017, https://www.youtube .com/watch?v=QChEAd3aa3M.

43. See History Task Force Implementation Team, Clemson University, "Final Report" (October 2019), https://www.clemson.edu/about/history/taskforce/documents/HistoryProjectFinalReport .pdf.

44. "Slaves Who Built USC are Virtually Unknown-Now College is Trying to Fix That," *State* (Columbia), December 6, 2017.

45. "New Markers Cite the Role of Slaves at University of South Carolina," ABC 4 News, December 5, 2017, https://abcnews4.com/news/local/new-markers-cite-the-role-of-slaves-at-university -of-south-Carolina.

46. Chris Horn, "History Unveiled," November 30, 2017, updated December 5, 2017, https:// www.sc.edu/USC/posts/2017/12/history_unveiled.php#.XsKJ8JNKg_V.

47. "South Carolina Wills and Probate Records, 1670–1980," Richland County, South Carolina, Box 40, Package 997, Thomas Cooper (1839), images 415–466.

48. 1830 US Federal Census, Richland County, South Carolina, Tho[ma]s Cooper, images 23–24.

49. 1850 US Federal Census-Slave Schedule, Richland County, South Carolina, Matthew J. Williams, Francis Lieber, Maximillian LaBorde, image 1; Richard T. Brumby, image 23; Maximillian LaBorde, William C. Preston, Charles P. Pelham, James H. Thornwell, Robert Henry, image 32. Each member of the 1850 faculty enslaved people. See Green, *A History of the University of South Carolina,* 452.

50. Snyder, discussion with authors.

51. "USC Class Reflects on History of Slavery," *Gamecock,* January 12, 2020.

52. USC, "Our History," accessed July 16, 2020, https://sc.edu/about/our_history/index.php.

53. J. L. Reynolds, "Memoir of Maximilian LaBorde, M.D.," in *History of the South Carolina College*, by LaBorde, 2nd ed. (Charleston: Walker, Evans & Cogswell Printers, 1874), xvi.

54. Reynolds, "Memoir of Maximilian LaBorde, M.D.," xv. On Reynolds, see Hollis, *University of South Carolina*, vol. 2, 65. Reynolds was replaced by none other than Richard T. Greener following his firing in 1873.

55. John Schreiner Reynolds, *Reconstruction in South Carolina, 1865–1877* (1905), repr. in Hollis, *University of South Carolina*, vol. 2, 411–15. See also John Schreiner Reynolds, *Reconstruction in South Carolina, 1865–1877* (Columbia: The State Co., Publishers, 1905), 415.

56. Hollis, *University of South Carolina*, vol. 2, 44.

57. Hollis, *University of South Carolina*, 79. See Wrighten v. Board of Trustees, F. Supp. 948 (1947).

58. The others are located on Greene Street in front of Thomas Cooper Library and on Bull Street.

59. Kaley Brown, Stephanie Gilbert, Justin Harwell, Zoie Horecny, Maclane Hull, Kira Lyle, Helen Marodin, Jennifer Melton, Hannah Patton, Ragan Ramsey, Kate Schoen, Carlie Todd, Paige Weaver, "A Layered History: Interpreting Cultural Resources at Sesquicentennial State Park" (Public History Program, University of South Carolina, Spring 2019), 33.

60. For the full text of this marker and all others established by the commission, see SC Department of Archives and History, *South Carolina Historical Markers: A Guidebook* (Winter 2019).

61. Although the university did not fund or determine the highway markers, it did sanction their placement and even replaced at least one of the signs after it was stolen in the late 1970s. See Campbell, "Monumental Memory," 31.

62. Description of project submitted to Buildings and Grounds Committee, Board of Trustees, USC, January 2012.

63. Katherine Chaddock, email to Greener Memorial Committee, September 2, 2011.

64. Chaddock, email to Lydia Brandt, November 17, 2011.

65. Jessica McCormick, email sent on behalf of Chaddock to Greener Memorial Committee, September 29, 2011.

66. See "Richard T. Greener Symposium & Memorial Ideas Competition," press release, January 26, 2012; competition guidelines, February 8, 2012.

67. The jury included Robin Waites (director, Historic Columbia), Kenny Vinson (president, Black Alumni Association), Susan Schramm (faculty, College of Education), and Bobby Donaldson (faculty, History).

68. Chaddock, email sent to winners of the Richard T. Greener Memorial Ideas Competition, March 28, 2012.

69. Shawn M. Glover, Richard T. Greener Memorial Ideas Competition entry, March 2, 2012.

70. Cooper's name was attached to the library in 1976. See Robert R. Weyeneth, Richard T. Greener Memorial Ideas Competition entry, March 1, 2012.

71. Chaddock, email to Brandt, November 8, 2011; Brandt, email to Chaddock et al., October 15, 2012.

72. Denise Wellman, discussion with Brandt, April 15, 2020.

73. Derek Gruner, discussion with authors, April 21, 2020. On the transformation and preservation of the Horseshoe in the 1970s, see Hal Brunton, *Renovation and Restoration of the USC Horseshoe* (Columbia: Caroline McKissick Dial Endowment, 2002).

74. The choice of Thomas Cooper Library as the site for Greener's statue was concurrent with the discovery and purchase of Greener's law diploma, a rare surviving document from the university's Reconstruction period. See Megan Sexton, "First African-American professor's diploma comes home, October 14, 2013, https://www.sc.edu/uofsc/posts/2013/greener_diploma_2013.php#.X0j752dKia6.

75. Administrators added Cooper's name to the library in 1976. See Weyeneth, Greener Memorial Ideas Competition entry.

76. Chaddock, email to Brandt, May 17, 2012; Chaddock, email to Brandt et al., December 6, 2012; Dean McNally, discussion with Greener Memorial Committee, September 27, 2012; Chaddock, email to Brandt et al., January 14, 2013.

77. See McNally, discussion with committee, September 27, 2012; Brandt, email to Chaddock, October 1, 2012; Brandt, email to Chaddock et al., October 15, 2012.

78. Chaddock, email to Greener committee, February 21, 2013; Jane Przbysz, email to Brandt, May 17, 2013. Conversations with Jane Przybysz, director of the McKissick Museum, and the university's purchasing department determined that the committee did not have to go through the university's strict procurement process if it used unrestricted funds for the monument, but it planned a formal RFP anyway to ensure rigor in the proposals.

79. Request for Proposals: Memorial for Richard T. Greener at the University of South Carolina, Columbia, September 2015.

80. The jury consisted of Amanda Mathis (undergraduate art student), Derek Gruner (university architect), Elizabeth Muth (alumni), John Dozier (diversity officer), Henry Fulmer (director of the South Caroliniana Library). Brandt, personal notes on the jury meeting, December 11, 2013.

81. Jon Hair Studio of Fine Art, LLC, "Request for Proposals, Memorial for Richard T. Greener at the University of South Carolina, Columbia," November 10, 2013. Hair proposed three figurative sculptures and the committee settled on a standing option, a lower base that anticipated climbing students, and a maximum scale of one-and-one-half times life-size after consulting with McNally and Gruner. Brandt, email to Derek Gruner, January 14, 2014; Chaddock, email to Brandt, December 16, 2013; Brandt, email to Jon Hair, February 26, 2014.

82. Chaddock to Anderson et al., April 17, 2014.

83. Brandt, email to Chaddock, April 16, 2014.

84. Thad Moore, "Bronze Cocky Statue Could Cost $100,000," *Daily Gamecock*, November 16, 2012; Denise Wellman, conversation with Brandt; Chaddock, email to Brandt, June 9, 2014.

85. Elaine Delk (formerly of the USC Foundations), discussion with Brandt, April 17, 2020.

86. Chaddock, email to Jane Przybysz, April 10, 2014; Christian Anderson, email to Chaddock and Brandt, February 6, 2014.

87. Anderson, email to Brandt and Chaddock, November 10, 2014.

88. Chaddock, email to Przybysz and Brandt, April 30, 2013; Chaddock, email to Brandt, May 23, 2013.

89. Chaddock, email to Brandt, May 16, 2013.

90. The committee first met with Jancy Houck, then director of development, in October 2014. See Chaddock, email to Brandt and Anderson, October 1, 2014; Chaddock, email to Jancy Houck, March 14, 2015; Buildings and Grounds Committee, Board of Trustees, USC, minutes, February 20, 2015; Board of Trustees, USC, minutes, February 20, 2015.

91. Polly Laffitte (development coordinator), email to Chaddock et al., August 12, 2015; Anderson, email to Brandt and Chaddock, December 2, 2015; "The Richard T. Greener Memorial: A Place of Honor at the Right Time in History," fundraising brochure, May 2016.

92. Chaddock, email to Brandt and Anderson, September 13, 2016.

93. Brittany Franceschina, "Black History Month Kicks Off with Statue Unveiling," *Daily Gamecock*, February 2, 2017. See also Buildings and Grounds Committee, Board of Trustees, USC, minutes, September 16, 2016; Avery Wilks, "Large Gamecock Sculpture planned for Williams-Brice Stadium," *State* (Columbia), September 16, 2016; Rodney Welch, "USC Approves Statue to School's First Black Professor," *Free Times* (Columbia), October 5, 2016. At the same meeting, the board approved a $995,000 statue of a Gamecock, to be placed in front of Williams-Brice Stadium (also "funded with gifts" and by artist Jon Hair).

94. Program, Inaugural Richard T. Greener Symposium, USC, February 21, 2018.

95. Alexis Frazier, "USC Unveils Statue of First African-American Professor," ABC Columbia, February 21, 2018, https://www.abccolumbia.com/2018/02/21/usc-unveils-statue-first-african-american-professor/.

96. Chaddock, email to Elizabeth West et al., February 12, 2018.

97. "The Richard T. Greener Memorial: A Place of Honor at the Right Time in History."

98. Katherine Reynolds Chaddock, *Uncompromising Activist: Richard Greener, First Black Graduate of Harvard College* (Baltimore: Johns Hopkins University Press, 2017).

99. Anderson, email to Chaddock and Brandt, July 26, 2014.

100. Christian K. Anderson and Lydia Mattice Brandt, "Excellence Initiative Proposal to create the Richard T. Greener Symposium Series," February 1, 2018.

101. Office of the Provost, University of South Carolina, "Excellence Initiative," accessed August 27, 2020, https://www.sc.edu/about/offices_and_divisions/provost/academicpriorities/special_initiatives/excellenceinitiative/index.php; Jeff Stensland, "USC's Excellence Initiative launches 8 high-impact projects," *USCToday*, April 2, 2019, https://www.sc.edu/uofsc/posts/2019/03/excellence_initiative_launces_eight_new_projects.php#.XqB2atNKimk.

102. Harris Pastides, "A Different Approach to the Confederate Statue Debate," *Charlotte Observer*, March 13, 2018.

103. One exception was the student symposium, conceived by Valinda W. Littlefield, that followed the unveiling of the Desegregation Commemorative Garden. Some of those papers appear in expanded form in this volume. See also https://www.sc.edu/desegregation/docs/AfricanAmerican ExperiencesAtUSC-StudentPresentations.pdf.

104. Hilary Green, "The Burden of the University of Alabama's Hallowed Grounds," *Public Historian* 42, no. 4 (November 2020): 28–40. Green undertook this work in earnest in 2015 and did so despite the emotional and physical toll that this type of labor entailed for her as a scholar of color. As she notes, her work was not compensated or considered part of her service requirement for tenure.

105. Katharine Thompson Allen, conversation with Hannah White, February 25, 2021. White created a tour of African American history available at https://hannahjw456.wixsite.com/uofscaatour. White's tour is one of the only known campus tours to include the Tree of Knowledge on Green Street in front of Russell House, a meeting place for Black students on campus 1968. The Association for African American students dedicated the tree in 1995 and received approval from the board of trustees for a new plaque in 2018. See "Hannah White plans African American history tour of USC, partners with Visitor Center," *Daily Gamecock*, July 12, 2020.

106. University of South Carolina, "Presidential Commission on University History," accessed August 27, 2020, https://sc.edu/about/our_history/presidential_commission.php. https://sc.edu/about/our_leadership/president/presidential_communications/2020_sotu.php

107. Wayback machine, June 24, 2020, https://sc.edu/about/offices_and_divisions/housing/residence-halls/womens_quad/index.php. The university also uses acronyms for the names of the Wade Hampton dormitory, McClintock dormitory, and Strom Thurmond Fitness Center.

CONCLUSION

1. Reggie Anderson, "A'ja Wilson says Grandmother Wasn't Even Allowed to Walk on USC Campus," *News19*, January 19, 2021.

2. "Interim Report," https://www.sc.edu/about/our_history/university_history/presidential_commission/commission_reports/interim_report/index.php, posted February 26, 2021, accessed March 8, 2021.

3. "Interim Report," accessed March 8, 2021.

4. One example of groundbreaking research in this direction can be found in the Andrew W. Mellon grant-supported "Invisible Histories Project." "Queer Southern History: Building

Community Archives to Preserve a Diverse LGBTQ+ Legacy," https://mellon.org/shared-experiences-blog/queer-southern-history-building-community-archives-preserve-diverse-lgbtq-legacy/, accessed March 8, 2021.

5. "Interim Report," accessed March 8, 2021.

6. Audrey Williams June, "U. of South Carolina Wants Its Share of Black Students to Mirror Black Population in the State," June 25, 2020.

AFTERWORD

1. Deirdre Cooper Owens, *Medical Bondage: Race, Gender, and the Origins of Medical Gynecology* (Athens, GA: University of Georgia Press, 2017).

Selected Bibliography

ARCHIVES

Cambridge, Massachusetts
Harvard University

Harvard Class of 1870 Class Book

Columbia, South Carolina
South Carolina Department of Archives and History

Report of Committee on Schools on Certain, Representations Made by the Trustees and Faculty of
the South Carolina College Asking that Jack, a Slave, may be Purchased for the Institution's Use.

South Caroliniana Library, University of South Carolina

Accounts and Receipts
Fisk P. Brewer Papers
James Carroll LaBorde Papers
Minutes of the Board of Trustees of the South Carolina College
Minutes of the Faculty of the South Carolina College
Miscellaneous 19th and 20th Century materials
Oral History Project
Peculiarly Suited for the Services of the Institution, 2006 [typescript]
Records of the Office of the President, Thomas F. Jones
Records of the Vice President of Finance and Office of the Treasurer
Report of the Professors of the South Carolina College Respecting the Commons
Richard Theodore Greener Papers
Steward's Hall Box 1, Commons Folder
South Carolina Council of Human Relations
Treasurer's records

South Carolina Political Collections, University of South Carolina

Luther Battiste Papers

University of South Carolina, Digital Libraries

Moving Images and Research Collection, Quest for Civil Rights Collection

New Orleans, Louisiana
Amistad Research Center, Tulane University

Edward Franklin Williams Papers

Selected Bibliography

Raleigh, North Carolina
North Carolina State Archives

S. P. Smith Will

PUBLISHED PRIMARY SOURCES

Acts of the State of Tennessee, Passed at the Second Session of the Thirty-Fourth General Assembly, for the Years 1865–66. Nashville, TN: S. C. Mercer, 1866.

Afro-American Encyclopedia; or, the Thoughts, Doings, and Sayings of the Race. Nashville, TN: Haley and Florida, 1895.

Annual Catalogue of the Normal and Preparatory Department of Howard University, Washington, DC, 1867. Washington, DC: Gibson Brothers, n.d.

Arnett, Benjamin W. *The Budget: Containing the Annual Reports of the General Officers of the African M. E. Church of the United States of America.* Xenia, OH: Torchlight Printing Company, 1881.

Brewer, Fisk Parsons, and William P. Vaughn. "South Carolina University—1876 of Fisk Parsons Brewer." *The South Carolina Historical Magazine* 76 (4) (1975): 225–31.

By-Laws of the South Carolina College: Revised and Adopted by the Board of Trustees at the Regular Meeting in May, 1853."

Catalogue of the Officers and Students of Howard University, District of Columbia, 1868–69. Washington, DC: Judd & Detweiler, 1869.

Catalogue of the Officers and Students of Howard University, District of Columbia, 1869–70. Washington, DC: Judd & Detweiler, 1870.

Catalogue of the Officers and Students of Howard University for the Academic Year 1873–74. Washington, DC: O. H. Reed, 1874.

The Congregational Year-Book, 1893. Boston: Congregational Sunday School and Publishing Society, 1893.

The Congregational Year-Book, 1894. Boston: Congregational Sunday School and Publishing Society, 1894.

The Congregational Year-Book, 1895. Boston: Congregational Sunday School and Publishing Society, 1895.

Cooper, Thomas. *Statutes at Large of South Carolina*, Volume 5. Columbia, SC: A.S. Johnston, 1970.

First Presbyterian Church of Columbia, Session Book, 1820–1821

Greener, Richard Theodore. *Charles Sumner: The Idealist, Statesman and Scholar, An Address Delivered on Public Day, June 29, 1874 at the Request of the Faculty of the University of South Carolina.* Columbia, SC: Republican Printing Company, 1874.

Greener, Richard T. "The White Problem." *Lend a Hand: A Record of Progress* 12 (May 1894): 366.

Heard, William Henry. *From Slavery to the Bishopric in the A.M.E. Church, An Autobiography.* Philadelphia: A.M.E. Book Concern, 1928.

LaBorde, Maximilian. *History of the South Carolina College from its Incorporation December 19, 1801, to Nov. 25, 1857, Including Sketches of its Presidents and Professors with an Appendix.* Columbia, SC: Peter B. Glass, 1859.

LaBorde, Maximilian. *History of the South Carolina College with an Appendix Prefaced by a Life of the Author by J.L. Reynolds, D.D.* Charleston, SC: Walter, Evans, and Cogswell, 1874.

Laws of the South Carolina College: Adopted by the Board of Trustees at their Annual Meeting in Dec. 1835. Chapter XV: Of the Marshall, and the College Buildings, Columbia, SC.

Laws of the South Carolina College: Provisionally Adopted by the Trustees at their Annual Meeting in Dec. 1806. Columbia, SC: D. and J.J. Faust, 1807.

Majors, Monroe Alphus. *Noted Negro Women: Their Triumphs and Activities.* Chicago: Donohue and Henneberry, 1893.

Meriwether, Colyer. "Collegiate Education." In *History of Higher Education in South Carolina, With a Sketch of the Free School System.* Washington; Bureau of Education, 1889.

The Sixty-Fourth Report of the American Home Missionary Society, Presented to the Executive Committee, at the Annual meeting, June 3, 1890. New York: The American Home Missionary Society, 1890.

United States Census, 1800, 1810, and 1820

US House of Representatives, *Testimony Taken by the Select Committee on the Recent Election in South Carolina,* 44th Congress, 2nd Session.

Woodruff, J. *Proceedings of the Constitutional Convention of South Carolina; Including the Debates and Proceedings.* Charleston, SC: Denny and Perry, 1868.

SECONDARY BOOKS AND ACADEMIC ARTICLES

Anderson, Christian K. "The South Carolina Military Academy During the Civil War: Training Ground for the Confederacy." In *Persistence Through Peril: Episodes of College Life and Academic Endurance in the Civil War South,* ed. R. Eric Platt and Holly Foster (Jackson: University Press of Mississippi, 2021).

Anderson, James D. *The Education of Blacks in the South, 1860–1935.* Chapel Hill: University of North Carolina Press, 1988.

Ardizzone, Heidi. *An Illuminated Life: Belle da Costa Greene's Journey from Prejudice to Privilege.* New York: W.W. Norton, 2007.

Bass, Jack, and Jack Nelson, *The Orangeburg Massacre,* 2002. Macon, GA: Mercer University Press, 2002.

Bass, Jack, and Scott Poole, eds. *The Palmetto State: The Making of Modern South Carolina.* Columbia: University of South Carolina Press, 1999.

Beaulieu, Elizabeth Ann, ed. *Writing African American Women: An Encyclopedia of Literature by and about Women of Color, Volume 1: A-J.* Westport, CT: Greenwood Press, 2006.

Bethell, John T., Richard M. Hunt, and Robert Shenton. *Harvard: A to Z.* Cambridge, MA: Harvard University Press, 2004.

Bond, Horace Mann. *The Education of the Negro in the American Social Order.* New York: Octagon Books, 1934.

Bradley, Stefan. *Harlem Vs. Columbia: Black Student Power in the Late 1960s.* Urbana: University of Illinois Press, 2009.

———. *Upending the Ivory Tower: Civil Rights, Black Power, and the Ivy League.* New York: New York University Press, 2019.

Brooks, F. Erik. *Pursuing a Promise: A History of African Americans at Georgia Southern University.* Macon, GA: Mercer University Press, 2006.

Buell, Duncan A., and Heidi Rae Cooley. "Critical Interactives: Improving Public Understanding of Institutional Policy." *Bulletin of Science, Technology & Society* 20, no. 10 (Spring 2012): 1–8.

Burke, W. Lewis, Jr. *All for Civil Rights: African American Lawyers in South Carolina 1868–1968.* Athens: University of Georgia Press, 2017.

Burton, Orville Vernon. "Dining with Harvey Gantt: Myths and Realities of 'Integration with Dignity,'" *Matthew J. Perry: The Man, His Times, and His Legacy,* ed. W. Lewis Burke and Belinda F. Gergel; Introduction by Randall L. Kennedy. Columbia: University of South Carolina Press, 2004.

Butchart, Ronald E. *Schooling the Freed People: Teaching, Learning, and the Struggle for Black Freedom, 1861–1876.* Chapel Hill: University of North Carolina Press, 2010.

Butchart, Ronald E., and Amy F. Rolleri. "Secondary Education and Emancipation: Secondary Schools for Freed Slaves in the American South, 1862–1875," *Paedagogica Historica* 40, no. 1–2 (2004): 157–81.

Catalogue of the Officers and Students of the Chicago Theological Seminary. Chicago, IL, 1877–78.

Catalogue of the Officers and Students of the Chicago Theological Seminary. Chicago, IL, 1878–79.

Catalogue of the Officers and Students of Howard University, District of Columbia, 1869–70. Washington, DC: Judd & Detweiler, 1870.

Catalogue of the Officers and Students of Howard University, District of Columbia, 1871–72. Washington, DC: Reed & Woodward, Printers, 1872.

Catalogue of the Officers and Students of Howard University, District of Columbia, 1874–76. Washington, DC: O. H. Reed, 1876.

Chaddock, Katherine Reynolds. *Uncompromising Activist: Richard Greener, First Black Graduate of Harvard College.* Baltimore, MD: Johns Hopkins University Press, 2017.

Cha-Jua, Sundiata, and Lang, Clarence "The 'Long Movement' As Vampire: Temporal and Spatial Fallacies in Recent Black Freedom Studies," *Journal of African American History* 92, no. 2 (2007): 265–88.

Charron, Katherine Mellen. *Freedom's Teacher: The Life of Septima Clark.* Chapel Hill: University of North Carolina Press, 2009.

Cohen, Michael David. *Reconstructing the Campus: Higher Education and the American Civil War.* Charlottesville, VA: University of Virginia Press, 2012.

Conlan, Timothy J. *Intergovernmentalizing the Classroom: Federal Involvement in Elementary and Secondary Education.* Advisory Commission on Intergovernmental Relations, 1981.

Constad, Alyssa. "Antagonistic Describes the Scene:" Local News Portrayals of the New Left and the Escalation of Protest at the University of South Carolina, 1970" (master's thesis, University of South Carolina, 2016).

Cooper, William J. *The Conservative Regime: South Carolina, 1877–1890.* Columbia: University of South Carolina Press, 2005.

Cornelius, Janet Duitsman. *When I Can Read My Title Clear: Literacy, Slavery, and Religion in the Antebellum South.* Columbia: University of South Carolina Press, 1991.

Crofts, Daniel W. "The Black Response to the Blair Education Bill." *Journal of Southern History* 37, no. 1 (1971): 41–65.

Cromwell, Adelaide M. *Unveiled Voices, Unvarnished Memories: The Cromwell Family in Slavery and Segregation, 1692–1972.* Columbia: University of Missouri Press, 2006.

Daniels, Maurice C. *Ground Crew: The Fight to End Segregation at Georgia State.* Athens: University of Georgia Press, 2019.

Du Bois, W. E. B. *Black Reconstruction in America.* New York: The Free Press, 1935/1998.

Edgar, Walter. *South Carolina: A History.* Columbia: University of South Carolina Press, 1998.

Eelman, Bruce W. *Entrepreneurs in the Southern Upcountry: Commercial Culture in Spartanburg, South Carolina, 1845–1880.* Athens: University of Georgia Press, 2008.

Egerton, Douglas R. *The Wars of Reconstruction: The Brief, Violent History of America's Most Progressive Era.* New York: Bloomsbury Press, 2014.

Fitchett, E. Horace. "The Influence of Claflin College on Negro Family Life." *Journal of Negro History* 29, no. 4 (1944): 429–60.

Foner, Eric. *Reconstruction: America's Unfinished Revolution, 1863–1877.* New York: Harper and Row, 1988.

Fordman, Damon L. *Voices of Black South Carolina: Legend and Legacy.* Charleston, SC: History Press, 2009.

Fulmer, Henry G. "Richard T. Greener and the Radical University Library." *Ex-Libris.* University of South Carolina Libraries, 1995.

Gates, Henry Louis, Jr. *Stony the Road: Reconstruction, White Supremacy, and the Rise of Jim Crow.* New York: Penguin Press, 2019.

Ginsberg, Benjamin. *Moses of South Carolina: A Jewish Scalawag During Radical Reconstruction.* Baltimore, MD: Johns Hopkins University Press, 2010.

Gordon, Asa H. *Sketches of Negro Life and History in South Carolina* [Second Edition]. Columbia: University of South Carolina Press, 1929/1971.

Gore, Blinzy L. *On a Hilltop High: The Origin and History of Claflin College to 1984.* Spartanburg, SC: The Reprint Company Publishers, 1993.

Green, Edwin Luther. *A History of the University of South Carolina.* Columbia, SC: The State Company, 1916.

Green, Hilary. "The Burden of the University of Alabama's Hallowed Grounds," *Public Historian* 42, no. 4 (2020): 28–40.

Grose, Philip. *South Carolina at the Brink: Robert McNair and the Politics of Civil Rights.* Columbia: University of South Carolina Press, 2006.

Hall, Jacquelyn Dowd. "The Long Civil Rights Movement and the Political Uses of the Past." *Journal of American History* 91, no. 4 (2005): 1233–63.

Harney, Stefano, and Fred Moten. *The Undercommons: Fugitive Planning & Black Study.* Wivenhoe, England: Minor Compositions, 2013.

Harris, Leslie M., James T. Campbell, and Alfred L. Brophy, eds. *Slavery and the University: Histories and Legacies.* Athens: University of Georgia Press, 2015.

Harter, Dale F. "For the Love of Books: Richard T. Greener's Brief Career as the University of South Carolina's First African-American University Librarian." *Proceedings of the South Carolina Historical Association* (1997): 54–60.

Hartmut, Keil. "Francis Lieber's Attitudes on Race, Slavery, and Abolition." *Journal of American Ethnic History* 28, no. 1 (2008): 13–33.

Hicks, Brian. *In Darkest South Carolina: J. Waties Waring and the Secret Plan That Sparked a Civil Rights Movement.* Charleston, SC: Evening Books, 2018.

Hine, William C. "Black Politicians in Reconstruction Charleston, South Carolina: A Collective Study." *The Journal of Southern History* 49, no. 4 (1983): 555–84.

———, *South Carolina State University: A Black Land-Grant College in Jim Crow America.* Columbia: University of South Carolina Press, 2018.

Hollars, B. J. *Opening the Doors: The Desegregation of the University of Alabama and the Fight for Civil Rights in Tuscaloosa.* Tuscaloosa: University of Alabama Press, 2013.

Hollis, Daniel Walker. *University of South Carolina: Volume 1, South Carolina College.* Columbia: University of South Carolina Press, 1951.

Hollis, Daniel Walker. *University of South Carolina: Volume 2, South Carolina College.* Columbia: University of South Carolina Press, 1956.

Holt, Thomas. *Black Over White: Negro Political Leadership in South Carolina during Reconstruction.* Urbana: University of Illinois Press, 1977.

Kantrowitz, Stephen. *Ben Tillman and the Reconstruction of White Supremacy.* Chapel Hill: University of North Carolina Press, 2000.

Kean, Melissa. *Desegregating Private Higher Education in the South: Duke, Emory, Rice, Tulane, and Vanderbilt.* Baton Rouge: Louisiana State University Press, 2008.

Kimball, Bruce A. "The Langdell Problem: Historicizing the Century of Historiography, 1906–2000s." *Law and History Review* 22, no. 2 (2004): 277–337.

Knight, Edgar Wallace. "The Schools in South Carolina from 1870 to 1876." In *The Influence of Reconstruction on Education in the South.* New York: Teachers College, Columbia University, 1913.

Lau, Peter F., *Democracy Rising: South Carolina and the Fight for Black Equality Since 1865.* Lexington: University Press of Kentucky, 2006.

Lesesne, Henry H. *A History of the University of South Carolina, 1940–2000*. Columbia: University of South Carolina Press, 2001.

Levin, Kevin M. *Searching for Black Confederates: The Civil War's Most Persistent Myth*. Chapel Hill: University of North Carolina Press, 2019.

Link, William A. *The Paradox of Southern Progressivism, 1880–1930*. Chapel Hill: University of North Carolina Press, 2000.

Litwack, Leon F. *Trouble in Mind: Black Southerners in the Age of Jim Crow*. New York: Vintage, 1999.

Logan, Rayford W. *Howard University: The First Hundred Years 1867–1967*. New York: New York University Press, 1969.

McCormick, Jacob L. "The Extracurriculum of the University of South Carolina: The First Century, 1805–1906" (PhD diss., University of South Carolina, 2005).

McInnis, Maurie D., and Lois P. Nelson, eds. *Educated in Tyranny: Slavery at Thomas Jefferson's Virginia*. Charlottesville: University of Virginia Press, 2019.

McPherson, James M. *The Abolitionist Legacy: From Reconstruction to the NAACP*. Princeton, NJ: Princeton University Press, 1975.

Mancini, Matthew J. "Francis Lieber, Slavery, and the 'Genesis' of the Laws of War." *Journal of Southern History* 77, No. 2 (May 2011): 325–48.

Martin, Jonathan D. *Divided Mastery: Slave Hiring in the American South*. Cambridge, MA: Harvard University Press, 2004.

Matalene, Carolyn B., and Katherine Chaddock Reynolds, eds. *Carolina Voices: Two Hundred Years of Student Experiences*. Columbia: University of South Carolina Press, 2001.

Merchant, Bristow. "The Slaves Who Built USC Are Virtually Unknown. How the College Is Trying to Fix That." *State*, https://www.thestate.com/news/local/education/article188153414.html. December 5, 2017.

Miller, Rebecca L. "Raised for Activism: Henrie Monteith and the Desegregation of the University of South Carolina." *The South Carolina Historical Magazine* 109, No. 2 (April 2008): 121–47.

Moore, John Hammond. *Columbia & Richland County: A South Carolina Community, 1740–1990*. Columbia: University of South Carolina Press, 1993.

Morison, Samuel Eliot. *Three Centuries of Harvard*. Cambridge, MA: The Belknap Press of Harvard University Press, 1936.

Mounter, Michael Robert. "Richard Theodore Greener: The Idealist, Statesman, Scholar and South Carolinian" (PhD diss., University of South Carolina, 2002).

Nolen, Claude H. *African American Southerners in Slavery, Civil War and Reconstruction*. Jefferson, NC: McFarland, 2005.

Padgett, James A. "Ministers to Liberia and their Diplomacy." *Journal of Negro History* 22, no. 1 (1937): 50–92.

Page, Yolanda, ed. *Encyclopedia of African American Women Writers*, Volume 1. Westport, CT: Greenwood Press, 2007.

Parry, Tyler D. "The Radical Experiment of South Carolina: The History and Legacy of a Reconstructed University." *Journal of African American History* 105, no. 4 (2020): 539–66.

Potts, John F., Sr. *A History of the Palmetto Education Association*. Washington, DC: National Education Association, 1978.

Powers, Bernard F., Jr. *Black Charlestonians: A Social History, 1822–1885*. Fayetteville: University of Arkansas Press, 1994.

Pratt, Robert A. *We Shall Not Be Moved: The Desegregation of the University of Georgia*. Athens: University of Georgia Press, 2002.

Quint, Howard H., *Profile in Black and White: A Frank Portrait of South Carolina*. Washington, DC: Public Affairs Press, 1958.

Randall, Claire. "Rise Up: 2020 Vision and a New Era of Intersectional Grassroots Activism" (senior thesis, University of South Carolina, 2017).

Reynolds, Jason S. *Reconstruction in South Carolina, 1865–1877.* Columbia, SC: The State Company, 1905.

Rogers, Ibram (Ibram X. Kendi), *The Black Campus Movement: Black Students and the Racial Reconstitution of Higher Education, 1965–1972.* New York: Palgrave Macmillan, 2012.

———, "The Black Campus Movement and the Institutionalization of Black Studies, 1965–1970," *Journal of African American Studies* 16, no. 1, 2012.

Roper, John H. "A Reconsideration: The University of South Carolina During Reconstruction (1974)." In *South Carolina in the Civil War and Reconstruction Eras: Essays from the Proceedings of the South Carolina Historical Society,* ed. Michael Brem Bonner and Fritz Hamer (Columbia: University of South Carolina Press, 2016), 184–94.

———, "The Radical Mission: The University of South Carolina in Reconstruction" (master's thesis, University of North Carolina at Chapel Hill, 1973).

Schlesinger, Andrew. *Veritas: Harvard College and the American Experience.* Chicago: Ivan R. Dee, 2005.

Scully, Amy. "Josiah Morse, The First Jewish Professor at the University of South Carolina: The Role of Mixed Bias in the American University System" (master's thesis, University of South Carolina, 2011).

Shields Davis S., ed. *Pioneering American Wine: Writings of Nicholas Herbemont, Master Viticulturist.* Athens: University of Georgia Press, 2009.

Simms, William Gilmore. *The History of South Carolina.* Columbia, SC: The State Company, 1918.

Slater, Robert Bruce. "The Blacks who First Entered the World of White Higher Education," *Journal of Blacks in Higher Education,* No. 4 (summer, 1994): 47–56.

Slater, Robert Bruce. "The First Black Graduates of the Nation's 50 Flagship State Universities." *Journal of Blacks in Higher Education* 13 (Autumn, 1996): 72–85.

Sollors, Werner, Caldwell Titcomb, Thomas A. Underwood, and Randall Kennedy, eds. *Blacks at Harvard: A Documentary History of African-American Experience at Harvard and Radcliffe.* New York: New York University Press, 1993.

Sproat, John H., "Firm Flexibility: Perspectives on Desegregation in South Carolina," in Robert H. Abzug and Stephen Maizlish, eds. *New Perspectives on Race and Slavery in America: Essays in Honor of Kenneth M. Stampp.* Lexington: University Press of Kentucky, 1986.

Sterling, Dorothy, ed. *The Trouble They Seen: Black People Tell the Story of Reconstruction.* Garden City, NY: Doubleday, 1976.

Sternhell, Yael A. *Routes of War: The World of Movement in the Confederate South.* Cambridge, MA: Harvard University Press, 2012.

Synott, Marcia G. "Protesting the History of Slavery and Segregation on University Campuses," *The Proceedings of the South Carolina Historical Association,* 2017, pp. 79–91.

———, "Desegregation in South Carolina, 1950–1963: Sometime 'Between "Now" and "Never,"'" in *Looking South: Chapters in the Story of An American Region,* ed. Winfred B. Moore, Jr. & Joseph F. Tripp. Contributions in American History, No. 136. New York; Westport, CT: London: Greenwood Press, 1989.

———, "African American Women Pioneers in Desegregating Higher Education," Chapter 7, in Peter Wallenstein, ed., *Higher Education and the Civil Rights Movement, White Supremacy, Black Southerners, and College Campuses.* Gainesville: University Press of Florida, 2008.

———, "Moderate White Activists and the Struggle for Racial Equality on South Carolina Campuses." In Robert Cohen and David Snyder, eds., *Rebellion in Black and White: Southern Student Activism in the 1960s.* Baltimore, MD: Johns Hopkins University Press, 2013.

Sugrue, Michael. "'We Desired Our Future Rulers to Be Educated Men': South Carolina College, the Defense of Slavery, and the Development of Secessionist Politics." In Roger Geiger (ed.), *The American College in the Nineteenth Century.* Nashville, TN: Vanderbilt University Press, 2000.

Sullivan, Patricia. *Days of Hope: Race and Democracy in the New Deal Era.* Chapel Hill: University of North Carolina Press, 1996.

————, *Lift Every Voice: The NAACP and the Making of the Civil Rights Movement.* New York: The New Press, 2010.

Taylor, Amy Murrell. *Embattled Freedom: Journeys through the Civil War's Slave Refugee Camps.* Chapel Hill: University of North Carolina Press, 2018.

Thomas, Rhondda Robinson. *Call My Name, Clemson.* Iowa City: University of Iowa Press, 2020.

Tindall, George Brown. "Negroes in Politics." In *South Carolina Negroes, 1877–1900.* Columbia: University of South Carolina Press, 1952.

Tuttle, Jon. *Two South Carolina Plays.* Spartanburg, SC: Hub City Writers Project, 2009.

Underwood, James Lowell, and W. Lewis Burke, eds. *At Freedom's Door: African American Founding Fathers and Lawyers in Reconstruction South Carolina.* Columbia: University of South Carolina Press, 2000.

Vaughn, William P. "Integration in Public Higher Education." In *Schools for All: The Blacks and Public Education in the South, 1865–1877.* Lexington: University of Kentucky Press, 1974.

Walker, Richard Lee. "Ghosts of the Horseshoe: A Mobilization of a Critical Interactive" (PhD diss., University of South Carolina, 2014).

Ward, Jason Morgan. *Defending White Democracy: The Making of a Segregationist Movement and the Remaking of Racial Politics, 1936–1965.* Chapel Hill: University of North Carolina Press, 2011.

Weisberger, Bernard A. "The Dark and Bloody Ground of Reconstruction Historiography." *The Journal of Southern History* 25, no.4 (November 1959): 427–47.

Weiss, Gerhard. "The Americanization of Franz Lieber and the Encyclopedia Americana." In Lynne Tatlock and Matt Erlin, Eds. *German Culture in Nineteenth-Century America Book Subtitle: Reception, Adaptation, Transformation.* Rochester, NY: Camden House, 2005.

West, Elizabeth Cassidy, and Katharine Thompson Allen. *On the Horseshoe: A Guide to the Historic Campus of the University of South Carolina.* Columbia: University of South Carolina Press, 2015.

White, Pamela Mercedes. "Free and Open: The Radical University of South Carolina, 1873–1877" (master's thesis, University of South Carolina, 1975).

Wilder, Craig Steven. *Ebony and Ivy: Race, Slavery, and the Troubled History of America's Universities.* New York: Bloomsbury, 2013.

Williamson, Joel. *A Rage for Order: Black-White Relations in the American South Since Emancipation.* New York: Oxford University Press, 1986.

Williamson, Joel. *After Slavery: The Negro in South Carolina During Reconstruction, 1861–1877.* New York: W.W. Norton, 1975.

Williamson, Joel. *The Crucible of Race: Black-White Relations in the American South since Emancipation.* New York: Oxford University Press, 1984.

Willis, Arthur Clifton. *Cheyney: Mother of Higher Education of African-Americans, 1837–1981.* Philadelphia: Arthur C. Willis, 1994.

Wynes, Charles E. "T. McCants Stewart: Peripatetic Black South Carolinian." *The South Carolina Historical Magazine* 80, no. 4 (October 1979): 311–17.

Index